Problem-Solving Strategies for *Efficient* and *Elegant* Solutions

Grades 6–12

Second Edition

Problem-Solving Strategies for *Efficient* and *Elegant* Solutions

Grades 6–12

A Resource for the Mathematics Teacher

Alfred S. Posamentier
Stephen Krulik
Afterword by Nobel Laureate Herbert A. Hauptman

Second Edition

CORWIN PRESS
A SAGE Company
Thousand Oaks, CA 91320

For information:

Corwin Press
A SAGE Company
2455 Teller Road
Thousand Oaks, California 91320
www.corwinpress.com

SAGE India Pvt. Ltd.
B 1/I 1 Mohan Cooperative
    Industrial Area
Mathura Road, New Delhi 110 044
India

SAGE Ltd.
1 Oliver's Yard
55 City Road
London EC1Y 1SP
United Kingdom

SAGE Asia-Pacific Pte. Ltd.
33 Pekin Street #02–01
Far East Square
Singapore 048763

Printed in the United States of America

Library of Congress Cataloging-in-Publication Data

Posamentier, Alfred S.
Problem-solving strategies for efficient and elegant solutions, grades 6–12:
a resource for the mathematics teacher / Alfred S. Posamentier, Stephen Krulik;
afterword by nobel laureate Herbert A. Hauptman. —2nd ed.
    p. cm.
Includes bibliographical references and index.
ISBN 978-1-4129-5969-8 (cloth)
ISBN 978-1-4129-5970-4 (pbk.)
    1. Problem solving. I. Krulik, Stephen. II. Title.

QA63.P67 2008
510.71'2—dc22   2007040296

This book is printed on acid-free paper.

08 09 10 11 12 10 9 8 7 6 5 4 3 2 1

Acquisitions Editor:	Cathy Hernandez
Editorial Assistants:	Megan Bedell, Ena Rosen
Production Editor:	Melanie Birdsall, Cassandra Margaret Seibel
Copy Editor:	QuADS Prepress (P) Ltd.
Typesetter:	C&M Digitals (P) Ltd.
Proofreader:	Charlotte J. Waisner
Cover Designer:	Michael Dubowe

Contents

Preface

Over the years, problem solving has emerged as one of the major concerns at all levels of school mathematics. In fact, the National Council of Supervisors of Mathematics (NCSM) points out that "learning to solve problems is the principal reason for studying mathematics" (NCSM, 1977, p. 1). Furthermore, the National Council of Teachers of Mathematics (NCTM) in their *Professional Standards for Teaching Mathematics* state rather boldly that "problem solving, reasoning and communication are processes that should pervade all mathematics instruction and should be modeled by teachers" (NCTM, 1991, p. 95). This is further buttressed in their *Principles and Standards for School Mathematics*, where they explicitly say that "problem solving is an integral part of all mathematics learning" (NCTM, 2000, p. 52). We are in complete agreement! In fact, we would go one step further: We feel that problem solving is not only a skill to be taught in mathematics but also a skill that will be carried over to everyday "problems" and serve a person well throughout his or her life.

In many cases, students seem to feel that a problem can only be solved in a single way, specific to the "type" of problem being taught (i.e., motion problems, age problems, mixture problems, etc.). Students often feel that an algebraic approach is the only procedure that will "work." But where does this misconception come from?

In fact, it is often the teachers who themselves are not even aware of the many problem-solving strategies that can be used to provide efficient and elegant solutions to many problems. It is often they who unconsciously convey to their students the notion that problems can only be solved using an algebraic approach. While we would agree that algebra is a most powerful tool, it is still only one of the many approaches students should be made aware of when it comes to problem solving. This book is a result of our many years of efforts to make teachers and students aware of this most important aspect of teaching mathematics. Furthermore, it is designed for the classroom teacher who has a sincere desire to help students succeed as problem solvers both in mathematics and beyond. This is not to say that the book cannot be used by students directly; quite the contrary! However, its "tone" is directed to the teacher, who "should engage students in mathematical discourse about problem-solving—(which) includes discussing different solutions and solution-strategies for a given problem, (and) how solutions can be extended and generalized" (NCTM, 1991, p. 95).

In this book, we examine 10 strategies that are widely used in problem solving both in mathematics and real-life situations. In the mathematics classroom, these strategies provide an alternate plan for resolving many problem situations that arise within the curriculum. We have selected about 200 problems to illustrate these strategies realizing that teachers will apply these strategies to their regular instructional program. To do this, we recommend a careful review and study of the examples provided for each strategy so that the strategy eventually becomes a genuine part of the teacher's thinking processes or, one might say, a part of the teacher's arsenal of problem-solving tools.

While it is true that most of the problems can be solved using the tried-and-true techniques of algebra and geometry (and we *do* show these solutions as well), the purely "mechanical" approach often masks some of the efficiency, beauty, and elegance of mathematics. In many cases, the problem-solving strategies presented make the solution of a problem much easier, much "neater," and much more understandable and, thereby, enjoyable!

Throughout the book we try to show how each of these strategies occurs and ought to be consciously used in real-life situations. Many people already make use of these strategies without realizing it. This carry-over into life outside of the school adds importance to the mathematics our students study and will ultimately improve their everyday performances. We believe that you and your students alike can profit from a careful reading (and working along) of this book. As you examine each problem, take the time to solve it in any way you wish, or perhaps in a variety of ways. Compare your solutions to the ones provided. (Naturally, we welcome any clever alternatives to those in the book.) Most important, try to absorb the impact of the application of the problem-solving strategies and how they contribute to the beauty and power of mathematics. All the better if you can carry this motivated feeling over to your students.

Understand our feeling that problem solving must be the cornerstone of any successful mathematics program and then try to infuse this same enthusiastic feeling and attitude in your daily teaching. This concentrated effort will make you a better problem solver and in turn help your students to also become better problem solvers. Not only will their attitude toward mathematics improve but so will their skills and abilities. This is our ultimate goal.

REFERENCES

National Council of Supervisors of Mathematics. (1977). *Position paper on basic mathematical skills.* Golden, CO: Author.

National Council of Teachers of Mathematics. (1991). *Professional standards for teaching mathematics.* Reston, VA: Author.

National Council of Teachers of Mathematics. (2000). *Principles and standards for school mathematics.* Reston, VA: Author.

Acknowledgments

A book such as this one requires extensive criticism and suggestions from professionals. We therefore sought input from a number of people from the international community. We sincerely thank Dr. Gerd Baron* (Professor Emeritus of Mathematics, Technical University of Vienna, Austria), Linda Berman (Chairman, ret., Mathematics Department, Bronx High School of Science, Bronx, NY), Jacob Cohen (Chairman, ret., Mathematics Department, Theodore Roosevelt High School, Bronx, NY), Ira Ewen (Mathematics specialist, ret., New York City public schools), Dr. Hans K. Kaiser* (Professor of Mathematics, and Vice Rector, Vienna University of Technology, Vienna, Austria), Dr. Ingmar Lehmann* (Doz., Mathematics Education, Humboldt University of Berlin, Germany), Dr. Stephen Moresh (Associate Professor of Mathematics Education, ret., City College of the City University of New York), the late Dr. Hans-Christian Reichel (Professor of Mathematics, University of Vienna, Austria), Dr. Jesse A. Rudnick (Professor of Mathematics Education, Emeritus, Temple University, Philadelphia, PA), and Dr. Wolfgang Schulz* (Professor of Mathematics Education, Humboldt University of Berlin, Germany). Those listed with an asterisk (*) not only read the manuscript but also made several substantive contributions in the form of problem suggestions and offered alternate solutions, for this we are doubly grateful. We are especially honored and grateful for the advice and the afterword provided by Dr. Herbert A. Hauptman, the first mathematician to win the Nobel Prize (for chemistry, 1985).

We also wish to acknowledge the many high school teachers, too numerous to mention, from New York, New Jersey, Philadelphia, Vienna (Austria), Berlin (Germany), and Klagenfurt (Austria), who have played a most important role reading various parts of the manuscript evaluating it for content and appropriateness for the secondary schools and for usefulness in the instructional program. In particular, the continuous help and support provided by Gladys Krulik and Barbara Lowin is most appreciated.

PUBLISHER'S ACKNOWLEDGMENTS

Corwin Press gratefully acknowledges the contributions of the following reviewers:

Nancy Foote, Mathematics Teacher
Desert Hills High School, Gilbert, AZ

Alex Jaffurs, Twelfth Grade Mathematics Teacher
Patuxent High School, Leonardtown, MD

Charlotte Kenney, Eighth Grade Mathematics and Science Teacher
Browns River Middle School, Jericho, VT

Mary Kollmeyer, Mathematics Teacher
Lejeune High School, Camp Lejeune, NC

Manfred Kronfellner, Professor of Mathematics
Vienna University of Technology, Vienna, Austria

Suzanna Laughland, Mathematics Teacher
Kennett High School, Conway, NH

Lyneille Meza, Mathematics Teacher
Strickland Middle School, Denton, TX

About the Authors

Alfred S. Posamentier is Dean of the School of Education and Professor of Mathematics Education at the City College of the City University of New York (CCNY). He is author and coauthor of more than 40 mathematics books for teachers, secondary and elementary school students, and the general public. Dr. Posamentier is also a frequent commentator in newspapers on topics relating to education.

After completing his AB degree in mathematics at Hunter College of the City University of New York, he took a position as a teacher of mathematics at Theodore Roosevelt High School (Bronx, NY), where he focused his attention on improving the students' problem-solving skills and at the same time enriching their instruction far beyond what the traditional textbooks offered. He also developed the school's first mathematics teams (both at the junior and senior levels). He is still involved in working with mathematics teachers and supervisors, nationally and internationally, to help them maximize their effectiveness. As Dean of the CCNY School of Education, his scope of interest covers the full gamut of educational issues.

Immediately on joining the CCNY faculty in 1970 (after having received his master's degree there in 1966), he began to develop new in-service courses for secondary school mathematics teachers in special areas such as recreational mathematics and problem solving in mathematics.

In 1973, Dr. Posamentier received his PhD from Fordham University (New York) in mathematics education and has since extended his reputation in mathematics education to Europe. He has been visiting professor at several European universities in Austria, England, Germany, and Poland; while at the University of Vienna he was Fulbright Professor (1990).

In 1989, he was awarded the position of *Honorary Fellow* at the South Bank University (London, England). In recognition of his outstanding teaching, the

CCNY Alumni Association named him *Educator of the Year* in 1994, and New York City had the day, May 1, 1994, named in his honor by the President of the New York City Council. In 1994, he was also awarded the *Grand Medal of Honor* from the Republic of Austria, and in 1999, on approval of Parliament, the President of the Republic of Austria awarded him the title of *University Professor of Austria*. In 2003, he was awarded the title of *Ehrenbürger* (Honorary Fellow) of the Vienna University of Technology, and in 2004, he was awarded the *Austrian Cross of Honor for Arts and Science, First Class* from the President of the Republic of Austria. In 2005, he was inducted into the Hunter College Alumni Hall of Fame, and in 2006, he was awarded the *Townsend Harris Medal* by the CCNY Alumni Association.

He has taken on numerous important leadership positions in mathematics education locally. He was a member of the New York State Education Commissioner's Blue Ribbon Panel on the Math-A Regents Exams and the Commissioner's Mathematics Standards Committee, which redefined the Mathematics Standards for New York State, and he also serves on the New York City schools' Chancellor's Math Advisory Panel.

Now in his 38th year on the faculty of the CCNY, he is still a leading commentator on educational issues and continues his longtime passion of seeking ways to make mathematics interesting to teachers, students, and the general public—as can be seen from some of his more recent books from among the more than 40 he has written: *The Art of Problem Solving: A Resource for the Mathematics Teacher* (Corwin Press, 1996), *Tips for the Mathematics Teacher: Research-based Strategies to Help Students Learn* (Corwin Press, 1998), *Advanced Euclidean Geometry: Excursions for Secondary Teachers and Students* (2002), *Math Wonders: To Inspire Teachers and Students* (2003), *Math Charmers: Tantalizing Tidbits for the Mind* (2003), *π, A Biography of the World's Most Mysterious Number* (2004), *Teaching Secondary School Mathematics: Techniques and Enrichment Units* (Seventh Edition, 2006), *101+ Great Ideas to Introduce Key Concepts in Mathematics* (Corwin Press, 2006), *What Successful Math Teachers Do: Grades 6–12* (Corwin Press, 2006), *What Successful Math Teachers Do: Grades K–5* (Corwin Press, 2007), *Exemplary Practices for Math Teachers* (2007), and *The Fabulous Fibonacci Numbers* (2007).

Stephen Krulik is Professor Emeritus of Mathematics Education at Temple University in Philadelphia. While at Temple University, Dr. Krulik was responsible for the undergraduate and graduate preparation of mathematics teachers for grades K–12, as well as the in-service alertness training of mathematics teachers at the graduate level. He teaches a wide variety of courses including the history of mathematics, methods of teaching mathematics, and the teaching of problem solving. This latter course grew out of his interest in problem solving and reasoning in the mathematics classroom. His concern that students understand the beauty and value of problem solving as well as the ability to reason led to this book.

Dr. Krulik received his BA degree in mathematics from Brooklyn College of the City University of New York and his MA and EdD in mathematics education from Columbia University's Teachers College. Before coming to Temple University, he taught mathematics in the New York City public schools for 15 years. At Lafayette High School in Brooklyn, he created and implemented several courses designed to prepare students for the SAT examination, while stressing the art of problem solving as opposed to rote memorization of algorithms.

Nationally, Dr. Krulik has served as a member of the committee responsible for preparing the *Professional Standards for Teaching Mathematics* of the National Council of Teachers of Mathematics. He was also the editor of NCTM's 1980 Yearbook *Problem Solving in School Mathematics.* Regionally, he served as president of the Association of Mathematics Teachers of New Jersey, was a member of the editorial team that produced the 1993 publication, *The New Jersey Calculator Handbook,* and was the editor for their 1997 monograph, *Tomorrow's Lessons.*

His major areas of interest are the teaching of problem solving and reasoning, materials for teaching mathematics, as well as comprehensive assessment in mathematics. He is author and coauthor of more than 30 books for teachers of mathematics, including the *Roads to Reasoning* (*Grades 1–8*) and *Problem Driven Math* (*Grades 3–8*). Dr. Krulik is also the senior problem-solving author for a major basal textbook series. Dr. Krulik is a frequent contributor to professional journals in mathematics education. He has also served as a consultant, and has conducted many workshops for school districts throughout the United States and Canada, as well as delivering major presentations in Vienna (Austria), Budapest (Hungary), Adelaide (Australia), and San Juan (Puerto Rico). He is in great demand as a speaker at both national and international professional meetings, where his major focus is on preparing *all* students to reason and problem solve in their mathematics classrooms, as well as in life.

In memory of my parents,
Ernest and Alice Posamentier,
who encountered some of the most extraordinary problems
of the twentieth century and confronted them with
"efficient and elegant" solutions.

—Alfred S. Posamentier

To my wife and life partner,
Gladys,
who, in her own "efficient" way, develops
"elegant" solutions to the problems I seem to create.

—Stephen Krulik

1

Introduction to Problem-Solving Strategies

Before we can discuss what problem solving is, we must first come to grips with what is meant by a problem. In essence, a problem is a situation that confronts a person, that requires resolution, and for which the path to the solution is not immediately known. In everyday life, a problem can manifest itself as anything from a simple personal problem, such as the best strategy for crossing the street (usually done without much "thinking"), to a more complex problem, such as how to assemble a new bicycle. Of course, crossing the street may not be a simple problem in some situations. For example, Americans become radically aware of what is usually a subconscious behavior pattern while visiting a country such as England, where their usual strategy for safely crossing the street just will not work. The reverse is also true; the British experience similar feelings when visiting the European continent, where traffic is oriented differently than that in Britain. These everyday situations are usually resolved "subconsciously," without our taking formal note of the procedures by which we found the solution. A consciousness of everyday problem-solving methods and strategies usually becomes more evident when we travel outside of our usual cultural surroundings. There the usual way of life and habitual behaviors may not fit or may not work. We may have to consciously adapt other methods to achieve our goals.

Much of what we do is based on our prior experiences. As a result, the level of sophistication with which we attack these problems will vary with the individual. Whether the problems we face in everyday life involve selecting a daily wardrobe, relating to friends or acquaintances, or dealing with professional issues or personal finances, we pretty much function automatically, without considering the method or strategy that best suits the situation. We go about addressing life's challenges with an algorithmic-like approach and can easily become a bit frustrated if that approach suddenly doesn't fit. In these situations, we are required to find a solution to the problem. That is, we must search our previous experiences to find a way we solved an analogous problem in the past. We could also reach into our bag of problem-solving tools and see what works.

When students encounter problems in their everyday school lives, their approach is not much different. They tend to tackle problems based on their previous experiences. These experiences can range from recognizing a "problem" as very similar to one previously solved to taking on a homework exercise similar to exercises presented in class that day. The student is not doing any problem solving—rather, he or she is merely mimicking (or practicing) the earlier encountered situations. This is the behavior seen in a vast majority of classrooms. In a certain sense, repetition of a "skill" is useful in attaining the skill. This can also hold true for attaining problem-solving skills. Hence, we provide ample examples to practice the strategy applications in a variety of contexts.

This sort of approach to dealing with what are often seen as artificial situations, created especially for the mathematics class, does not directly address the idea of problem solving as a process to be studied for its own sake, and not merely as a facilitator. People do not solve "age problems," "motion problems," "mixture problems," and so on in their real lives. Historically, we always have considered the study of mathematics topically. Without a conscious effort by educators, this will clearly continue to be the case. We might rearrange the topics in the syllabus in various orders, but it will still be the topics themselves that link the courses together rather than the mathematical procedures involved, and this is not the way that most people think! Reasoning involves a broad spectrum of thinking. We hope to encourage this thinking here.

We believe that there can be great benefits to students in a mathematics class (as well as a spin-off effect in their everyday lives) by considering problem solving as an end in itself and not merely as a means to an end. Problem solving can be the vehicle used to introduce our students to the beauty that is inherent in mathematics, but it can also be the unifying thread that ties their mathematics experiences together into a meaningful whole. One immediate goal is to have our students become familiar with numerous problem-solving strategies and to practice using them. We expect this procedure will begin to show itself in the way students approach problems and ultimately solve them. Enough practice of this kind should, for the most part, make a longer-range goal attainable, namely, that students naturally come to use these same problem-solving strategies not only to solve mathematical problems but also to resolve problems in everyday life. This transfer of learning (back and forth) can be best realized by introducing problem-solving strategies in both mathematical and real-life situations concomitantly. This is a rather large order and an ambitious goal as well. Changing an instructional program by relinquishing some of its time-honored emphasis on isolated topics and concepts, and devoting the time to a procedural approach, requires a great deal of teacher "buy-in" to succeed. This must begin by convincing the teachers that the end results will prepare a more able student for this era, where the ability to think becomes more and more important as we continue to develop and make use of sophisticated technology.

When we study the history of mathematics, we find breakthroughs that, although simple to understand, often elicit the reaction, "Oh, I would never have thought about that approach." Analogously, when clever solutions to certain problems are found and presented as "tricks," they have the same effect as the great breakthroughs in the history of mathematics. We must avoid this sort of rendition and make clever solutions part of an attainable problem-solving strategy knowledge base that is constantly reinforced throughout the regular instructional program.

You should be aware that, in the past few decades, there has been much talk about problem solving. While many new thrusts in mathematics last a few years, then disappear leaving some traces behind to enrich our curriculum, the problem-solving movement has endured for more than a quarter of a century and shows no sign of abatement. If anything, it shows signs of growing stronger. The National Council of Teachers of Mathematics (NCTM), in its *Agenda for Action* (1980), firmly stated that "problem solving must be the focus of the (mathematics) curriculum." In their widely accepted *Curriculum and Evaluation Standards for School Mathematics* (1989), the NCTM offered a series of process Standards, in addition to the more traditional content Standards. Two of these four Standards (referred to as the "Process Standards"), Problem Solving and Reasoning, were for students in all grades, K through 12. In their *Principles and Standards for School Mathematics* (2000), the NCTM continued this emphasis on problem solving throughout the grades as a major thrust of mathematics teaching. All these documents have played a major role in generating the general acceptance of problem solving as a major curricular thrust. Everyone seems to agree that problem solving and reasoning are, and must be, an integral part of any good instructional program. In an effort to emphasize this study of problem solving and reasoning in mathematics curricula, most states are now including problem-solving skills on their statewide tests. Teachers sometimes ask, "If I spend time teaching problem solving, when will I find the time to teach the arithmetic skills the children need for the state test?" In fact, research has shown that students who are taught via a problem-solving mode of instruction usually do as well, or better, on state tests than many other students who have spent all their time learning only the skills. After all, when solving a problem, one must dip into his or her arsenal of arithmetic skills to find the correct answer to the problem. Then why has the acceptance of problem solving as an integral part of the mathematics curriculum not come to pass? In our view, the major impediment to a successful problem-solving component in our regular school curriculum is a weakness in the training teachers receive in problem solving, as well as the lack of attention paid to the ways in which these skills can be smoothly incorporated into their regular teaching program. Teachers ought not to be forced to rely solely on their own resourcefulness as they attempt to move ahead without special training. They need to focus their attention on what problem solving is, how they can use problem solving to teach the skills of mathematics, and how problem solving should be presented to their students. They must understand that problem solving can be thought of in three different ways:

1. Problem solving is a subject for study in and of itself.

2. Problem solving is an approach to a particular problem.

3. Problem solving is a way of teaching.

Above all, teachers must focus their attention on their own ability to become competent problem solvers. It is imperative that they know and understand problem solving if they intend to be successful when they teach it. They must learn which problem-solving strategies are available to them, what these entail, and when and how to use them. They must then learn to apply these strategies, not only to mathematical situations but also to everyday life experiences whenever possible. Often, simple problems can be used in clever ways to demonstrate these strategies. Naturally, more challenging problems will show the power of the problem-solving strategies. By learning the strategies, beginning with simple applications and then progressively moving to more challenging and complex problems, the students will have opportunities to grow in the everyday use of their problem-solving skills. Patience must be used with students as they embark on, what is for most of them, this new adventure in mathematics. We believe that only after teachers have had the proper immersion in this alternative approach to mathematics in general and to problem solving in particular, and after they have developed sensitivity toward the learning needs and peculiarities of students, then, and only then, can we expect to see some genuine positive change in students' mathematics performance.

We will set out with an overview of those problem-solving strategies that are particularly useful as tools in solving mathematical problems. From the outset, you should be keenly aware that it is rare that a problem can be solved using all 10 strategies we present here. Similarly, it is equally rare that only a single strategy can be used to solve a given problem. Rather, a combination of strategies is the most likely occurrence when solving a problem. Thus, it is best to become familiar with all the strategies and to develop facility in using them when appropriate. The strategies selected here are not the only ones available, but they represent those most applicable to mathematics instruction in the schools. The user will, for the most part, determine appropriateness of a strategy in a particular problem. This is analogous to carpenters, who, when called on to fix a problem with toolbox in hand, must decide which tool to use. The more tools they have available and the better they know how to use them, the better we would expect the results to be. However, just as not every task carpenters have to do will be possible using the tools in their toolbox, so, too, not every mathematics problem will be solvable using the strategies presented here. In both cases, experience and judgment play an important role.

We believe that every teacher, if he or she is to help students learn and use the strategies of problem solving, must have a collection from which to draw examples. Throughout the book, we make a conscious effort to label the strategies and to use these labels as much as possible so that they can be called on quickly, as they are needed. This is analogous to the carpenter deciding which tool to use in constructing something; usually, the tool is referred to by name (i.e., a label). For you to better understand the strategies presented in this book, we begin each section with a description of a particular strategy, apply it to an everyday problem situation, and then present examples of how it can be applied in mathematics. We follow this with a series of mathematics problems from topics covered in the schools, which can be used with your students to practice the strategy. In each case, the illustrations are not necessarily meant to be typical but are presented merely to best illustrate the use of the particular strategy under discussion. The following strategies will be considered in this book:

1. Working backwards

2. Finding a pattern

3. Adopting a different point of view

4. Solving a simpler, analogous problem (specification without loss of generality)

5. Considering extreme cases

6. Making a drawing (visual representation)

7. Intelligent guessing and testing (including approximation)

8. Accounting for all possibilities (exhaustive listing)

9. Organizing data

10. Logical reasoning

As we have already mentioned, there is hardly ever one unique way to solve a problem. Some problems lend themselves to a wide variety of solution methods. As a rule, students should be encouraged to consider alternative solutions to a problem. This usually means considering class-mates' solutions and comparing them with the "standard" solution (i.e., the one given in the textbook or supplied by the teacher). Indeed, it has been said that it is far better to solve one problem in four ways than to solve four problems, each in one way. In addition, we must again state that many problems may require more than one strategy for solution. Furthermore, the data given in the problem statement, rather than merely the nature of the problem, can also determine the best strategy to be used in solving the problem. All aspects of a particular problem must be care-fully inspected before embarking on a particular strategy.

Let's consider a problem that most people can resolve by an intuitive (or random) trial-and-error method, but that might take a considerable amount of time. To give you a feel for the use of these problem-solving strategies, we will approach the problem by employing several of the strat-egies listed.

Problem 1.1

Place the numbers from 1 through 9 into the grid below so that the sum of each row, column, and diagonal is the same. (This is often referred to as a magic square.)

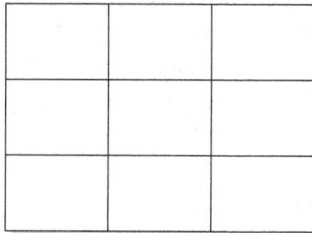

Figure 1.1

Solution

A first step to a solution would be to use *logical reasoning*. The sum of the numbers in all nine cells would be $1+2+3+ \cdots +7+8+9=45$. If each row has to have the same sum, then each row must have a sum of $\frac{45}{3}$ or 15.

The next step might be to determine which number should be placed in the center cell. Using *intelligent guessing and testing* along with some addi-tional *logical reasoning*, we can begin by trying some *extreme cases*. Can 9 occupy the center cell? If it did, then 8 would be in some row, column, or diagonal along with the 9, making a sum greater than 15. Therefore, 9 cannot be in the center cell. Similarly, 6, 7, or 8 cannot occupy the center cell, because then they would be in the same row, column, or diagonal with 9 and would not permit a three number sum of 15. Consider now the other extreme. Could 1 occupy the center cell? If it did, then it would be in some row, column, or diagonal with 2, thus requiring a 12 to obtain a sum of 15. Similarly, 2, 3, or 4 cannot occupy the center cell. Having *accounted for all the possibilities*, this leaves only the 5 to occupy the center cell.

	5	

Figure 1.2

Now, using *intelligent guessing and testing*, we can try to put the 1 in a corner cell. Because of symmetry, it does not matter which corner cell we use for this guess. In any case, this forces us to place the 9 in the opposite corner, if we are to obtain a diagonal sum of 15.

1		
	5	
		9

Figure 1.3

With a 9 in one corner, the remaining two numbers in the row with the 9 must total 6; that is, 2 and 4. One of those numbers (the 2 or the 4) would then also be in a row or a column with the 1, making a sum of 15 impossible in that row or column. Thus, 1 cannot occupy a corner. Placing it in a middle cell of one outside row or column forces the 9 into the opposite cell so as to get a sum of 15.

	1	
	5	
	9	

Figure 1.4

The 7 cannot be in the same row or column with the 1, because a second 7 would then be required to obtain a sum of 15.

7	1	?
	5	
	9	

Figure 1.5

In this way, we can see that 8 and 6 must be in the same row or column (and at the corner positions, of course) with the 1.

8	1	6
	5	
	9	

Figure 1.6

This then determines the remaining two corner cells (4 and 2) to allow the diagonals to have a sum of 15:

8	1	6
	5	
4	9	2

Figure 1.7

To complete the magic square, we simply place the remaining two numbers, 3 and 7, into the two remaining cells to get sums of 15 in the first and third columns.

8	1	6
3	5	7
4	9	2

Figure 1.8

In this solution to the problem, observe how the various strategies were used for each step of the solution.

We stated earlier that problems can (and should) be solved in more than one way. Let's examine an alternative approach to solving this same problem. Picking up the solution from the point at which we established that the sum of every row, column, or diagonal is 15, list all the possibilities of three numbers from this set of nine that have a sum of 15 (*accounting for all the possibilities*). By *organizing the data* in this way, the answer comes rather quickly:

	5	

Figure 1.9

We now *adopt a different point of view* and consider the position of a cell and the number of times it is counted into a sum of 15 (*logical reasoning*). The center square must be counted four times: twice in the diagonals and once each for a row and a column. The only number that appears four times in the triples we have listed below is 5. Therefore, it must belong in the center cell.

1, 5, 9	2, 6, 7
1, 6, 8	3, 4, 8
2, 4, 9	3, 5, 7
2, 5, 8	4, 5, 6

The corner cells are each used three times. Therefore, we place the numbers used three times (the even numbers, 2, 4, 6, and 8) in the corners.

8		6
	5	
4		2

Figure 1.10

The remaining numbers (the odd numbers) are each used twice in the above sums and, therefore, are to be placed in the peripheral center cells (where they are only used by two sums) to complete our magic square:

8	1	6
3	5	7
4	9	2

Figure 1.11

This *logical reasoning* was made considerably simpler by using a *visual representation* of the problem. It is important to have students realize that we solved the same problem in two very different ways. They should try to develop other alternatives to these, and they might also consider using consecutive numbers other than 1 to 9. An ambitious student might also consider the construction of a 4 × 4 or a 5 × 5 magic square.

As we stated before, it is extremely rare to find a single problem that can be efficiently solved using each of the 10 problem-solving strategies we listed. There are times, however, when more than one strategy can be used, either alone or in combination, with varying degrees of efficiency. Of course, the level of efficiency of each method may vary with the reader. Let's take a look at one such problem. It's a problem that is well known, and you may have seen it before. We intend, however, to approach its solution with a variety of different strategies.

Problem 1.2

In a room with 10 people, everyone shakes hands with everybody else exactly once. How many handshakes are there?

Solution A

Let's use our *visual representation* strategy, by drawing a diagram. The 10 points (no 3 points of which are collinear) represent the 10 people. Begin with the person represented by point *A*.

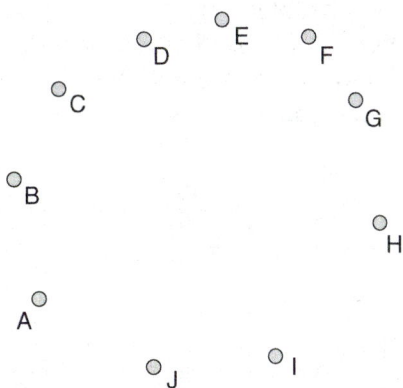

Figure 1.12

We join *A* to each of the other 9 points, indicating the first 9 handshakes that take place.

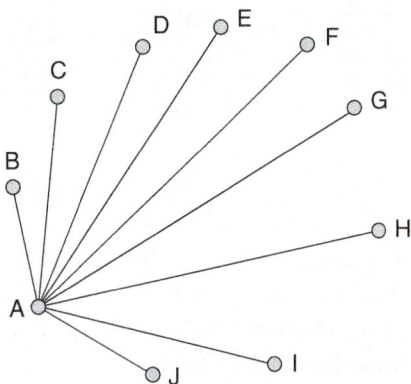

Figure 1.13

Now, from B there are 8 additional handshakes (since A has already shaken hands with B and $\overline{AB}$ is already drawn). Similarly, from C there will be 7 lines drawn to the other points ($\overline{AC}$ and $\overline{BC}$ are already drawn), from D there will be 6 additional lines or handshakes, and so on. When we reach point I, there is only one remaining handshake to be made, namely, I with J, since I has already shaken hands with $A, B, C, D, E, F, G,$ and H. Thus, the sum of the handshakes equals $9+8+7+6+5+4+3+2+1=45$. In general, this is the same as using the formula for the sum of the first n natural numbers, $\frac{n(n+1)}{2}$, where $n \geq 2$. (Notice that the final drawing will be a decagon with all its diagonals drawn.)

Solution B

We can approach the problem by *accounting for all the possibilities.* Consider the grid shown in Figure 1.14, which indicates persons A, B, $C, \dots, H, I, J$ shaking hands with one another. The diagonal with the Xs indicates that people cannot shake hands with themselves.

	A	B	C	D	E	F	G	H	I	J
A	X									
B		X								
C			X							
D				X						
E					X					
F						X				
G							X			
H								X		
I									X	
J										X

Figure 1.14

The remaining cells indicate doubly all the other handshakes (i.e., A shakes hands with B, and B shakes hands with A). Thus, we take the total number of cells (10^2) minus those on the diagonal (10) and divide the result by 2. In this case, we have $\frac{100-10}{2}=45$.

In a general case for the $n \times n$ grid, the number would be $\frac{n^2-n}{2}$, which is equivalent to the formula $\frac{n(n-1)}{2}$.

Solution C

Let's now examine the problem by *adopting a different point of view*. Consider the room with 10 people, each of whom will shake 9 other people's hands. This seems to indicate that there are 10×9 or 90 handshakes, but we must divide by 2 to eliminate the duplication (since when A shakes hands with B, we may also consider that as B shaking hands with A); hence, $\frac{90}{2} = 45$.

Solution D

Let's try to solve the problem by *looking for a pattern*. In the table shown in Figure 1.15, we list the number of handshakes occurring in a room as the number of people increases.

Number of People in Room	Number of Handshakes for Additional Person	Total Number of Handshakes in Room
1	0	0
2	1	1
3	2	3
4	3	6
5	4	10
6	5	15
7	6	21
8	7	28
9	8	36
10	9	45

Figure 1.15

The third column, which is the total number of handshakes, gives a sequence of numbers known as the *triangular numbers*, whose successive differences increase by 1 each time. It is therefore possible to simply continue the table until we reach the corresponding sum for the 10 people. Alternatively, we note that the pattern at each entry is one half the product of the number of people on that line and the number of people on the previous line.

Solution E

We can approach the problem by a careful use of the *organizing data* strategy. The chart in Figure 1.16 shows each of the people in the room and the number of hands they have to shake each time, given that they have already shaken the hands of their predecessors and don't shake their own hands. Thus, person number 10 shakes 9 hands, person number 9 shakes 8 hands, and so on, until we reach person number 2, who only has one person's hand left to shake, and person number 1 has no hands to shake because everyone already shook his hand. Again the sum is 45.

Organizing Data										
No. of people	10	9	8	7	6	5	4	3	2	1
No. of handshakes	9	8	7	6	5	4	3	2	1	0

Figure 1.16

Solution F

We may also combine *solving a simpler problem* with *visual representation (drawing a picture)*, *organizing the data*, and *looking for a pattern*. Begin by considering a figure with 1 person, represented by a single point. Obviously, there will be 0 handshakes. Now, expand the number of people to 2, represented by 2 points. There will be 1 handshake. Again, let's expand the number of people to 3. Now, there will be 3 handshakes needed. Continue with 4 people, 5 people, and so on.

Number of People	Number of Handshakes	Visual Representation
1	0	A
2	1	 A — B
3	3	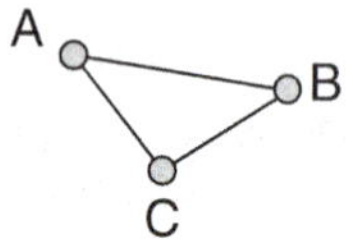 A, B, C triangle
4	6	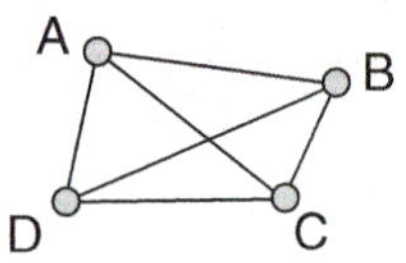 A, B, C, D complete graph
5	10	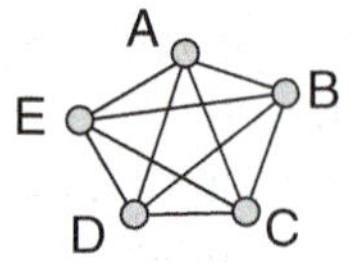 A, B, C, D, E complete graph

Figure 1.17

The problem has now become a geometry problem, in which the answer is the number of sides and diagonals of an "*n*-gon." Thus, for 10 people we have a decagon, and the number of sides, $n = 10$. For the number of diagonals, we may use the formula

$$d = \frac{n(n-3)}{2}, \text{ where } n > 3.$$

Hence,

$$d = \frac{(10)(7)}{2} = 35.$$

Thus, the number of handshakes equals $10 + 35 = 45$.

Solution G

Of course, some students might simply recognize that this problem could be resolved easily by applying the combinations formula of 10 things taken 2 at a time:

$$_{10}C_2 = \frac{10 \times 9}{1 \times 2} = 45.$$

Although this solution is quite efficient, brief, and correct, it uses hardly any mathematical thought (other than application of a formula), and it avoids the problem-solving approach entirely. Although it is a solution that should be discussed, we must call the other solutions to the students' attention.

Notice that we continually differentiate between the terms *answer* and *solution*. The *solution* is the entire problem-solving process, from the moment the problem is encountered, until we leave it as completed. The *answer* is something that appears along the way. While we insist on correct answers, it is the solution that is most important in the problem-solving process.

To help you teach problem solving, you might want to begin to create a Problem Deck. Take a package of large (5" × 9") file cards. Use a separate card for each problem. Write the problem on one side of the card. On the other side, write the solution or solutions, the strategy or strategies used to solve the problem, the correct answer, and where the problem may fit into your curriculum. Problems may be used in several ways:

1. As a means of introducing a topic

2. As a means of reviewing a topic taught earlier

3. As a means of summarizing a lesson just completed

4. As an enrichment of a topic taught

5. To dramatize a problem-solving technique

6. To demonstrate the power and beauty of mathematics

As you teach problem solving, you will encounter many problems that fit into one or more of these categories. Continue to add them to your problem cards collection. In this way, you will be constantly increasing your resource of problem-solving materials with which to teach mathematics.

We suggest that you read the book through, become familiar with all the strategies, practice them, and then begin to present them to your students. In this way, you and they can develop facility with the basic tools of problem solving.

In addition, we suggest that you begin to format more and more of your teaching in a problem-solving mode. That is, encourage your students to be creative in their approach to problems, encourage them to solve problems in a variety of ways, and encourage them to look for more than one method of solution to a problem. Have your students work together in small groups solving problems and communicating their ideas and work to others. The more students talk about problems and problem solving, the better they will become in this vital skill. Referring to the various problem-solving methods or strategies by name will ensure better and more efficient recollection when they are needed. Remember that the concept of metacognition (i.e., being aware of one's own thought processes) is an important factor in problem solving. Encouraging students to talk to themselves when tackling a problem is another way to help the students become aware of their problem-solving success.

REFERENCES

National Council of Teachers of Mathematics. (1980). *An agenda for action: Recommendations for school mathematics of the 1980s.* Reston, VA: Author.

National Council of Teachers of Mathematics. (1989). *Curriculum and evaluation standards for school mathematics.* Reston, VA: Author.

National Council of Teachers of Mathematics. (2000). *Principles and standards for school mathematics.* Reston, VA: Author.

2

Working Backwards

On the surface, the very title of this problem-solving strategy sounds confusing. This stems from a lack of familiarity with the procedure. From their earliest days in school, students are typically taught to solve problems in the most straightforward way possible. This is the way typical mathematics textbook problems are intended to be solved. Unfortunately, a substantial portion of this supposed "problem solving" is done by rote. Students struggle through one problem in a section, the teacher then usually reveals a "model solution," and the remaining "problems" in the section are solved in a similar manner. Little imaginative thinking is required of the students. In fact, we do not even consider these as *problems*; instead, we refer to them as *exercises*, whose purpose is simply to reinforce a particular method of solution via repeated use. In the typical high school geometry course, when students are first required to write proofs, they once again look for ways in which they can merely repeat previous procedures to solve successive problems. We seek to enable students to question the value of learning mathematics merely by rote. Such students then are more receptive to the problem-solving strategy offered here, namely, *working backwards*.

Developing a time schedule is another real-life example of using the working backwards strategy. When people develop a schedule for various tasks that must be completed by a certain time, they often start with what has to be done, the time at which all the work must be completed, and how long each task should take. They then *work backwards* to assign time "slots" to each task to arrive at the appropriate time to begin the work.

The working backwards strategy also is widely used every day in traffic investigations. When the police are confronted by an automobile accident, they must begin to *work backwards* from the time of the accident to determine the causes, which car swerved immediately before the collision, who hit whom, which driver was at fault, what the weather condition was at the time of the accident, and so on as they attempt to reconstruct the accident.

When we look at the procedures that are shown in many typical textbook exercises, some very useful techniques are sometimes presented. Unfortunately, however, techniques are often taken for granted and not called to the students' attention. Students may be required to reason in reverse order, even though they have not been told to do so. An obvious example, once again, is the procedure students should use when writing proofs in the high school geometry course. They should begin by examining what they are trying to prove before doing anything else. Thus, an attempt to prove line segments congruent might stem from proving a pair of triangles congruent. This, in turn, should suggest that the students look for the parts necessary to reach this triangle congruence. Continuing in this manner, students will be led to examine the given information. They are, in essence, *working backwards*. When the goal is unique, but there are many possible starting points, a clever problem solver begins to work backwards from the desired conclusion to a point where the given information is reached.

We must stress that when there is a unique endpoint (here, that which is to be proved) and a variety of paths to get to the starting point, the working backwards strategy may be desirable. The "working forward" method is still the most natural method for solving the problem. In fact, working in the forward direction is used to solve *most* problems. We are not saying that the solving of all problems should be attempted by the working backwards strategy. Rather, after a natural approach (usually "forward") has been examined, a backwards strategy might be tried to see if it provides a more efficient, more interesting, or more satisfying solution to the problem.

THE *WORKING BACKWARDS* STRATEGY IN EVERYDAY LIFE PROBLEM-SOLVING SITUATIONS

The best approach to determine the most efficient route from one city to another depends on whether the starting point or the destination (endpoint) has more access roads. When there are fewer roads leading from the starting point, the forward method is usually superior. However, when there are many roads leading from the starting point and only one or two from the destination, an efficient way to plan the trip is to locate this final destination on a map, determine which roads lead most directly back toward the starting position, and then determine to which larger road that "last" access road leads. Progressively, by continuing in this way (i.e., *working backwards*), one reaches a familiar road that is easily reachable from the starting point. At this step, you will have mapped out the trip in a very systematic way.

A salesman or an executive who has an appointment in a distant city must determine the flight he will take to arrive comfortably on time for his meeting, yet not too far in advance. He begins by examining the airline schedule, starting with the arrival time closest to his appointment. Will he arrive in time? Is he "cutting it too close"? If so, he examines the next earlier arrival time. Is this time all right? What if there is a weather delay? When is the next earlier flight? Thus, by *working backwards*, the executive can decide the most appropriate flight to take to get to his appointment on time.

When a high school freshman announces to a guidance counselor the desire to be admitted to a major Ivy League school and wants to know what courses to take, the counselor will usually look at what the potential college requires. At that point, the counselor begins to build the student's program for the next 4 years by working backwards from the Advanced Placement courses that are usually taken in the senior year. However, to be prepared to take these courses, the student must first take some of the more basic courses as a freshman, sophomore, and junior. For example, to take the Advanced Placement examination in calculus during senior year, the student must take functions as a junior, geometry as a sophomore, and algebra as a freshman. As we have stated previously, when there is a single final goal and we are interested in discovering the path to a starting point, we have a good opportunity to use the working backwards strategy.

The strategy game of Nim is another excellent example of when it is appropriate to use the *working backwards* strategy. In one version of the game, two players are faced with 32 toothpicks placed in a pile between them. Each player in turn takes 1, 2, or 3 toothpicks from the pile. The player who takes the final toothpick is the winner. Players develop a winning strategy by working backwards from 32 (i.e., to win, the player must pick up the 28th toothpick, the 24th toothpick, etc.). Proceeding in this manner from the final goal of #32, we find that the player who wins picks the 28th, 24th, 20th, 16th, 12th, 8th, and 4th toothpicks. Thus, a winning strategy is to permit the opponent to go first and proceed as we have shown. (See Problem 2.12 for a more extensive discussion.)

APPLYING THE *WORKING BACKWARDS* STRATEGY TO SOLVE MATHEMATICS PROBLEMS

Although many problems may require some reverse reasoning (even if only to a small extent), there are some problems whose solutions are dramatically facilitated by working backwards. Consider the following problem. Be aware that it is not typical of the school curriculum but rather a dramatic illustration of the power of *working backwards*.

The sum of two numbers is 12, and the product of the same two numbers is 4. Find the sum of the reciprocals of the two numbers.

Most students will immediately generate two equations, $x + y = 12$ and $xy = 4$, where x and y represent the two numbers. They have been taught to solve this pair of equations simultaneously by substitution. If, in this complicated example, the students do not make any algebraic errors, they will arrive at a pair of rather unpleasant looking values for x and y, that is, $x = 6 \pm 4\sqrt{2}$ and $y = 6 \pm 4\sqrt{2}$. They must then find the reciprocals of these numbers and, finally, their sum. Can this problem be solved in this manner? Yes, of course! However, this rather complicated solution process can be made much simpler by starting from the end of the problem, namely, what we wish to find, $\frac{1}{x} + \frac{1}{y}$. The students might now ask themselves, "What do we usually do when we see two fractions to be added? How do we add them?" If we compute the sum in the usual way, we obtain $\frac{x+y}{xy}$. However, since $x + y$ was given as 12 and xy was given as 4, this fraction becomes $\frac{12}{4} = 3$. (Notice that students were never asked to find the specific values of x and y; rather, they were asked for the sum of their reciprocals.[1])

Special care must be taken to avoid having students, discouraged by their frustrations, take the attitude that "I would never have been able to come up with that 'trick' solution." In fact, they should be encouraged to see that this valuable and unusual problem-solving strategy is one with which they should become familiar and that its use is indeed attainable with some additional practice.

Still another use of the *working backwards* strategy in mathematics is the indirect proof or proof by contradiction. Euclid's proof of the infinitude of primes and Aristotle's proof of the irrationality of $\sqrt{2}$ are two excellent examples. In both cases, we assume the opposite of what we wish to prove and then work backwards from this assumption until we arrive at a contradiction.

---

1. It may be useful at times to consider other versions of the problems, where the more elegant solution, such as the one used here, bypasses other potential difficulties. For example, had we chosen to formulate the problem with the equations $x + y = 2$ and $xy = 3\sqrt{2}$, then the resulting values for x and y would have been complex. Might this then be useful in the instructional program?

PROBLEMS USING THE
WORKING BACKWARDS STRATEGY

Problem 2.1

Find a path on the adjoining grid beginning at "start" and ending at "end," where the sum of the cells is 50. You may pass through any open gate, after which the gate closes.

Start

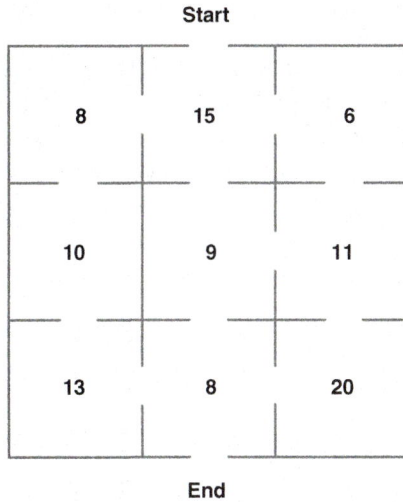

End

Figure 2.1

Solution

Naturally, by a trial-and-error method you should eventually stumble onto the right path. However, by using the *working backwards* strategy you can simplify the problem significantly. You should be quick to realize that regardless of the path you will have to pass through the 15 and 8 cells near the start and end, respectively. This means that $15 + 8 = 23$ will have to be used. This leaves us with a sum of $50 - 23 = 27$ that still needs to be visited. It should not be too difficult now to see that $8 + 10 + 9 = 27$, and thus, the required path is

$$\text{Start } 15 \rightarrow 8 \rightarrow 10 \rightarrow 9 \rightarrow 8 \text{ End.}$$

It was the working backwards strategy that makes this problem far more manageable than originally.

Problem 2.2

Evelyn, Henry, and Al play a certain game. The player who loses each round must give each of the other players as much money as each player has at that time. In Round 1, Evelyn loses and gives Henry and Al as much money as they each then have. In Round 2, Henry loses and gives Evelyn and Al as much money as they each then have. Al loses in Round 3 and gives Evelyn and Henry as much money as they each have. They decide to quit at this point and discover that they each have $24. How much money did they each start with?

Solution

Students usually begin this problem by setting up a system of three equations in three variables. Can it be done? Of course! When teaching this topic in an algebra class, you should have the students do exactly that. However, because the problem requires a great deal of subtraction and simplification of parenthetical expressions, the final set of equations is likely to be incorrect. Even if the correct set of equations is obtained, they must then be solved simultaneously:

Round	Evelyn	Henry	Al
Start	x	y	z
1	$x - y - z$	$2y$	$2z$
2	$2x - 2y - 2z$	$3y - x - z$	$4z$
3	$4x - 4y - 4z$	$6y - 2x - 2z$	$7z - x - y$

which leads us to the system of equations

$$4x - 4y - 4z = 24$$
$$-2x + 6y - 2z = 24$$
$$-x - y + 7z = 24.$$

Solving the system leads to $x = 39, y = 21$, and $z = 12$. Thus, Evelyn began with $39, Henry began with $21, and Al began with $12.

Students should understand that the problem stated the situation at the end of the story ("They each have $24.") and asked for the starting situation ("How much money did they each start with?"). This is almost a sure sign that the *working backwards* strategy could be employed. Let's see how this makes our work easier. We begin at the end with each having $24:

	Evelyn	Henry	Al
End of round 3	24	24	24
End of round 2	12	12	48
End of round 1	6	42	24
Start	39	21	12

Evelyn started with $39, Henry with $21, and Al with $12—the same answers we arrived at by solving the problem algebraically.

You should encourage your students to solve the problem *both ways*. One of the aims in problem solving and reasoning is to have students use their creative skills to find as many ways as they can to solve a problem. This activity keeps the given conditions of the problem completely intact and allows students to focus on the thought processes needed to solve the problem.

Problem 2.3

Candis has an 11-liter can and a 5-liter can. How can she measure out exactly 7 liters of water?

Solution

Most students simply guess at the answer and keep "pouring" back and forth in an attempt to arrive at the correct answer, a sort of "unintelligent" guessing and testing. However, the problem can be solved in a more organized manner by using the *working backwards* strategy. We need to end up with 7 liters in the 11-liter can, leaving a total of 4 empty liters in the can. But where do 4 empty liters come from?

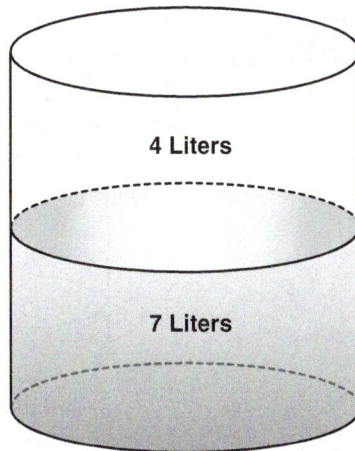

4 Liters

7 Liters

Figure 2.2

To obtain 4 liters, we must leave 1 liter in the 5-liter can. Now, how can we obtain 1 liter in the 5-liter can? Fill the 11-liter can and pour from it twice into the 5-liter can, discarding the water. This leaves 1 liter in the 11-liter can. Pour the 1 liter into the 5-liter can.

Now, fill the 11-liter can and pour off the 4 liters needed to fill the 5-liter can. This leaves the required 7 liters in the 11-liter can.

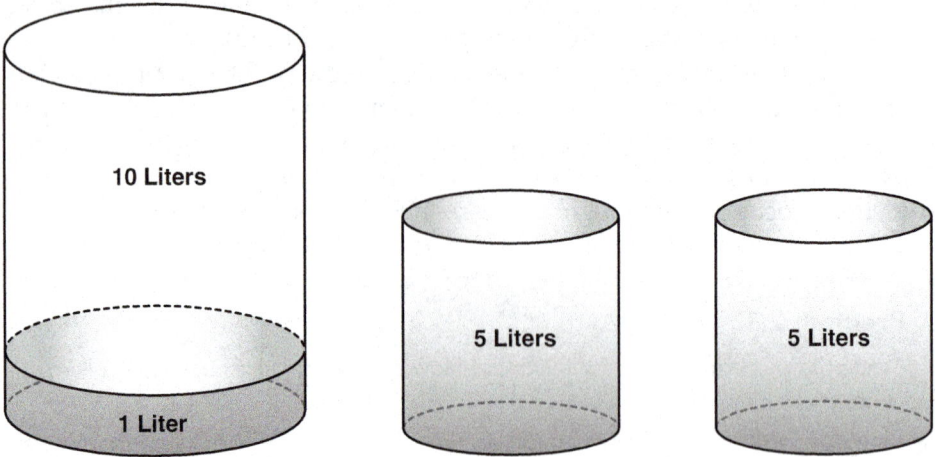

Figure 2.3

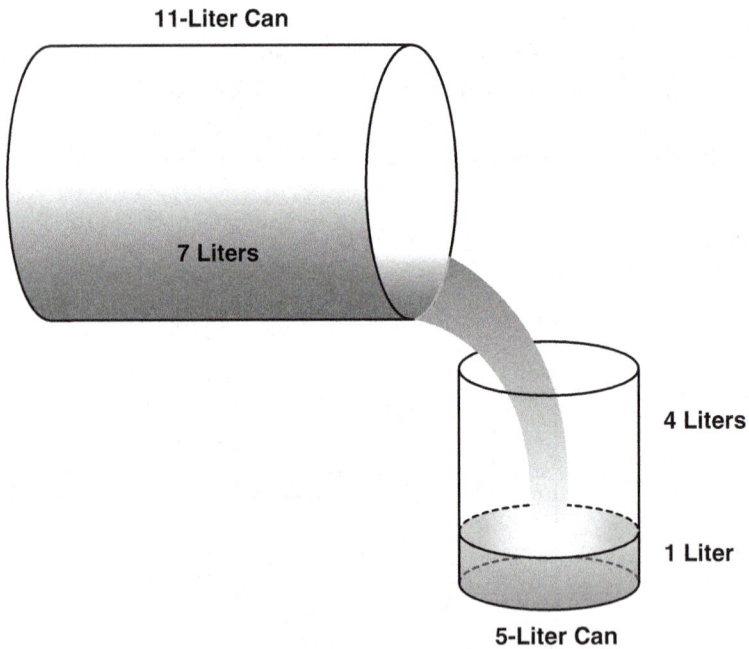

Figure 2.4

Note that problems of this sort do not always have a solution. That is, if you wish to construct additional problems of this sort, you must bear in mind that a solution exists only when the difference of multiples of the capacities of the two given cans can be made equal to the desired quantity. In this problem, $2(11) - 3(5) = 7$.

This concept can lead to a discussion of parity. We know that the sum of two like parities will always be even (i.e., even + even = even and odd + odd = even), whereas the sum of two unlike parities will always be odd, odd + even = odd. Thus, if two even quantities are given, they can never yield an odd quantity. Further discussion can be particularly fruitful because it gives the students a much-needed insight into some valuable number properties and concepts.

Problem 2.4

Barbara visited the games-of-chance at the New Jersey State Fair on three consecutive days. On the first day, she doubled her money and spent $30. On the second day, she tripled her money and spent $54. On the third day, she quadrupled her money and spent $72. She found that she had $48 when she left the fair. How much money did Barbara start with?

Solution

The typical solution presented by students is algebraic. Let $2x - 30$ represent the amount of money she had at the end of the first day. Then,

$$3(2x - 30) - 54 = 6x - 144$$
$$= \text{the amount of money she had at the end}$$
$$\text{of the second day}$$

$$4(6x - 144) - 72 = 24x - 648$$
$$= \text{the amount of money she had at the end}$$
$$\text{of the third day}$$

$$24x - 648 = 48$$
$$24x = 696$$
$$x = 29.$$

Barbara started with $29. The students must, however, be extremely careful in formulating the equations, because it is quite easy to make an error and forget to double, triple, or quadruple *all* the previous money.

Let's approach the problem using the *working backwards* strategy. Notice that by working backwards we are also using inverse operations:

Third day	$48 + 72 = 120$
	$120 \div 4 = 30$
Second day	$30 + 54 = 84$
	$84 \div 3 = 28$
First day	$28 + 30 = 58$
	$58 \div 2 = 29$

She started with $29.

Problem 2.5

Jeanette and Ruth breed French poodles as a hobby. They sold half of the puppies and half a puppy from the latest litter to the local pet shop. Then they sold half of the puppies that were left in the litter and half a puppy to the Poodle Palace. They then decided to give the one remaining puppy to their friend, Gladys. How many puppies were originally in the litter?

Solution

The traditional, most obvious solution is to set up with a series of expressions following the action in the problem, until we arrive at an equation. Thus, if x represents the number of puppies originally in the litter, we obtain

$$\text{First sale: } \frac{x}{2} + \frac{1}{2},$$

which leaves

$$\left[x - \left(\frac{x}{2} + \frac{1}{2} \right) \right] \text{ or } x - \frac{x}{2} - \frac{1}{2}.$$

$$\text{Second sale: } \frac{\left(x - \frac{x}{2} - \frac{1}{2} \right)}{2} + \frac{1}{2},$$

which leaves

$$x - \left(\frac{x}{2} + \frac{1}{2} \right) - \left[\frac{\left(x - \frac{x}{2} - \frac{1}{2} \right)}{2} + \frac{1}{2} \right].$$

Thus,

$$x - \left(\frac{x}{2} + \frac{1}{2} \right) - \left[\frac{x - \left(\frac{x}{2} + \frac{1}{2} \right)}{2} + \frac{1}{2} \right] = 1,$$

which ultimately yields $x = 7$.

To obtain this equation and then to solve it is quite difficult for most students. However, because we know they finished with one puppy, let's *work backwards*.

First of all, since it is impossible to sell half a puppy, we reason that all the numbers at each sale must be odd, to account for the extra "half puppy." Thus, if they had one puppy left, but gave half a puppy ($1\frac{1}{2}$) and sold half, there were two puppies sold to the Poodle Palace. (That is, $\left(\frac{1}{2} \right)(3) = 1\frac{1}{2}$ plus $\frac{1}{2} = 2$. This leaves one puppy.) Similarly, this $3 + \frac{1}{2}$ then doubled tells us that there were seven puppies in the original litter.

Once again, we can check our work by examining the problem from the beginning to see if our answer is correct. They began with seven puppies.

They sold half the litter $(3\frac{1}{2} + \frac{1}{2}$ puppy; $3\frac{1}{2} + \frac{1}{2} = 4)$, leaving them with three puppies. Now they sell half of the three puppies $(1\frac{1}{2})$ plus half a puppy $(1\frac{1}{2} + \frac{1}{2} = 2)$, leaving them with one puppy. Our answer of seven puppies in the litter is correct.

Problem 2.6

Jeremy's average (arithmetic mean) for 11 math tests is 80. His teacher announced that the students could eliminate any one of their test grades and then recompute their average. Jeremy eliminated the 30 he received on his first test. What is Jeremy's new average?

Solution

Frequently, students begin by guessing what the scores might have been to yield an average of 80 for 11 tests. Obviously, this technique is quite tedious, because so many different possibilities exist, and it may never yield the correct set of scores. Let's *work backwards* from the average to the sum of the 11 scores. Because the original arithmetic mean was 80, the sum of Jeremy's 11 scores must have been 880. We subtract the 30 from this total. Thus, his new average is $850 \div 10$ or 85.

Problem 2.7

Nancy breeds New Zealand rabbits as a hobby. During April, the number of rabbits increased by 10%. In May, 10 new rabbits were born, and at the end of May, Nancy sold one third of her herd. During June, 20 new rabbits were born, and at the end of June, Nancy sold one half of her total herd. So far in July, 5 rabbits have been born, and Nancy now has 55 rabbits. How many rabbits did Nancy start with on April 1?

Solution

We can begin with an algebraic approach. Let x represent the number of rabbits Nancy started with on April 1. Then,

$$x + \frac{x}{10} = \frac{11x}{10} = \text{ the number of rabbits at the end of April}$$

$$\left(\frac{2}{3}\right)\left(\frac{11x}{10} + 10\right) = \frac{22x}{30} + \frac{20}{3}$$

$$= \text{ the number of rabbits at the end of May}^2$$

---

2. Because Nancy sold one third of her herd, two thirds remained; hence, the leftmost term.

$$\left(\frac{1}{2}\right)\left(\frac{22x}{30}+\frac{20}{3}+20\right) = \text{the number of rabbits at the end of June}$$

$$\left(\frac{1}{2}\right)\left(\frac{22x}{30}+\frac{20}{3}+\frac{20}{1}\right)+5=55=\text{Nancy's total rabbits in July}$$

$$\left(\frac{1}{2}\right)\left(\frac{22x}{30}+\frac{20}{3}+20\right)=50$$

$$\left(\frac{22x}{30}+\frac{20}{3}+20\right)=100$$

$$\frac{22x}{30}+\frac{20}{3}=80$$

$$22x=2200$$

$$x=100.$$

Nancy started with 100 rabbits.

Notice that the problem tells us how many rabbits Nancy had at the end of the situation and we are asked to find how many she began with. Let's apply our *working backwards* strategy. We perform the inverse operations consecutively, working backwards:

$55-5=50$	(start of July)
$50 \times 2 = 100$	(June—sold $\frac{1}{2}$; therefore, must have been 100)
$100-20=80$	(20 were born in June—must have been 80)
120	(sold $\frac{1}{3}$; thus the 80 represents the $\frac{2}{3}$ she had, so we multiply by $\frac{3}{2}$)
110	(10 were born in May, so we subtract 10)
100	(to get to the start, we need to find the number, which when increased by 10% is 110; that number is 100).

Therefore, Nancy started with 100 rabbits. Be certain that your students check the accuracy of their work by working the problem forward from 100 rabbits to see if they do get 55 as the number she now has.

Problem 2.8

Using two egg timers, one of which runs for exactly 7 min and the other for exactly 11 min, show how to time the cooking of an egg for exactly 15 min.

Solution

The usual way that most students attempt to solve this problem is by trial and error. They aimlessly try various combinations of the 7- and 11-min timers to see how they can arrive at exactly 15 min. Although this might eventually yield the correct result, it is a difficult and time-consuming procedure to use.

To solve the problem, we will use the *working backwards* strategy. Consider the end result, 15 min. This can be obtained from consecutive timings of 11 and 4 min. We have an 11-min timer, but the 4 min presents a possible difficulty. How can we measure exactly 4 min? Since $11 - 7 = 4$, we begin the timing by starting both timers at the same time. When the 7-min timer rings, begin cooking the egg. This leaves exactly 4 min on the 11-min timer. After the 4 min have elapsed, restart the 11-min timer. When it finally rings, the egg will have cooked for exactly 15 min.

Problem 2.9

The RW Society has 100 members. One member has been notified that the Society's meeting place must be changed. This member activates the Society's telephone squad by telephoning 3 other members, each of whom then telephones another 3 members, and so on until all 100 RW Society members have been notified of the meeting place change. What is the greatest number of members of the RW Society who do not need to make a telephone call?

Solution

The typical response to this question is to simulate the action in the problem by counting. Students will begin to count systematically:

Member #1 calls 3 other members; total members contacted $= 4$.

Members #2, #3, and #4 each make three calls; total members contacted $= 4 + 9 = 13$.

Members #5 through #13 each make three calls; total members contacted $= 4 + 9 + 27 = 40$.

Members #14 through #33 each make three calls; total members contacted $= 4 + 9 + 27 + 60 = 40$.

Since 33 members had to make telephone calls to reach all 100 members, there were 67 members who did not have to make any calls.

This problem can be solved in a simpler way by *working backwards*. We know that after the first member has been contacted, there are 99 additional members who have to be contacted. This requires 33 members each making three telephone calls. This leaves 67 members who need not make any calls.

Problem 2.10

Frosia delivers prescriptions for the local pharmacy. On Tuesday, she delivered $\frac{5}{9}$ of the prescriptions already in the delivery van and then $\frac{3}{4}$ of the remaining prescriptions. After picking up 10 more prescriptions at the store, she delivered $\frac{2}{3}$ of those she had with her. She then picked up an additional 12 prescriptions and delivered $\frac{7}{8}$ of those she had in the van. Finally, she picked up 3 more and then delivered the remaining 5 prescriptions. How many prescriptions did she deliver?

Solution

The traditional solution is to formulate a series of equations by following through the action in the problem. This procedure is quite cumbersome and quite difficult.

A better approach is to use our *working backwards* strategy. If Frosia picked up 3 additional prescriptions and then had 5 prescriptions to deliver, there must have been 2 left in the van (this is the $\frac{1}{8}$ after delivering $\frac{7}{8}$). Thus, she delivered 14 (the $\frac{7}{8}$) and had a total of 16. Since she picked up 12, she had 4 (the $\frac{1}{3}$) remaining. This makes the $\frac{2}{3}$ a total of 8. This gives a total of 12 after she picked up 10. This result means that 2 (the $\frac{1}{4}$) remained, and the $\frac{3}{4}$ must have been 3 times as much or 6 prescriptions. Since she delivered $\frac{5}{9}$ of the prescriptions at first, there must have been $\frac{4}{9}$ or 8 remaining, and the $\frac{5}{9}$ was 10 prescriptions. If $\frac{5}{9}$ was 10, then $\frac{9}{5}$ of 10 is 18, the number of prescriptions Frosia started with. [In general, if $\frac{5}{9}x = 10$, then $x = \frac{9}{5}(10) = 18$.] Thus, Frosia picked up 10, 12, and 3, so the total delivered must have been $18 + 10 + 12 + 3 = 43$ prescriptions.

Problem 2.11

Parsifal came to a drawbridge that had a sign stating that the toll taker would double his money each time he crossed the bridge, but Parsifal would have to pay a fee of $1.20 per crossing. Parsifal decided to cross the bridge three times and see how the system worked. Sure enough, each time Parsifal crossed the bridge, the toll taker doubled his money, and then took $1.20 in toll charges. After the third crossing, Parsifal was surprised when he paid the $1.20 fee and found himself with no money. How much money did Parsifal start with?

Solution

Students would start with an algebraic approach as follows:

1. Let x represent the amount of money Parsifal started with.

2. Then, after the first crossing he would have $2x$ and pay 1.20, giving him $2x - 1.20$.

3. After the second crossing, he doubles his money, giving him $4x - 2.40$ and pays 1.20, giving him $4x - 3.60$.

4. After the third crossing, he again doubles his money, giving him $8x - 7.20$ and then pays 1.20, giving him $8x - 8.40$, which must equal 0;

$$8x - 8.40 = 0$$
$$8x = 8.40$$
$$x = 1.05.$$

Parsifal started with $1.05.

Of course, this approach requires a good background in algebra and the ability to keep careful track of each transaction as it occurs. Let's take another approach, namely, using the *working backwards* strategy. We set up a table to keep track of our work as we go through the transactions in reverse:

Transaction	Amount Left After Paying the Fee	Amount After Doubling Plus Fee	Amount He Started This Trip Across With
3	0	1.20	0.60
2	0.60	1.80	0.90
1	0.90	2.10	1.05

Thus, Parsifal started with $1.05 in his pocket.

Problem 2.12

An egg vendor delivering a shipment of eggs to a local store had an accident, and all his eggs were broken. He could not remember how many eggs he had in the delivery. However, he did remember that when he tried to pack them into packages of 2, he had one left over; when he tried to pack them in packages of 3, he had one left over; when he tried to pack them into packages of 4, he had one left over; when he tried to pack them into packages of 5, he had one left over; and when he tried to pack them into packages of 6, he had one left over. Nonetheless, when he packed them into packages of 7, he had none left over. What is the smallest number of eggs he could have had in the shipment?

Solution

A student typically begins by using a trial-and-error method, without much planning or forethought. Using the strategy of *working backwards*, however, may give structure and meaning to a problem, which may not be the case with a straightforward solution.

We should realize that if there is a remainder of 1 when dividing, then the number of eggs had to be a multiple of that divisor plus 1. Because we are looking for the smallest possible quantity of eggs the vendor had, we want to take the least common multiple of 2, 3, 4, 5, and 6, and then add 1 to it. If that number is exactly divisible by 7, our problem is solved.

The least common multiple of 2, 3, 4, 5, and 6 is 60, yet 61 is not divisible by 7. Consider the next larger common multiple, 121 (i.e., $2 \times 60 + 1$), and test its divisibility by 7. Continue this process sequentially with $3 \cdot 60 + 1 = 181, 4 \cdot 60 + 1 = 241$, and $5 \cdot 60 + 1 = 301$, which *is* finally divisible by 7. This solves our original problem: The merchant had 301 eggs.

Problem 2.13

Nim-type games are a broad category of games in which players alternately take away chips from a given "pot" and try to be the one who removes the final chip. Suppose the game is as follows: 32 chips are placed on the table between the two players. Each player, in turn, removes 1, 2, or 3 chips from the pot. The player who removes the final chip is the winner. What would be your strategy to win the game?

Solution

Students will usually begin this game by guessing the number of chips to remove each time it is their turn and testing their guesses to see if they actually win. This so-called strategy is not very helpful; it certainly does not guarantee success.

Instead, let's examine this problem using our *working backwards* strategy. Start at the end. Put yourself in the position of being the player whose turn it is to move, and there are 1, 2, or 3 chips left on the table. Obviously, you can take all of them and win the game. Now work backwards from this point. You should confront your opponent with 4 chips when it is his or her move; no matter how many are removed, you will have the 1, 2, or 3 chips you require to win. You cannot confront your opponent with 4 chips on your first move, so you must again work backwards from this point. If you leave your opponent with 8 chips on the previous turn, no matter how many are taken, you can take the correct number of chips to bring the number down to 4. Continuing in this manner, we see that to win the game you must leave your opponent with 12, 16, 20, 24, and 28 chips each time it is your turn. The *working backwards* strategy readily reveals the correct "play" to win the game.

Note that if we change the number of chips in the original problem to 31, then the first player can win by developing a similar strategy.

Problem 2.14

A merchant has five sections of a chain, each consisting of three silver links. He wishes to form one straight length of chain by connecting the five sections. It costs him 30¢ to open a link and 70¢ to close a link. Can he form the straight length of chain for just $3.00? If so, how? If not, why not?

Solution

At first glance, the problem appears to be impossible to solve, because it usually requires four links to connect five sections of a chain. Students begin by attempting various open-close combinations to see if they can fulfill the requirements of the problem. Notice, too, that the money is basically a distraction. We can *work backwards*, however, and ask ourselves the question, "Where is the merchant to get the links that will be used as the connectors for the sections of the chain?" These can only be obtained by using some of the links he already has. Thus, if he uses the three links that form one section as the connectors, they can be used to connect the four sections that will remain. Thus, he opens three links, costing him $3 \times 30\cancel{c} = 90\cancel{c}$, and then closes three links as follows:

One link connects sections 1 and 2 (cost: $70\cancel{c}$).

One link connects section 3 to 1-2 (cost: $70\cancel{c}$).

One link connects section 4 to 1-2-3 (cost: $70\cancel{c}$).

This completes the chain for the required $3.00 ($3 \times 70\cancel{c} + 3 \times 30\cancel{c} = \$3.00$).

Note: A slightly different version of this problem can be simply solved by using another strategy. Refer to Problem 4.16.

Problem 2.15

Construct a triangle (using a straightedge and compasses) given the lengths of its three medians.

Solution

This problem was selected from a list of 179 such possible constructions of triangles given three of its "parts."[3] Our reason for selecting this particular problem is not that it is the most typical or that it is the easiest of the lot; rather, we selected it because it demonstrates the *working backwards* strategy of problem solving quite dramatically. In addition, the solution is rather interesting as an example that shows some useful geometric thinking.

When we consider the problem, that is, the triangle to be constructed, it is natural to look at the finished (or end) product.

---

3. By "parts" of a triangle, we refer to its sides, angles, medians, angle bisectors, altitudes, in radius, and circumradius. In some cases, the triangle can be determined by using sets of three of these parts. For a more complete discussion of this sort of construction problem, as well as many other types of geometric constructions, see Posamentier, A. S. (2002). *Advanced Euclidean Geometry.* Emeryville, CA: Key College Publishing.

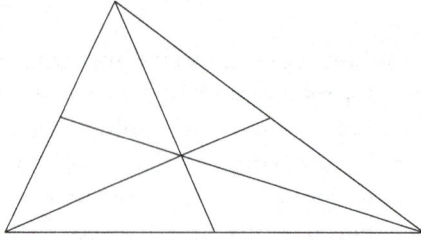

Figure 2.5

We can draw each of the three medians, because we are given their length, but we have no way to determine at which angle they meet the side to which they are drawn or what angle size they make with each other. Here, we can use a clever scheme, namely, extending one of the three medians one third of its length through the midpoint of the side to which it is drawn.

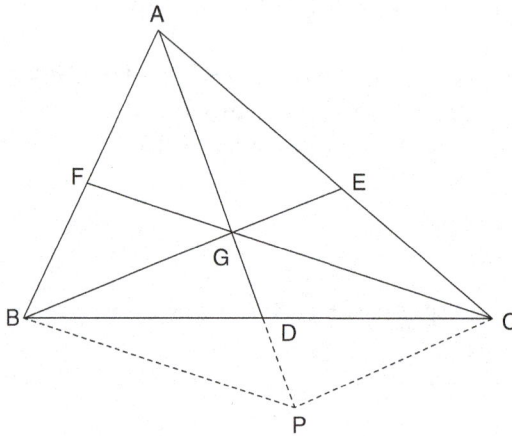

Figure 2.6

This creates quadrilateral BGCP, which is a parallelogram because its diagonals bisect each other. △ GPC is easily constructable because each of its sides is two thirds the length of each of the three medians. Using the traditional method, we construct this triangle and then extend $\overline{CG}$ by half its own length to locate point F. Then, extend $\overline{PG}$ by its own length to point A. Finally, we can construct △ ABC by drawing $\overline{AF}$ and extending it by its own length to locate point B. Now having located the points A, B, and C, we have essentially constructed the triangle, the length of whose medians were given.

The *working backwards* approach was essential in this problem, as it is in many such geometric construction problems, which, by the way, provide a very rich source of genuine problem-solving experiences.

Problem 2.16

The rational fraction in lowest terms, $\frac{N}{D}$, is equivalent to the infinitely repeating decimal $1.26\overline{6}$. Find the fraction $\frac{N}{D}$.

Solution

Rather than puzzle out the fraction that yields the given infinitely repeating decimal, we *work backwards* by "dismantling" the decimal expression[4]:

$$1.26\overline{6} = 1.2 + 0.06\overline{6} = 1.2 + \frac{6}{90} = \frac{6}{5} + \frac{6}{90}$$
$$= \frac{(6)(18)}{(5)(18)} + \frac{6}{90} = \frac{(6)(19)}{90} = \frac{19}{15}.$$

Problem 2.17

Jimmy, Ronald, George, and Bill spent the afternoon picking apples, which they put into a large box. They were so tired from their labors that they went to sleep early that evening. During the night, Jimmy awoke, took $\frac{1}{4}$ of the apples from the box, put them into his pack, and went back to sleep. Later, Ronald awoke, took $\frac{1}{4}$ of the apples from the box, put them into his pack, and went back to sleep. Later, George awoke, took $\frac{1}{4}$ of the apples in the box, and put them into his pack. He, too, went back to sleep. Finally, just before daylight, Bill awoke, took $\frac{1}{4}$ of the apples from the box, put them into his pack, and woke the other three boys. They counted the apples and found 81 apples in the box. How many apples had they picked?

Solution

We can write an equation to find the number of apples as follows:

We let x represent the number of apples originally picked and placed in the box.

Then Jimmy took $\frac{1}{4}$ of x, leaving $\frac{3}{4}$ of x in the box.

Ronald then took $\frac{1}{4}$ of the $\frac{3}{4}$ of x that remained, leaving $\frac{3}{4}$ of $\frac{3}{4}$ of x.

Then George took $\frac{1}{4}$ of the $\frac{3}{4}$ of the $\frac{3}{4}$ of x that remained.

---

4. Students should be familiar with the traditional way to convert infinitely repeating decimals to common fractions. In this case, let $x = 0.06\overline{6}$. Then, $10x = 0.6\overline{6}$ and $100x = 6.6\overline{6}$. By subtraction, we get $90x = 6$ and $x = \frac{6}{90}$.

Finally, Bill took $\frac{1}{4}$ of the $\frac{3}{4}$ of the $\frac{3}{4}$ of the $\frac{3}{4}$ of x that remained.

Thus,

$$\frac{3}{4}\frac{3}{4}\frac{3}{4}\frac{3}{4}(x) = 81$$

$$\frac{81x}{256} = 81$$

$$x = 256.$$

They picked 256 apples.

Although this procedure seems satisfactory, finding the correct equation can prove difficult for some students. Let's use the *working backwards* strategy.

Bill left 81 apples after taking $\frac{1}{4}$. This was $\frac{3}{4}$ of the apple sum; therefore, $\frac{4}{4} = 108$.

George left 108 apples after taking $\frac{1}{4}$. This was $\frac{3}{4}$ of the apple sum; therefore, $\frac{4}{4} = 144$.

Ronald left 144 apples after taking $\frac{1}{4}$. This was $\frac{3}{4}$ of the apple sum; therefore, $\frac{4}{4} = 192$.

Jimmy left 192 apples after taking $\frac{1}{4}$. This was $\frac{3}{4}$ of the apple sum; therefore, $\frac{4}{4} = 256$.

They began with 256 apples.

Problem 2.18

Which is larger, $\sqrt[9]{9!}$ or $\sqrt[10]{10!}$?

Solution

Using an algebraic method to prove the general case for this situation entails proving that $\sqrt[n+1]{(n+1)!} > \sqrt[n]{n!}$. Although it is a bit tedious, we provide this proof here (also you can then better compare it with the problem-solving strategy we offer as an alternative). Whereas $\sqrt[n+1]{n+1} > \sqrt[n+1]{n}$, $\sqrt[n+1]{n!(n+1)} > \sqrt[n+1]{n!n}$ (multiplying by $\sqrt[n+1]{n!}$); that is, $\sqrt[n+1]{(n+1)!} > \sqrt[n+1]{n!n}$.

Whereas $n^n > n!$ for $n > 1$, $n > \sqrt[n]{n!}$. Therefore, $n!n > n!(n!)^{1/n} = (n!)^{(n+1)/n}$ and $\sqrt[n+1]{n!n} > \sqrt[n]{n!}$. Thus, $\sqrt[n+1]{(n+1)!} > \sqrt[n+1]{n!n} > \sqrt[n]{n!}$.

As an alternative to this rather difficult proof, we can *work backwards*, that is, we begin with what we want to establish. Let us start by taking both terms to a common power, namely, the 90th power:

$$\left(\sqrt[9]{9!}\right)^{90} \quad ? \quad \left(\sqrt[10]{10!}\right)^{90}$$
$$(9!)^{10} \quad ? \quad (10!)^9$$
$$(9!)^9(9!) \quad ? \quad (9!)^9(10)^9$$
$$9! < 10^9.$$

Therefore, $\sqrt[9]{9!} < \sqrt[10]{10!}$.

Problem 2.19

Consider a scalene triangle with a 120° angle and all three of its angle bisectors drawn as seen in the figure below. We must prove that the segments joining the feet of the angle bisectors, $\overline{FE}$ and $\overline{DE}$, are perpendicular.

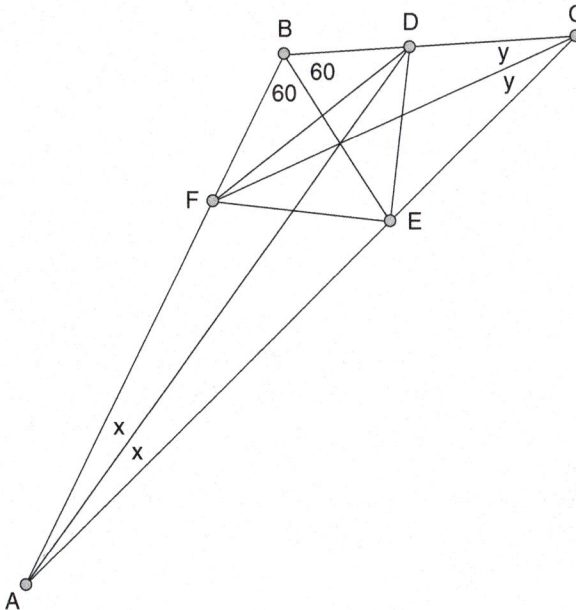

Figure 2.7

Solution

We leave this as the last problem in the section, since without the *working backwards* strategy, the problem is exceedingly difficult. Moreover, it is not typical of the type of problem offered in the high school geometry course, because it does not involve congruence.

Let us begin by inspecting the end result and then work backwards in our analysis. Only then can we write our conclusion in the forward direction. The segments $\overline{FE}$ and $\overline{DE}$ would be perpendicular if they each would bisect the two supplementary angles ∠AEB and ∠CEB. But how can we show that either one is an angle bisector? Could we show that a point say, F, is equidistant from the sides of the angle AEB? Let's pursue this tack.

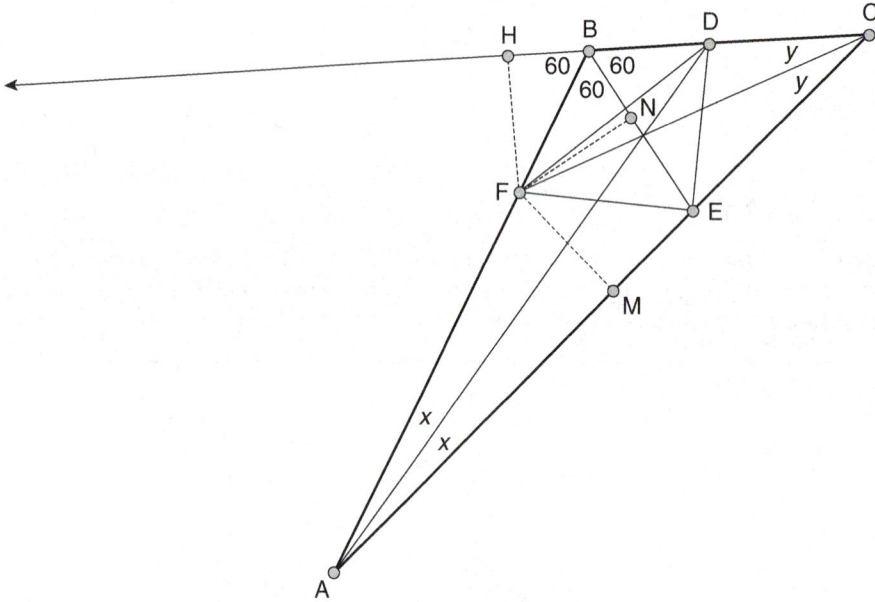

Figure 2.8

Extend $\overline{CB}$ to point H where $\overline{FH} \perp \overline{CH}$. Because of the angle bisector property for ∠EBH, $FH = FN$ (where $\overline{FN} \perp \overline{BE}$). We shall draw $\overline{FM} \perp \overline{AC}$, and since $\overline{FC}$ is the angle bisector of ∠ACB, then $FM = FH$. Therefore, $FM = FN$. Thus, $\overline{FE}$ is also an angle bisector, since one of its points, F, is equidistant from the sides of the angle.

In a similar manner, we can show that $\overline{DE}$ is the angle bisector of ∠BEC. It then follows that ∠FED is a right angle, since the sum of its two parts is one-half of a straight angle.

$$3$$

Finding a Pattern

One of the inherent beauties of mathematics is the logic and order that it exudes. This logic can be seen "physically" as a pattern or as a series of patterns. In fact, mathematician W. W. Sawyer once said that mathematics is a search for patterns. The nonmathematician often appreciates geometry for the patterns it provides. The mathematician uses patterns as an aid to solving problems in geometry, as well as in many other fields. In the secondary school curriculum, we see mathematics problems that clearly require pattern recognition for their solution. For example, to find the next two numbers[1] in the sequence 1, 3, 4, 7, 11, 18, _, _, we must first search for and then recognize a pattern. One possible pattern has each number after the first two as the sum of the two preceding numbers. Recognizing that this is an example of a Fibonacci-type sequence (known as the Lucas numbers) leads to the next two numbers, namely, 29 and 47. It is true that there may be more sophisticated (and more cumbersome) ways to find the immediate successors of 18 in the given sequence. Now consider finding the next two terms in the sequence 1, 10, 2, 7, 3, 4, 4, _, _. It is very unlikely that this can be resolved in any way other than by recognizing that this sequence is actually two separate sequences interwoven. One sequence is from the numbers in the odd positions: 1, 2, 3, and 4 (a difference of +1). The other is formed by the numbers in the even positions: 10, 7, 4 (a difference of −3). Thus, the next two terms would be 1 and 5.

---

1. Although our wording implies that there are specific numbers to be found, note that there may be sequences that may be correctly continued in a variety of ways. You will soon see this with the sequence 1, 2, 4, 8, 16, _, where both 32 and 31 can be used correctly.

These are problems whose resolution is, by their very nature, one of pattern recognition. In these cases, the use of pattern seeking was announced by the type of problem. We consider problems in this chapter, however, where pattern recognition is not expected, yet proves to be an invaluable aid to solving the given problem more simply than the traditional or common solution method.

We must caution our students that *finding a pattern* within a given sequence of numbers does not always lead to a unique "next term." For example, consider the sequence 1, 2, 4, 8, 16, ... The next number, according to most people, would be 32, which is obtained by doubling each number to arrive at its successor or by using the general term $2^{(n-1)}$ to generate the terms of the given sequence. However, we could argue mathematically (and legitimately, as well) that the next number could (or should) be 31, followed by 57 and 99. This sequence, embedded in the Pascal triangle (Figure 3.1), also represents the number of regions into which a circle may be partitioned by increasing the number of joined points on the circle.

```
                    1                          =   1
                  1   1                        =   2
                1   2   1                      =   4
              1   3   3   1                    =   8
            1   4   6   4   1                  =  16
          1   5  10  10   5   1                =  31
        1   6  15  20  15   6   1              =  57
      1   7  21  35  35  21   7   1            =  99
    1   8  28  56  70  56  28   8   1          = 163
  1   9  36  84 126 126  84  36   9   1        = 256
```

Figure 3.1

THE *FINDING A PATTERN* STRATEGY IN EVERYDAY LIFE PROBLEM-SOLVING SITUATIONS

We often use patterns or seek to form patterns to help us remember numbers (combination locks, license plates, telephone numbers, etc.). We may discover different patterns for the same set of numbers, yet these patterns (or mnemonic devices) are helpful tools to aid our memory. Discovering patterns can also be useful to navigate city streets by car. When driving through a city where most of the streets lie on a rectangular grid, an astute driver tries to avoid red lights as much as possible. Often pattern recognition is used to avoid these stoplights. Noting a pattern can be a way to minimize waiting time. If we assume that the lights are in synchronization either as a "green wave" or in groups of x lights at a time, we can determine when it is best to change paths or when to continue along the same one and when to speed up or when to slow down.

When searching for an address, we very often seek to establish a pattern among the house numbers along a street. Most streets have the odd-numbered houses on one side and the even-numbered houses on the other. This establishes a pattern. Furthermore, in one direction the numbers increase, and in the other direction the numbers decrease. Again, a pattern!

Another pattern is often sought when trying to determine how many blocks one has to travel to reach a particular address. That is, some address numbers are hyphenated where the cross street is the first part of the address number. Other types of patterns also exist, such as the dead-end street or courtyard, where the numbers begin on one side starting from the open end and continue around the dead end, back consecutively on the other side of the street. In all these situations, we are required to search for the various patterns so that we can find a sought-after address.

In most cities, when one of the local sports teams wins a championship, a parade is usually held in its honor. The police keep a record of previous parades, the patterns of alcohol consumption by those attending (depending on the time of year), patterns of crowd behavior, and the impact of the weather on the parade. As a result of these patterns, they are able to deploy their officers in such a way as to maximize crowd control.

The police often make use of the finding a pattern strategy in other ways too. For example, when the police are confronted by a series of crimes (e.g., robberies), they often try to find a pattern in the crimes: They look for a *modus operandi* that might lead them to a particular criminal.

Scientists involved in medical research often use the finding a pattern strategy to locate and isolate similar variables and, thus, draw conclusions about the particular virus or bacteria they are examining.

Even in everyday school situations, we are involved in finding patterns. We often see recurring patterns of behavior in certain children, which may indicate the need for extra attention or extra help. In some extreme cases, the patterns of behavior reveal the possible presence of attention deficit disorder, which requires special help or even medication.

A game that we have frequently played with children is the "likes... dislikes" game. In this game, the leader (usually the teacher) gives the students several items (in this case, food) that they "like" as well as several they "dislike." It is the students' task to determine where to place additional items, by discovering why certain items fall into their respective categories. Thus, we might say that we like apples, but dislike fruit; we like cookies, but dislike cake; we like pizza, but dislike tomatoes; we like vanilla ice cream, but dislike chocolate ice cream. We then ask the children to categorize roast beef, cabbage, duck, candy, rolls, bagels, strawberries, and so forth. The students must discover the pattern being used—in this case, foods with double letters are those liked.

The power of pattern recognition is best seen, however, when the strategy can be used to solve a problem where the nature of the problem is such that it is not obvious that the solution can be significantly simplified by seeking a pattern.

APPLYING THE *FINDING A PATTERN* STRATEGY TO SOLVE MATHEMATICS PROBLEMS

Consider the following problem:

> Determine the sum of the measures of the interior angles of an icosagon (a 20-sided polygon).

Aside from referring to a formula (the derivation of which is in itself dependent on pattern recognition), the most efficient way to solve this problem is to examine polygons of increasing number of sides and their corresponding angle measure sums. Do they form a pattern? Is it easily recognizable? Can we generalize it? Can we extend it? Let's begin with a triangle (interior angle sum 180°) and then consider each of the polygons with successively increased numbers of sides, that is, quadrilateral, pentagon, hexagon, and so forth. We find that we can triangulate the polygons by drawing lines from one vertex to each of the other vertices (see Figure 3.2). When we do this, we notice that each successive polygon includes one more triangle than its predecessor.

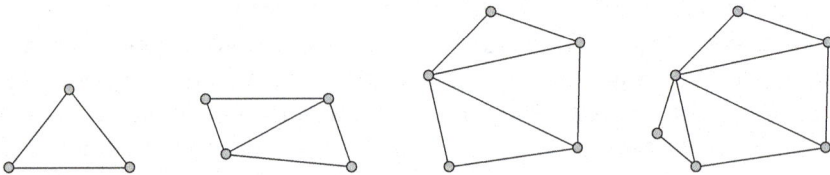

Figure 3.2

This yields a pattern that can help us to our desired goal. These angle sums should be put into tabular form so as to make it easier to recognize a pattern. This shows how a geometric pattern yields a numerical pattern (Figure 3.3).

Number of sides	3	4	5	6	7	8	9	...	20
Number of triangles	1	2	3	4	5	6	7	...	18
Angle measure sum	180	360	540	720	900	1,080	1,260	...	3,240

Figure 3.3

An inspection of the first seven entries (although we really didn't need that many) shows a pattern; namely, when the number of sides increased by 1, the number of triangles increased by 1 and the angle sum increased by 180°. Thus, for a nonagon (9-sided polygon), the number of triangles formed would be 7 and the angle sum would be $7 \times 180° = 1{,}260°$. Using this pattern, we could work our way up to the 20-sided polygon we seek using the pattern of increments of 180°. Alternatively, we could recognize the pattern as one that implies that the angle measure sum will always be 180 times a number that is 2 less than the number of sides. Thus, for the icosagon, the angle measure sum is $18 \times 180° = 3{,}240°$.

Although it was not obvious from the outset that *finding a pattern* was necessary or even useful, we have used this strategy to solve this problem. As with the earlier problems, identifying a pattern and then using it to discover the answer to the question asked proves to be very efficient. Notice also that solving the problem involves more than a single strategy. In addition to *recognizing a pattern*, we also used *visual representation (making a drawing)*, *organizing the data*, and *solving a simpler version* of the original problem. This should remind you that a single strategy is usually not sufficient to solve a problem.

Furthermore, we could have solved this problem by considering it from a *different point of view*. The sum of the exterior angles measures of any polygon is 360°. We can consider a simpler version of the problem without any loss of generality, namely, we can consider a *regular* icosagon. Here, each exterior angle has a measure $\frac{360°}{20} = 18°$. The interior angle is its supplement or 162°. To get the sum of the interior angles, we merely multiply by 20 to get $20 \times 162° = 3{,}240°$.

PROBLEMS USING THE
FINDING A PATTERN STRATEGY

Problem 3.1

Find the units digit of 8^{19}.

Solution

Many of your students will attack this problem by entering the powers of 8 into their calculators. Soon they will realize that most calculators do not permit them to arrive at an answer, because the display will run out of digit space before they reach their goal. Thus, we must look for another approach.

Let's examine the increasing powers of 8 and see if there is a *pattern* that we can use:

$$8^1 = \underline{8}$$
$$8^2 = 6\underline{4}$$
$$8^3 = 51\underline{2}$$
$$8^4 = 4{,}09\underline{6}$$
$$8^5 = 32{,}76\underline{8}$$
$$8^6 = 262{,}14\underline{4}$$
$$8^7 = 2{,}097{,}15\underline{2}$$
$$8^8 = 16{,}777{,}21\underline{6}.$$

Notice the pattern that emerges—the units digits repeat in cycles of four. Now we can apply this pattern rule to our original problem. The exponent we are interested in is 19, which gives a remainder of 3 when divided by 4. Thus, the terminal digit of 8^{19} should be the same as that of $8^{15}, 8^{11}, 8^7, 8^3$, which we recognize as 2.

Note: This same kind of problem can be used to illustrate the *solve a simpler analogous problem* strategy. This serves to reemphasize the fact that students often use more than one strategy to solve a problem.

Problem 3.2

Find the units digit for the sum $13^{25} + 4^{81} + 5^{411}$.

Solution

This problem is similar to the previous one. Again, some students will attempt to solve this problem by using their calculators. This is a formidable task, and a student error can usually be expected. Once again, let's use the *looking for a pattern* strategy. Students must examine the patterns that exist in the powers of three different sets of numbers. Practice in doing this will help familiarize them with the cyclical pattern for the final digits of the powers of numbers.

For powers of 13, we obtain

$$13^1 = 1\underline{3}$$
$$13^2 = 16\underline{9}$$
$$13^3 = 2{,}19\underline{7}$$
$$13^4 = 28{,}56\underline{1}$$
$$13^5 = 371{,}29\underline{3}$$
$$13^6 = 4{,}826{,}80\underline{9}$$

$$13^7 = 62{,}748{,}51\underline{7}$$
$$13^8 = 725{,}731{,}72\underline{1}.$$

The units digits for powers of 13 repeat as 3, 9, 7, 1, 3, 9, 7, 1,..., in cycles of four. Thus, 13^{25} has the same units digit as 13^1, which is 3.

For powers of 4, we obtain

$$4^1 = \underline{4}$$
$$4^2 = 1\underline{6}$$
$$4^3 = 6\underline{4}$$
$$4^4 = 25\underline{6}$$
$$4^5 = 1{,}02\underline{4}$$
$$4^6 = 4{,}09\underline{6}$$
$$4^7 = 16{,}38\underline{4}$$
$$4^8 = 65{,}53\underline{6}.$$

The units digits for powers of 4 repeat as 4, 6, 4, 6, 4, 6,..., in cycles of two. Thus, 4^{81} has the same units digit as 4^1, which is 4.

The units digit for powers of 5 must be 5 (i.e., $\underline{5}$, $2\underline{5}$, $12\underline{5}$, $62\underline{5}$, etc.).

The sum we are looking for is $3 + 4 + 5 = 12$, which has a units digit of 2.

You might suggest to your students that they examine the cyclical nature of the units digits when raising any number to powers. Are the powers of all single-digit numbers cyclical? What are the cycles?

Problem 3.3

We have a function machine that operates *only* on the given number and no other. Thus, if we input 3, the machine can operate only on 3s. The machine uses the four fundamental operations of arithmetic (addition, subtraction, multiplication, and division) either alone or in combination. Here are the first six outputs for inputs of $x = 1$ through 6:

Input (x)	Output
1	1
2	9
3	29
4	67
5	129
6	221

What is the value if we input 9?

Solution

Most students begin this problem by attempting to guess the function rule. This is a very difficult and time-consuming task. However, the problem can be solved by using the *looking for a pattern* strategy together with some reasoning to determine what the function machine is doing when we input a number. The output appears to be close to the cube of the input number. That is,

Input (x)	Output	x^3	Difference (From x^3)
1	1	1	0
2	9	8	$+1$ or $(2-1)$
3	29	27	$+2$ or $(3-1)$
4	67	64	$+3$ or $(4-1)$
5	129	125	$+4$ or $(5-1)$
6	221	216	$+5$ or $(6-1)$
$\vdots$	$\vdots$	$\vdots$	$\vdots$
x		x^3	$+(x-1)$

However, because our output can contain only the input number, we must express x^3 as $x \times x \times x$ and $(x-1)$ as $(x - \frac{x}{x})$. Thus, our output rule for input of x seems to be $x \times x \times x + (x - \frac{x}{x})$, and the answer to our problem is $9 \times 9 \times 9 + (9 - \frac{9}{9}) = 9^3 + 8 = 729 + 8 = 737$.

Problem 3.4

Find the sum of the first 20 odd numbers.

Solution

The 20th odd number is 39. Thus, we wish to find the sum of $1 + 3 + 5 + 7 + \cdots + 33 + 35 + 37 + 39$. Of course, some students may decide to solve this problem by simply writing out all the odd numbers from 1 through 39 and actually adding them. Alternatively, they can punch these same numbers into a calculator one at a time and arrive at the sum. At best, however, this method is extremely cumbersome and time consuming, and there are numerous possibilities for error.

Some students might apply the *looking for a pattern* strategy in a manner similar to the way we believe young Carl Friedrich Gauss did when he was in elementary school. This involves listing the 20 odd numbers as 1, 3, 5, 7, 9, ..., 33, 35, 37, 39. Now notice that the sum of the 1st and 20th numbers is $39 + 1 = 40$, the sum of the 2nd and 19th numbers is also $40(37 + 3)$, and so on. This then requires determining how many 40s to add. Because there were 20 numbers under consideration, we have 10 pairs, and we multiply $10 \times 40 = 400$ to get the answer.

We can examine this problem by *looking for a pattern*, but in a different manner:

Addends	Number of Addends	Sum
1	1	1
1 + 3	2	4
1 + 3 + 5	3	9
1 + 3 + 5 + 7	4	16
1 + 3 + 5 + 7 + 9	5	25
1 + 3 + 5 + 7 + 9 + 11	6	36

The table reveals quite clearly that the sum of the first n odd numbers is n^2. Thus, the answer to our problem is simply $20^2 = 400$.

Problem 3.5

Find the sum of the first 100 even numbers.

Solution

As we suggested in the previous problem, students may wish to write out the first 100 even numbers and add them in the order written:

$$2 + 4 + 6 + 8 + \cdots + 194 + 196 + 198 + 200.$$

This can be done with a calculator, or they can be clever and add in pairs, recognizing that there is a pattern:

$$2 + 200 = 202$$
$$4 + 198 = 202$$
$$6 + 196 = 202,$$

and so on. There will be 50 pairs whose sum is 202. Thus, the sum of the first 100 even numbers would be $50 \times 202 = 10,100$.

As an alternative approach, let's make use of the *looking for a pattern* strategy, but in a different and far less expected way. One might even say that this is looking at the problem from *a different point of view*:

Number of Even Numbers to Be Added		Sum	
1	2	= 2	= 1 × 2
2	2 + 4	= 6	= 2 × 3
3	2 + 4 + 6	= 12	= 3 × 4
4	2 + 4 + 6 + 8	= 20	= 4 × 5
⋮	⋮		
n	2 + 4 + 6 + 8 + ⋯ + n		= $n(n+1)$

Thus, for the first 100 even numbers, the sum would be $(100)(101) = 10,100$. In both cases, the notion of *looking for a pattern* was particularly useful for solving this problem.

Problem 3.6

A map of a local town is shown in Figure 3.4. Billy lives at the corner of 4th Street and Fairfield Avenue. Betty lives at the corner of 8th Street and Appleton Avenue. Billy decides that he will visit Betty once a day until he has tried every different route to her house. The streets only run east and north. How many different routes can Billy take to get to Betty's house if he can only go east or north?

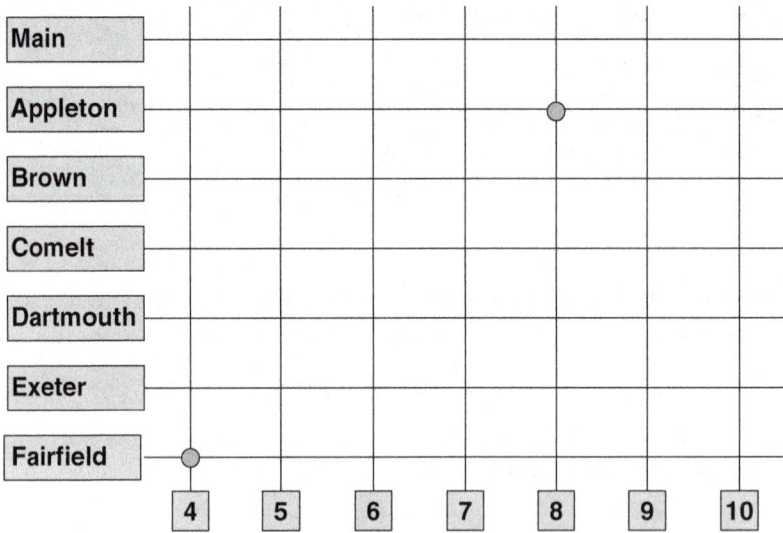

Figure 3.4

Solution

Traditionally, many students' first attempt is to try to draw all the possible routes and count how many there are. This will not be an easy task, and some ways are certain to be omitted. Other students may recognize that there are four east streets and five north streets to be traveled. Thus, they look for all the possible arrangements of the five north streets and the four east streets. At this point, many students begin to list them all:

EENNEENNN   NENENENEN   NNNENNEEE . . .

Obviously, there are too many to list.

Some students may recognize that this problem is similar to the traditional textbook exercise, "How many arrangements of the letters in the word 'Mississippi' are possible?" These students are trying to find how many arrangements of the letters EEEENNNNN (nine total, four Es, five Ns) are possible, and will set up the expression

$$\frac{9!}{4!5!},$$

which equals 126.

Let's see how we can solve this problem with the *looking for a pattern* strategy. To do this, we must combine this strategy with the strategy of *solving a simpler analogous problem*. Suppose we consider the simpler problem that Betty's house is at the corner of 5th and Fairfield. There is only one way for Billy to get there. Similarly, if Betty's house were "moved" to 6th and Fairfield, there would be only one way for Billy to get there. The same is true if we "move" Betty's house to any point on Fairfield or to any point on 4th—exactly one way. Now consider the number of different routes there are if we "move" Betty's house to Exeter and 5th—there are only two ways. "Move" the house to Exeter and 6th—three ways (the same as if it were "moved" to Dartmouth and 5th). We now consider how many routes there would be if Betty's house were "moved" to each of the grid points in turn (see Figure 3.5).

1	6	21	56	126
1	5	15	35	70
1	4	10	20	35
1	3	6	10	15
1	2	3	4	5
	1	1	1	1

Figure 3.5

Notice that these numbers form the coefficients of the Pascal triangle (see Figure 3.6). Once we recognize the pattern, the answer is readily found, namely, 126 ways.

```
                              1
                          1       1
                      1       2       1
                  1       3       3       1
              1       4       6       4       1
          1       5      10      10       5       1
      1       6      15      20      15       6       1
    1     7      21      35      35      21       7      1
  1     8     28      56      70      56      28      8     1
1     9     36     84     126    [126]    84      36     9     1
```

Figure 3.6

Problem 3.7

How many digits are there in the expression $(111,111,111)^2$? What is the middle digit?

Solution

Some students may attempt to "beat the problem to death," that is, actually perform the indicated multiplication. This can be done, but requires extreme care, because the typical student calculator does not accept a nine-digit number.

Let's see if we can solve this problem by *looking for a pattern*:

1 digit	1^2	$= 1$	$= 1$ digit; middle digit $= 1$
2 digits	11^2	$= 121$	$= 3$ digits; middle digit $= 2$
3 digits	111^2	$= 12321$	$= 5$ digits; middle digit $= 3$
4 digits	1111^2	$= 1234321$	$= 7$ digits; middle digit $= 4$
$\vdots$	$\vdots$	$\vdots$	$\vdots$
9 digits	$111,111,111^2$	$= 12345678987654321$	$= 17$ digits; middle digit $= 9$

There are 17 digits in the product; the middle digit is 9.

Although the symmetry of the original problem seemed to imply the presence of a pattern, it still was not an obvious method of approach. Only through practice will students try to find a pattern as a possible method of solution.

Problem 3.8

How many pairs of vertical angles are formed by 10 distinct lines, concurrent through a point?

Solution

Students often attempt to draw a large, accurate figure showing the 10 concurrent lines. They then attempt to actually count the pairs of vertical angles. This is rather confusing, however, and they can easily lose track of the pairs of angles under examination.

Instead, we can make use of our *search for a pattern* strategy. Let's start with a simpler case, gradually expand the number of lines, and see if a pattern emerges.

If we start with one line, we get 0 pairs of vertical angles.

Two lines produce 2 pairs of angles: 1-3 and 2-4 (Figure 3.7a).

Three lines produce 6 pairs of angles: 1-4; 2-5; 3-6; 1, 2-4, 5; 2, 3-5, 6; 1, 6-3, 4 (Figure 3.7b).

Four lines produces 12 pairs of vertical angles: 1-5; 2-6; 3-7; 4-8; 1, 2-5, 6; 2, 3-6, 7; 3, 4-7, 8; 4, 5-8, 1; 1, 2, 3-5, 6, 7; 2, 3, 4-6, 7, 8; 3, 4, 5-7, 8, 1; 4, 5, 6-8, 1, 2 (Figure 3.7c).

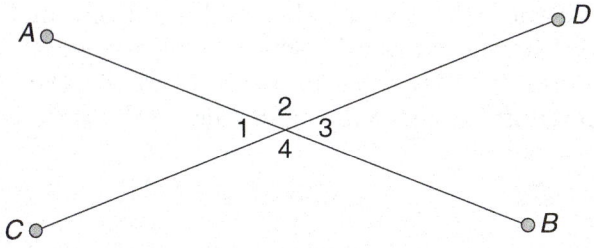

(a)

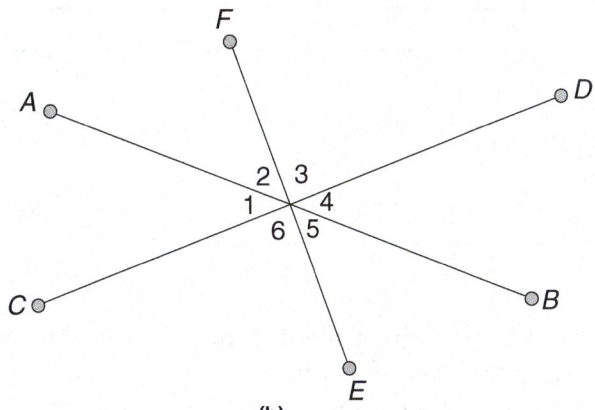

(b)

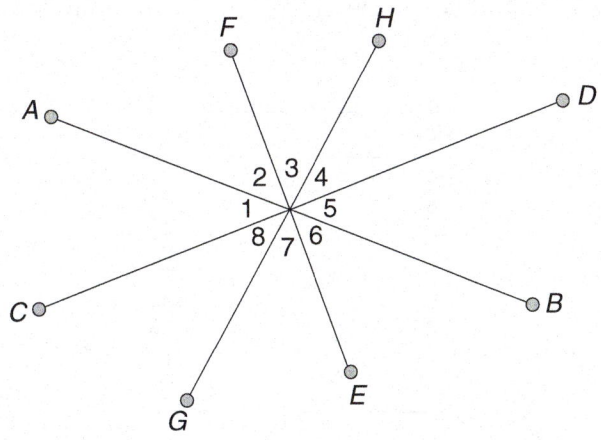

(c)

Figure 3.7

We can now summarize the data in a table:

Number of lines	1	2	3	4	5	$\cdots$	n
Pairs of vertical angles	0	2	6	12	20	$\cdots$	$n(n-1)$

Thus, for 10 distinct lines, there will be $10(9) = 90$ pairs of vertical angles.

Notice that we can also consider this problem from another point of view. Each pair of lines produces 2 pairs of vertical angles. Thus, we ask how many selections of 2 lines can be made from 10? The answer is, of course, $_{10}C_2 = 45$. Thus, we get 45×2 or 90 pairs of vertical angles.

Problem 3.9

What is the sum of the numbers in the 25th row of the following array?

```
                            1
                      3           5
                  7         9          11
             13        15        17        19
        21        23        25        27        29
   31        33        35        37        39        41
```

Solution

Students can continue writing the odd numbers in the array until they reach the 25th row, and then find the sum of the 25 addends. However, this is rather awkward and requires a great deal of patience (not to mention a great deal of paper!). It would be easier to examine this array and *look for a pattern* that governs the entries. Let's summarize each row with a table:

Row	Sum
1	1
2	8
3	27
4	64
5	125
6	216
$\vdots$	$\vdots$
n	n^3

Therefore, in the 25th row, the sum of the 25 entries would be $25^3 = 15{,}625$.

Problem 3.10

The first 6 "terms" in a sequence are shown in Figure 3.8. If the sequence continues in this manner, how many squares will there be in the 10th term and how many of these squares will be shaded?

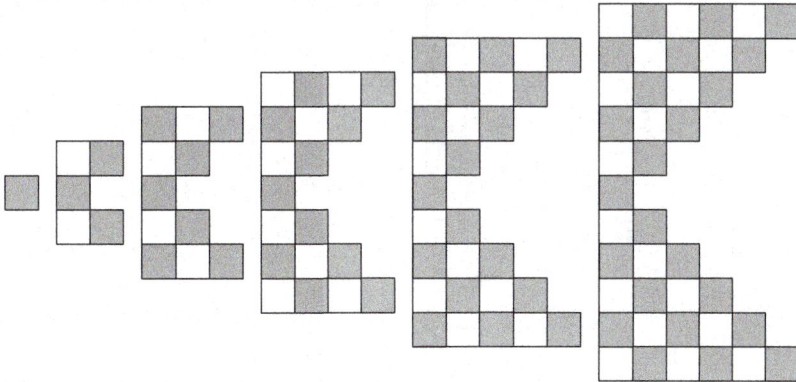

Figure 3.8

Solution

We could, of course, continue to draw the figures, adding rows on top and bottom as we do, until we obtain the 10th drawing in the sequence. We would then simply count how many squares there are and how many of them are shaded. However, if we organize our data in a table, we can use the strategy of *searching for a pattern* to see if a pattern exists that might help us solve the problem. Let's summarize the data we have in a table:

"Term" number	1	2	3	4	5	6
Total number	1	5	11	19	29	41
Number shaded	1	3	7	11	17	23

Let's first look at the total number of squares. There is a pattern here. The differences between the terms are 4, 6, 8, 10, ... In other words, $1+4=5$, $5+6=11$, $11+8=19$, $19+10=29$, and so on. Now let's examine the number shaded row. Note that the differences between the terms form a different pattern: 2, 4, 4, 6, 6, ... We can now complete our table up to 10 terms:

"Term" number	1	2	3	4	5	6	7	8	9	10
Total number	1	5	11	19	29	41	55	71	89	109
Number shaded	1	3	7	11	17	23	31	39	49	59
Differences		2	4	4	6	6	8	8	10	10

There will be 109 squares in the 10th figure and 59 of them will be shaded.

We can check our work by drawing the 7th figure and checking our pattern (see Figure 3.9). Do we, indeed, get 55 squares, 31 of which are shaded? Yes. Thus, we may conclude that the pattern we have found does work.

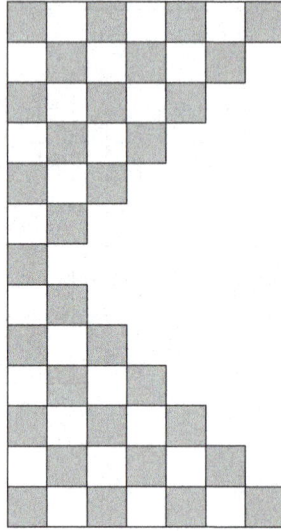

Figure 3.9

Problem 3.11

If we continue writing the integers from 2 through 1,000 in the following table, in which column will the number 1,000 fall?

A	B	C	D	E	F	G	H
	2		3		4		5
9		8		7		6	
	10		11		12		13
17		16		15		14	
	18		19		20		21
25		24		23		22	
	26		27		28		29
				...		30	

Solution

Students can solve this problem by continuing to place the numbers into the array until they reach 1,000. Assuming they make no errors in placement or in counting, they should arrive at the correct answer, namely, 1,000 occurs in column C. This is an extremely arduous task.

We will try to solve this problem in another way, by *looking for a pattern*. The numbers seem to be placed underneath the letters according to a pattern; let's try to figure out what this pattern is. There are 8 columns headed by 8 letters. What happens if we divide the numbers in each column by 8?

Every number in the *A* column leaves a remainder of 1.

Every number in the *B* column leaves a remainder of 2.

Every number in the *C* column leaves a remainder of 0.

Every number in the *D* column leaves a remainder of 3.

Every number in the *E* column leaves a remainder of 7.

Every number in the *F* column leaves a remainder of 4.

Every number in the *G* column leaves a remainder of 6.

Every number in the *H* column leaves a remainder of 5.

Let's divide our number, 1,000, by 8. Aha! One thousand leaves a remainder of 0. Thus, 1,000 will occur in the *C* column.

Note: This is an excellent place to discuss the concept of a modulo system. All the numbers fall into remainder categories from 1 through 7 when divided by 8. For example, we say that 5, 13, 21, 29, ... are all congruent to 5 modulo 8.

Problem 3.12

Solve for *x* and *y*:

$$x^3 + y^3 = 133$$
$$x^2 - xy + y^2 = 19.$$

Solution

The traditional solution involves a great many of the practical skills taught in algebra:

Complete the square of

$$x^2 - xy + y^2 = 19$$
$$x^2 - xy + y^2 + 3xy = 19 + 3xy$$
$$x^2 + 2xy + y^2 = 19 + 3xy$$
$$(x + y)^2 = 19 + 3xy. \qquad [3.1]$$

Multiply both sides by $(x + y)$:

$$(x + y)^3 = (19 + 3xy)(x + y) = 19(x + y) + 3xy(x + y). \qquad [3.2]$$

Consider

$$(x+y)^3 = x^3 + 3x^2y + 3xy^2 + y^3$$
$$= x^3 + 3xy(x+y) + y^3. \qquad [3.3]$$

Now, from Equations 3.2 and 3.3, we obtain

$$19(x+y) + 3xy(x+y) = x^3 + y^3 + 3xy(x+y)$$
$$19(x+y) = x^3 + y^3.$$

We know from the original equation that $x^3 + y^3 = 133$. Therefore,

$$19(x+y) = 133$$
$$(x+y) = 7. \qquad [3.4]$$

Substituting Equation 3.4 into 3.1, we obtain

$$(7)^2 = 19 + 3xy$$
$$10 = xy. \qquad [3.5]$$

If we now solve Equations 3.4 and 3.5 simultaneously, we obtain

$$x = 5, \quad x = 2,$$
$$y = 2, \quad y = 5.$$

Now let's examine this problem by *searching for a pattern*. In this case, the "pattern" is different: It entails recognizing algebraic specialties. This, of course, comes from experience. Nonetheless, it is an important aspect of problem solving. We have often said that part of becoming a good problem solver in both mathematics and everyday life is the ability to recall previous experiences and relationships.

Here, factoring the sum of cubes makes the problem much simpler:

$$x^3 + y^3 = 133$$
$$(x+y)(x^2 - xy + y^2) = 133. \qquad [3.6]$$

We know that

$$x^2 - xy + y^2 = 19. \qquad [3.7]$$

Thus, by substituting in Equation 3.6, we obtain

$$(x+y)(19) = 133$$
$$(x+y) = 7 \text{ and } y = 7 - x.$$

Substituting into Equation 3.7, we now get

$$x^2 - x(7-x) + (7-x)^2 = 19$$
$$x^2 - 7x + x^2 + 49 - 14x + x^2 = 19$$
$$3x^2 - 21x + 30 = 0$$
$$x^2 - 7x + 10 = 0,$$

$$x = 5, \quad x = 2,$$
$$y = 2, \quad y = 5,$$

which are the same answers as before.

Problem 3.13

How many angles are formed by 10 distinct rays with a common endpoint?

Solution

Traditionally, students begin by drawing a large figure composed of 10 distinct rays at a single endpoint. They use this to "count" the number of angles. However, the drawing soon becomes rather confusing because they lose track of the angles they are forming.

Students may also use combinatorics and realize that every pair of rays determines one angle. Therefore,

$$_{10}C_2 = \frac{10 \times 9}{1 \times 2} = 45.$$

We could also reason that with each additional ray, we form an angle with each of the existing rays, and so a sequence is established. Let's start with a simpler case and look for a pattern as we increase the number of cases.

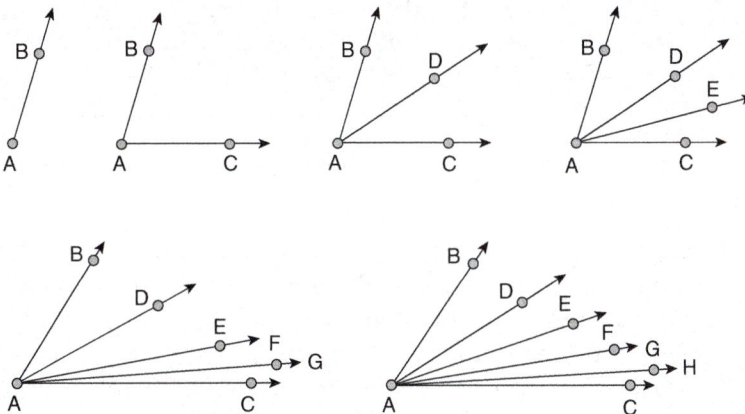

Figure 3.10

Let's summarize these data in a table:

Number of rays	1	2	3	4	5	6	7	8	...
Number of angles formed	0	1	3	6	10	15	21		

The students should not have to draw more than the case of 5 or 6 rays to see the emerging pattern:

$$0, 1, 3, 6, 10, 15, 21, \ldots .$$

This is a sequence whose differences form a simple arithmetic progression $1, 2, 3, 4, 5, 6, \ldots$. Continuing this sequence to 10 terms is simple:

$$0, 1, 3, 6, 10, 15, 21, 28, 36, 45.$$

You can also determine from this relationship a general term for the nth number in the sequence: $\frac{n(n-1)}{2}$. Thus, our strategy of finding a pattern enabled us to discover that the number of angles formed by the 10 rays is 45.

Note: These numbers are referred to as the "triangular" numbers because they can be represented geometrically in a triangular array:

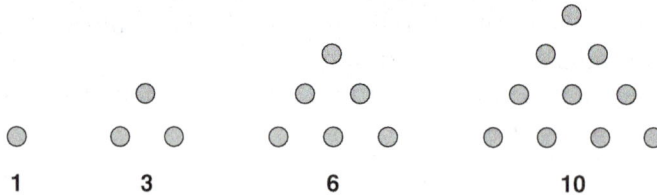

| 1 | 3 | 6 | 10 |

Figure 3.11

Problem 3.14

If you take the digit-sum of a number, that is, you add the digits in the number, how many three-digit numbers will have a digit-sum of 10? (For example, 262 is one, since $2 + 6 + 2 = 10$; 505 is another, since $5 + 0 + 5 = 10$.)

Solution

Students usually try to solve this problem by writing out all the numbers between 100 and 999 and then taking the digit-sum for each. This is obviously a correct solution and will yield the correct answer, but it is very cumbersome and time consuming.

Let's use our *looking for a pattern* strategy to see how we can solve the problem. We can make use of our *organizing data* strategy to help set up the lists of numbers with a digit-sum of 10 and then see if a pattern exists:

	100s		200s		300s		400s	
	109	190	208	280	307	370	406	460
	118	181	217	271	316	361	415	451
	127	172	226	262	325	352	424	442
	136	163	235	253	334	342	433	
	145	154	244					
Total	10		9		8		7	...

There does appear to be a pattern here. Let's move to the other end and examine the 800s and 900s to be certain:

	800s		900s	
	802	820	901	910
	811			
Total	3		2	

Our pattern is confirmed. There are $10+9+8+7+6+5+4+3+2=54$ numbers between 100 and 999 that have a digit-sum of 10.

Problem 3.15

Find the sum of the series

$$\frac{1}{1 \times 2} + \frac{1}{2 \times 3} + \frac{1}{3 \times 4} + \cdots + \frac{1}{49 \times 50}.$$

Solution

The traditional way to solve this problem is to compute the individual values for each of the fractions and then add the results. That is,

$$\frac{1}{2} + \frac{1}{6} + \frac{1}{12} + \cdots + \frac{1}{2,450}.$$

At best, this is a rather laborious task and is likely to lead to some error. Let's see if we can find some kind of *pattern* we can use:

$$\frac{1}{1 \times 2} = \frac{1}{2}$$

$$\frac{1}{1 \times 2} + \frac{1}{2 \times 3} = \frac{2}{3}$$

$$\frac{1}{1 \times 2} + \frac{1}{2 \times 3} + \frac{1}{3 \times 4} = \frac{3}{4}$$

$$\frac{1}{1 \times 2} + \frac{1}{2 \times 3} + \frac{1}{3 \times 4} + \frac{1}{4 \times 5} = \frac{4}{5}.$$

The pattern that emerges strongly suggests that the sum of this series, with its last term of $\frac{1}{49 \times 50}$, will be $\frac{49}{50}$. Here, the *finding a pattern* strategy was a bit hidden in the problem.

Another application of *recognizing a pattern* to help us to a solution can be seen if we consider these fractions as

$$\frac{1}{1 \times 2} = \frac{1}{1} - \frac{1}{2}$$
$$\frac{1}{2 \times 3} = \frac{1}{2} - \frac{1}{3}$$
$$\frac{1}{3 \times 4} = \frac{1}{3} - \frac{1}{4}$$
$$\frac{1}{49 \times 50} = \frac{1}{49} - \frac{1}{50}.$$

We seek the sum of the left side, which is equal to the sum of the right side, where every term drops out except for the first and the last terms:

$$\frac{1}{1} - \frac{1}{50} = \frac{49}{50}.$$

Problem 3.16

What is the quotient of 1 divided by 500,000,000,000?

Solution

This problem cannot be done on the calculator most of your students use, because the answer contains more places than the display permits. It can be done manually, although the computation often leads to an error due to the large number of zeros in the answer. We might, however, examine the answers we obtain by starting with a small divisor, increasing the divisor, and seeing if a usable pattern emerges. Notice that the *recognition of a pattern* strategy is used here.

	Number of 0s After the 5	Quotient	Number of 0s After the Decimal and Before the 2
$1 \div 5$	0	0.2	0
$1 \div 50$	1	0.02	1
$1 \div 500$	2	0.002	2
$1 \div 5000$	3	0.0002	3
$\vdots$	$\vdots$	$\vdots$	
$1 \div 500000000000$	11	0.000000000002	

The correct answer is found easily. The number of zeros after the decimal point and before the 2 is the same as the number of zeros in the divisor.

Problem 3.17

Find the next two terms in the sequence 1, 0, 2, 3, 3, 8, 4, 15, 5, ...

Solution

The type of problem offered here suggests that we *search for a pattern*. We have a sequence that appears to have terms going up and down in some "random" order. This might suggest a guess that there are possibly two interwoven sequences in the set of numbers. Using this possible pattern, let's examine the sequence further:

Sequence #1	1		2		3		4		5	(the odd-place terms)
Sequence #2		0		3		8		15		(the even-place terms)

Our conjecture was correct; there are indeed two interwoven sequences. The first sequence is simply the counting numbers. The second sequence is a bit more complex—the difference between successive terms is 3, 5, 7. The next term in Sequence #2 will differ from 15 by 9 and is 24. The next term in Sequence #1 is 6. Thus, the next two terms of the original sequence are 24 and 6. Once we find a pattern (if one exists), the problem should be solved easily.

Problem 3.18

In the sequence 1, 3, 2, ..., each term after the first two is found by taking the preceding term and subtracting the one preceding that. Thus, to find the next term in this sequence, we would take 2 − 3 or −1. Find the sum of the first 25 terms of this sequence.

Solution

The most obvious way to solve this problem is to write out the 25 terms and then add to find their sum. Many students prefer to sum all the positive terms, sum all the negative terms, and then add the two sums.

We solve the problem by extending the sequence for several more terms and then *looking for a pattern*. We continue the sequence:

$$1, 3, 2, -1, -3, -2, 1, 3, 2, -1, -3, -2, \ldots .$$

Aha! The pattern is easy to observe. The sequence has a cycle of six terms, after which the cycle repeats. Furthermore, the sum of the six terms in the cycle is 0. Thus, the sum of the first 24 terms will be 0 and the 25th term will be 1. The sum of the first 25 terms is 1.

Problem 3.19

A palindrome is a number that reads the same forward and backward, such as 747 or 1991. How many palindromes are there between 1 and 1,000, inclusive?

Solution

The traditional approach to this problem would be to write out all the numbers between 1 and 1,000 and then see which ones are palindromes. This is a cumbersome and time-consuming task at best, and some of the numbers could be omitted easily.

Range	Number of Palindromes	Total Number
1–9	9	9
10–99	9	18
100–199	10	28
200–299	10	38
300–399	10	48
⋮	⋮	⋮

Let's see if we can use the *looking for a pattern* strategy to solve the problem in a more direct fashion. There is a pattern: there are exactly 10 palindromes in each group of 100 numbers (after 99). Thus, there will be 9 sets of $10 = 90$, plus the 18 from 1 to 99, for a total of 108 palindromes between 1 and 1,000.

Another solution to this problem involves organizing the data in a favorable way. Consider all the single-digit numbers (self-palindromes), which number 9. The two-digit palindromes also number 9. The three-digit palindromes have 9 possible "outside digits" and 10 possible "middle digits," so there are 90 of these. In total, there are 108 palindromes between 1 and 1,000, inclusive.

Problem 3.20

In Figure 3.12a, four unit squares are drawn. Find the measure of the angle marked x.

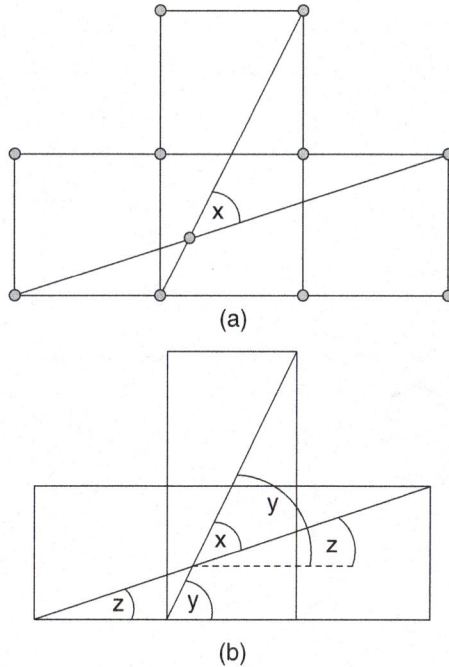

(a)

(b)

Figure 3.12

Solution

There are many ways to solve this problem. One could involve trigonometry. If we assume the length of the side of each of the squares (see Figure 3.12b) to be equal to 1, then tan $y = 2$, which implies that $y = 63.434949\ldots$.

Also tan $z = \frac{1}{3}$, which implies that $z = 18.434949\ldots$. Furthermore, from properties of parallel lines we get $x = y - z = 45$. We can use a more formal approach. Because

$$\tan x = \tan(y - z) = \frac{\tan y - \tan z}{1 + \tan y \tan z} = \frac{2 - \dfrac{1}{3}}{1 + 2 \times \dfrac{1}{3}} = \frac{\dfrac{5}{3}}{\dfrac{5}{3}} = 1,$$

$$x = 45°.$$

This solution can be made considerably simpler if we *search for a pattern* from the original problem diagram. If we consider the diagram in Figure 3.13 as an extension of the given diagram, we easily can see that the two angles marked x are the same measure because they are corresponding angles of parallel lines. Because the newly introduced angle of the two angles is formed by a diagonal of a square with its side, it must have a measure of 45°.

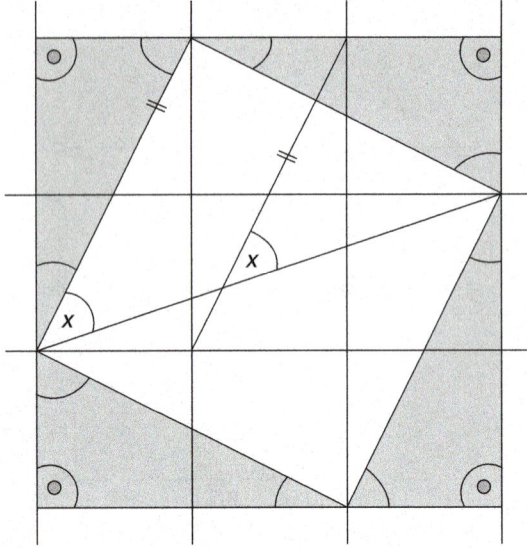

Figure 3.13

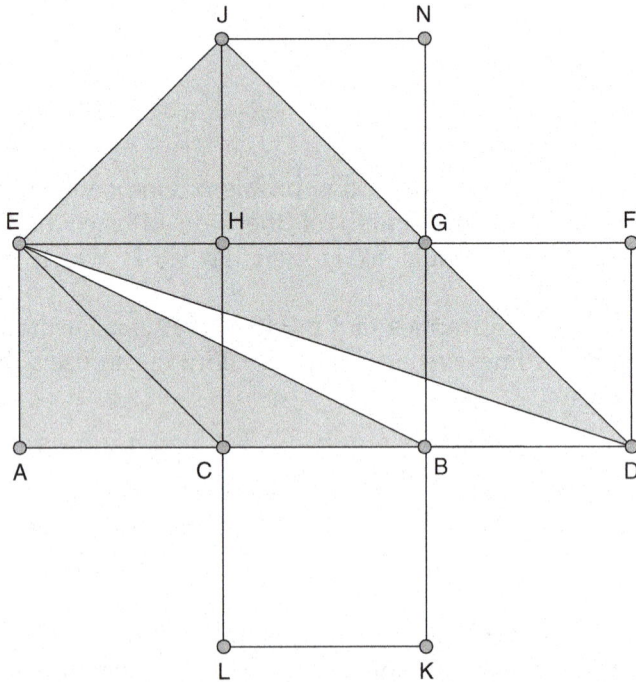

Figure 3.14

An interesting aspect of this problem is to notice (in Figure 3.14) that the sum of the measures of ∠ACE, ∠ABE, and ∠ADE equals 90°. These are the same angles we used in our previous solution. We can prove this relationship by considering the similar triangles *EJD* and *EAB*. Thus,

$\angle JDE \cong \angle ABE$. Because $m\angle JDE + m\angle ADE = 45°$ (since $\overline{GD}$ is a diagonal of a square), by substitution $m\angle ADE + m\angle ABE = 45°$. We already know that $m\angle ACE = 45°$. Thus, the sum of the three angles is $90°$.

We can look at this same problem from another point of view. Consider the circumscribed circle for the "cross":

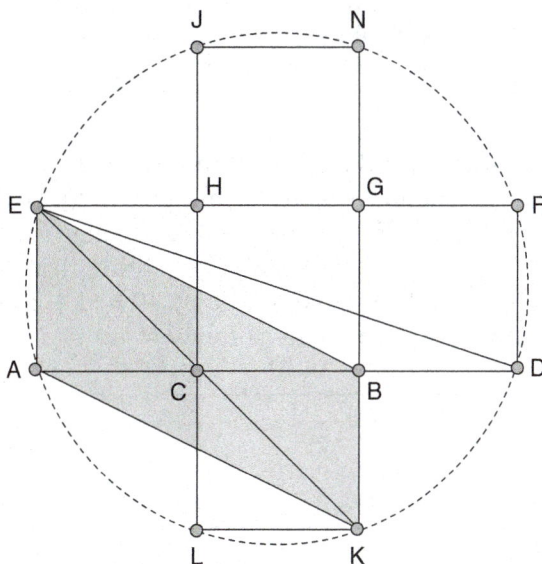

Figure 3.15

This time we focus on the shaded quadrilateral. We can show it is a parallelogram because the diagonals bisect each other ($AC = CB$ and $EC = KC$, because they are sides and diagonals, respectively, of congruent squares). Therefore, $\angle AKE \cong \angle BEK$ and because $\angle AKE$ and $\angle ADE$ both intercept the same arc (AE) of the circumcircle of the "cross," they, too, must be congruent. Thus, $\angle BEK \cong \angle ADE$. Consider $\angle ACE$ the exterior angle of $\triangle BCE$, where $m\angle BEC + m\angle CBE = m\angle ACE = 45°$. By substitution, we get $m\angle ADE + m\angle ABE + m\angle ACE = 90°$.

Problem 3.21

What is the sum of $1^3 + 2^3 + 3^3 + 4^3 + \cdots + 9^3 + 10^3$?

Solution

Students could actually cube all the integers from 1 through 10 and then take the sum. Carefully done with the aid of a calculator, this should yield the correct answer.

If we did not have a calculator handy, however, the multiplication and addition could prove quite cumbersome and messy! Let's see how we might solve the problem by the *search for a pattern* strategy. We organize our data (another strategy) with a table:

1^3	$= (1)$	$= 1$	$= 1^2$
$1^3 + 2^3$	$= (1 + 8)$	$= 9$	$= 3^2$
$1^3 + 2^3 + 3^3$	$= (1 + 8 + 27)$	$= 36$	$= 6^2$
$1^3 + 2^3 + 3^3 + 4^3$	$= (1 + 8 + 27 + 64)$	$= 100$	$= 10^2$

Notice that the numbers in the final column (namely, 1, 3, 6, 10, …) are the *triangular numbers*. The nth triangular number is formed by taking the sum of the first n integers. That is, the first triangular number, $1 = 1$; the second triangular number, $3 = (1 + 2)$; the third triangular number, $6 = (1 + 2 + 3)$; the fourth triangular number, $10 = (1 + 2 + 3 + 4)$; and so on. Thus, we can rewrite our problem as follows:

1^3	$= (1)^2$	$= 1^2$	$= 1$
$1^3 + 2^3$	$= (1 + 2)^2$	$= 3^2$	$= 9$
$1^3 + 2^3 + 3^3$	$= (1 + 2 + 3)^2$	$= 6^2$	$= 36$
$1^3 + 2^3 + 3^3 + \cdots + 9^3 + 10^3$	$= (1 + 2 + 3 + \cdots + 9 + 10)^2$	$= 55^2$	$= 13{,}025$

Problem 3.22

Solve the equation $(2x^2 - x + 4)^2 - 6(2x^2 - x) = 19$ for (real) x.

Solution

It is not unexpected that students begin to solve this equation by first clearing parentheses in the hope that many cumbersome terms will drop out. This is not the case here. As a matter of fact, clearing parentheses leaves a troublesome quartic equation for solution, something outside the scope of a secondary school student.

We ought to inspect the equation before simply plunging into a procedure without forethought and a bit of planning. It is often advantageous to *look for patterns*. In this case, we notice that the expression $2x^2 - x$ appears twice. Let us call this expression $2x^2 - x = u$. By appropriate substitution, we get

$$(u + 4)^2 - 6u = 19.$$

Then,

$$u^2 + 2u - 3 = 0 \text{ and } (u + 3)(u - 1) = 0,$$

where $u = -3$ and $u = 1$. Now substitute for u:

$$2x^2 - x = -3 \qquad 2x^2 - x = 1$$

$$2x^2 - x + 3 = 0 \qquad 2x^2 - x - 1 = 0$$

$$\text{Imaginary roots} \qquad x = -\frac{1}{2} \text{ and } x = 1$$

We must remember that "patterns" such as the one noticed in this problem do not always exist. However, when one does exist and we can identify it, it usually helps us tremendously toward an elegant solution.

Problem 3.23

The new school has 1,000 lockers. And, ironically, it has exactly 1,000 students. On the first day of school, the children met in the yard and came up with a plan. They peeked into the school and saw that all the lockers were closed. The first student would run through and open all the lockers. The second student would then run through and close all the lockers that are multiples of 2, beginning with Locker #2. Student number 3 would then run through and reverse every locker that is a multiple of 3, beginning with Locker #3. If it was open, he would close it. If it was closed, he would open it. The fourth student would change all the multiples of 4, and so on. When all 1,000 students have done their thing, how many lockers are left open? How many are closed?

Solution

This problem is well known. Most students start by trying to find an algebraic solution, but are forced to give up rather quickly. Of course, we could get 1,000 lockers and 1,000 students and actually perform the action. But that would be rather impractical. Let's attack a simpler, analogous problem and see what happens. Suppose there were 10 students and 10 lockers. Let's make a table and simulate the action.

Locker No.	1	2	3	4	5	6	7	8	9	10
St #1	**O**	O	O	O	O	O	O	O	O	O
St #2		C	O	C	O	C	O	C	O	C
St #3			C	C	O	O	O	C	C	C
St #4				**O**	O	O	O	O	C	C
St #5					C	O	O	O	C	O
St #6						C	O	O	C	O
St #7							C	O	C	O
St #8								C	C	O
St #9									**O**	O
St #10										C

Notice that lockers 1, 4, and 9 remain open. This suggests that the lockers with the perfect square numbers will be the open ones. This is an excellent opportunity to introduce the concept of factors. Factors usually come in pairs, except for the perfect squares, when the square root is its own "mate" factor. Thus, only the perfect squares have an odd number of factors and, consequently, will be "touched" an odd number of times, open, close, open. Since 32 squared = 1024 and 31 squared = 961, there will be 31 perfect squares less than 1,000 and 31 lockers left open. There will be 1,000 − 31 = 969 lockers remaining closed.

4

Adopting a Different Point of View

The typical training that students receive in school basically prepares them to solve problems in a single, straightforward fashion. This leads to a solution, but not always in the most efficient way. In fact, it is well known that once a student attempts to solve a problem in a particular manner and fails to resolve the situation, he or she will most likely attempt to solve the problem in exactly the same way. This is referred to as the Einstellung effect. After repeated attempts at this same approach, the student will often simply give up. It is sometimes beneficial to the problem solver to adopt a different point of view than that to which he or she was led initially by the problem. This sort of thinking was used when we discussed the *working backwards* strategy. The problem was inspected from a different point of view, namely, from the end back to the beginning. We use this sort of thinking automatically in everyday life. Consider the problem of being separated from and trying to find a friend in a crowd. It would be logical to stand on some sort of elevated platform so that your overview of the crowd is different (more advantageous); that is, you can *adopt a different point of view* (in this case, quite literally!).

Such a different point of view might be one where instead of focusing on the *winners* of a contest, we look at the *losers*. For example, suppose you were asked to determine how many games would have to be played in a single-elimination tennis tournament that began with 25 players. You would find it very cumbersome to work directly by setting up a diagram of the tournament, counting the winners in each round, following them through the hypothetical tournament, and arriving at a single winner. You would then have to count the number of games that had been played. Yes, the problem could be solved in this manner! It would be much more efficient, however, to look at this from a *different point of view*; that is, ask yourself how many losers this tournament must have. The answer is simply 24. Since 1 player is eliminated each time a game is played, there would have to be 24 games to have 24 losers!

We can look at this problem from still another point of view. Consider (hypothetically, of course) that you *know* who the winner will be. Then suppose that this "winner" plays each of the other contestants and defeats them (of course). Because this is a single-elimination tournament, players do not need to play each other. This "winner" must play 24 games to get 24 losers!

Many times the complexity of the setting in which a problem is placed impedes the students' ability to even understand what must be done. As a result, experienced problem solvers often adopt a slightly different point of view or setting in an attempt to simplify their understanding.

THE *ADOPTING A DIFFERENT POINT OF VIEW* STRATEGY IN EVERYDAY LIFE PROBLEM-SOLVING SITUATIONS

You are asked to determine the number of people in attendance at a meeting of an association. Counting the members present would be unwieldy, because there are many empty seats spread throughout the auditorium. Absentees all called in prior to the meeting to be excused. Therefore, you solve the problem of determining the number present by subtracting the number of absentees from the total membership of the association. This exemplifies approaching the problem from a point of view different from simply counting or systematically "estimating" the attendance.

In any competitive sports event, the immediate tendency is to plan to use your strengths or strategies directly. An alternative point of view would be to assess and evaluate your competitor's strengths and weaknesses and generate your strategy from that assessment. Rather than viewing the impending contest and developing your game plan from your own vantage point, you could just as easily *adopt a different point of view* and assess it by considering the competition.

It is interesting to note that in any form of negotiations, rather than considering only your own point of view, it is important to anticipate what position your "opponent" will take. Looking at the situation from this other point of view might help you find an appropriate direction for your own stance at these negotiations.

Another way to look at this problem-solving strategy is to consider a detective investigating a case. The detective can sometimes select the guilty party from among several suspects, not necessarily proving that this one person committed the crime, but rather by *adopting a different point of view*. This could be done by establishing that all the other suspects had valid alibis. Naturally, more substantial arguments would be necessary for a conviction, but at least this process establishes a direction for the investigation.

APPLYING THE *ADOPTING A DIFFERENT POINT OF VIEW* STRATEGY TO SOLVE MATHEMATICS PROBLEMS

Problems in spatial geometry usually cause trouble for most students, because the ability to visualize in three-dimensional space is not usually pursued; hence, most students have little practice. Consider, then, the following problem from spatial geometry.

> Determine the number of diagonals of a regular dodecahedron that do not lie on a face of the dodecahedron.

A first reaction to this problem is to count the diagonals called for in the statement of the problem itself. Quickly, we realize that this task is, at best, extremely confusing and complicated. Direct counting is not a viable procedure. At this point, it would be wise to approach this problem from a *different point of view*.

Rather than counting just the required diagonals, let us consider counting all the diagonals of the regular dodecahedron and then eliminating from that count those that lie on a face or an edge. This would leave us with the number of diagonals called for in the original problem. You will see that the task becomes much simpler than the counting required in our original approach.

Let us begin by mentally picturing a regular dodecahedron. It is a 12-faced regular polyhedron, which often is used as a calendar paperweight because it has exactly 12 faces; thus, each face can be used to represent a different month of the year. Each face is a regular pentagon. To determine the number of edges, we simply count the number of sides of these 12 pentagons and then divide by 2, because each edge was counted twice (once in each of two adjacent pentagons). Thus, there are $\frac{12 \times 5}{2} = 30$ edges. To find the number of vertices, we can use the famous (and extremely useful) Euler formula for the relationship involving the number of vertices, faces, and edges of a polyhedron: faces + vertices − edges = 2. We now calculate the number of vertices for the regular dodecahedron $(12 + v - 30 = 2)$, so there are 20 vertices.

We now reason inductively. A "first vertex" is connected to 19 other vertices, a "second vertex" is then connected to 18 other vertices, a "third vertex" to 17 others, and so on. Therefore, the connection of all vertices is achieved with $19 + 18 + 17 + 16 + \cdots + 3 + 2 + 1 = 190$ line segments. (Note: The same result could be obtained with the formula $_{20}C_2 = 190$.) Similarly, for each face pentagon, the vertices can be joined by $4 + 3 + 2 + 1 = 10$ (or $_5C_2$) line segments. Because there are 12 faces, we have 12×10 or 120 line segments joining vertices on the faces. Of these, we know that 30 lie on the edges and therefore were counted twice. Hence, of the line segments joining the vertices, $120 - 30 = 90$ must lie on a face or an edge of the dodecahedron. The remainder of the 190 line segments must, therefore, lie "in the interior" of the dodecahedron. There are, therefore, $190 - 90 = 100$ interior diagonals. Notice that we were able to find the number of interior diagonals of the dodecahedron by *adopting a different point of view*; this may be done by not counting them directly but rather arriving at the number by eliminating all except those required.

In geometry, we often can simplify a problem by considering it *from another point of view*, one that may be brought about by adding one or more auxiliary lines. Such is the case when we want to establish that the angle measure sum of a triangle is 180. We consider the line through one vertex, which is parallel to the opposite side, and then simply proceed to reach our goal.

PROBLEMS USING THE *ADOPTING A DIFFERENT POINT OF VIEW* STRATEGY

Problem 4.1

Mike was racing in a bike marathon. He was $\frac{3}{8}$ of the way across a narrow bridge, when he heard the whistle of the Wabash Cannonball train approaching the bridge from behind him at 60 miles per hour. Being an amateur mathematician as well as a marathon biker, Mike calculated that he could *just* reach either end of the bridge at the same time as the train. How fast was Mike pedaling his bike?

Solution

As we have said before, this problem, like many others, can be solved by using traditional algebra methods. In this case, the situation can be described as shown in Figure 4.1.

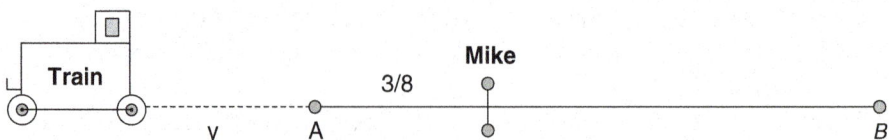

Figure 4.1

We can now set up a system of equations as follows:

Case 1

Mike rides to point A. Let x be Mike's speed in miles per hour and y be the distance of the train from the beginning of the bridge. Suppose the length of the bridge is 8 miles (a rather long bridge); we can choose any "convenient" length.

	Rate	Time	Distance
Train	60	$\dfrac{y}{60}$	y
Mike	x	$\dfrac{3}{x}$	3

By equating the two times, we obtain

$$\frac{y}{60} = \frac{3}{x} \text{ and then } xy = 180. \qquad [4.1]$$

Case 2

Mike rides to point B. Again, let x be Mike's speed in miles per hour and y be the distance of the train from the beginning of the bridge:

	Rate	Time	Distance
Train	60	$\dfrac{8+y}{60}$	$8+y$
Mike	x	$\dfrac{5}{x}$	5

By equating the two times, we obtain

$$\frac{8+y}{60} = \frac{5}{x}$$
$$8x + xy = 300. \qquad [4.2]$$

Solving Equations 4.2 and 4.2 simultaneously, we obtain

$$8x + xy = 300$$
$$8x + 180 = 300$$
$$8x = 120$$
$$x = 15.$$

Mike is cycling at 15 miles per hour.

Although this solution is perfectly satisfactory, we can examine the problem from *another point of view*. Because Mike can just reach point A (a distance $\frac{3}{8}$ of the length of the bridge) when the train reaches point A, let him pedal toward point B. When the train reaches point A, he will have covered exactly an additional $\frac{3}{8}$ of the bridge, for a total traveled by Mike of $\frac{6}{8}$ of the bridge. Now, he has $\frac{2}{8}$ or $\frac{1}{4}$ of the bridge remaining until he reaches point B, just as the train covers the entire bridge to point B. Hence, Mike can cycle $\frac{1}{4}$ as fast as the train, or 15 miles per hour.

Problem 4.2

Find the value of the following expression when $x = 6$:

$$(x - 10)(x - 9)(x - 8) \cdots (x - 3)(x - 2)(x - 1).$$

Solution

It is true that students can write out the 10 terms in the sequence, substitute 6 for x in each term, and then multiply the resulting 10 numbers. However, let's examine this problem from *another point of view*. Within the 10-term sequence, we find $(x - 6)$ as one of the factors. Because this factor will have the value 0 when we substitute 6 for x, the entire expression will have the value 0. Thus, the problem is easily solved.

Problem 4.3

Find the area of the shaded region between triangle ABC and triangle GHI, if the corresponding sides of the three triangles are parallel and 1 unit apart. Triangle DEF lies midway between the other two triangles. The lengths of the three sides of triangle DEF are 5, 6, and 7 units (see Figure 4.2).

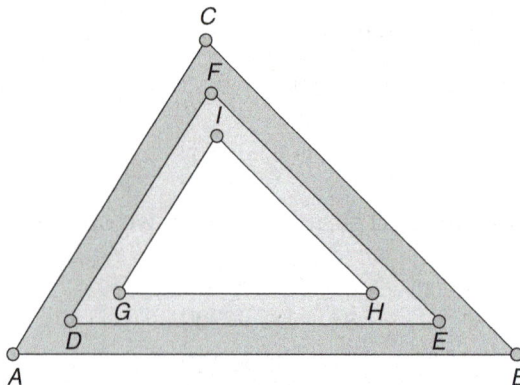

Figure 4.2

Solution

Students will initially try to find the area of triangles ABC and GHI, and then take the difference. Rather than pursue this method, let's look at the problem from *another point of view*. Consider the figure as cut into three trapezoids (*AGIC*, *AGHB*, and *BCIH*) as shown in Figure 4.3.

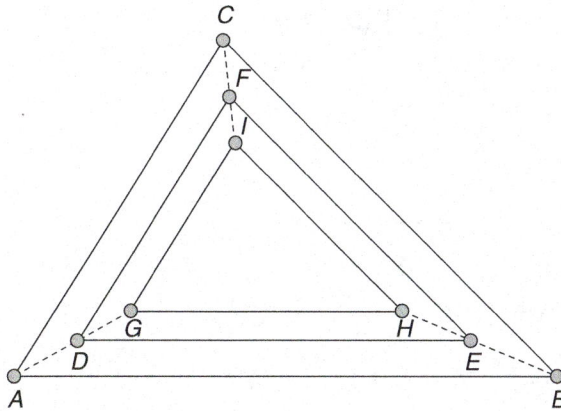

Figure 4.3

In each case, the altitude of the trapezoid is 2. The medians are 5, 6, and 7, respectively. Thus, we apply the formula for the area of a trapezoid, $A = \text{median} \times \text{height}$:

$$\text{Trapezoid } AGIC = 5 \times 2 = 10.$$

$$\text{Trapezoid } AGHB = 7 \times 2 = 14.$$

$$\text{Trapezoid } BCIH = 6 \times 2 = 12.$$

The total area of the shaded region is $10 + 14 + 12 = 36$ square units.

Problem 4.4

What is the greatest value of the expression

$$ab + bc + cd + ad$$

if a, b, c, and d have values 1, 2, 3, and 4, but not necessarily in that order?

Solution

We could list all possibilities for a, b, c, and d, and then for $ab + bc + cd + ad$, but this appears to be somewhat cumbersome. Let's consider this problem from *another point of view*. Can we possibly factor the expression?

$$\begin{aligned}
ab + bc + cd + ad &= b(a + c) + d(c + a) \\
&= b(a + c) + d(a + c) \\
&= (a + c)(b + d).
\end{aligned}$$

Now consider all possibilities for the two factors:

$$(1+2)(3+4) = 3 \times 7 = 21$$
$$(1+3)(2+4) = 4 \times 6 = 24$$
$$(1+4)(2+3) = 5 \times 5 = 25.$$

The largest sum is 25.

Problem 4.5

Correct to two decimal places, find the value of

$$3.1416 \times 2.7831 + 3.1416 \times 12.27 - 5.0531 \times 3.1416.$$

Solution

The most common and obvious method for solving this problem is to find the three separate products and then add or subtract as necessary. Using a calculator, we obtain

3.1416×2.7831	$=$	8.743387
$+\,3.1416 \times 12.27$	$=$	38.547432
	$=$	47.290819
-5.0531×3.1416	$=$	15.874818
	$=$	31.416001
	$=$	31.42 to the nearest hundredth

Notice that students must carefully arrange their work and keep track of the partial products. In addition, when using a calculator to solve the problem, students can easily press a wrong key and not even be aware of it, or be able to check it!

Let's examine this problem from *another point of view*. There is a common factor in each term, namely, 3.1416. If we factor out this term, we obtain

$$3.1416(2.7831 + 12.27 - 5.0531)$$
$$= 3.1416(10)$$
$$= 31.416$$
$$= 31.42 \text{ to the nearest hundredth,}$$

a much simpler procedure.

Note that this solution also involves *finding a pattern*, namely, recognizing that there is a common factor in each term. This sort of "pattern recognition" is worth highlighting.

Problem 4.6

In Figure 4.4, *ABCD* is a square, and *P* and *Q* are the midpoints of the sides. What is the ratio of the area of triangle *DPQ* to the area of the square?

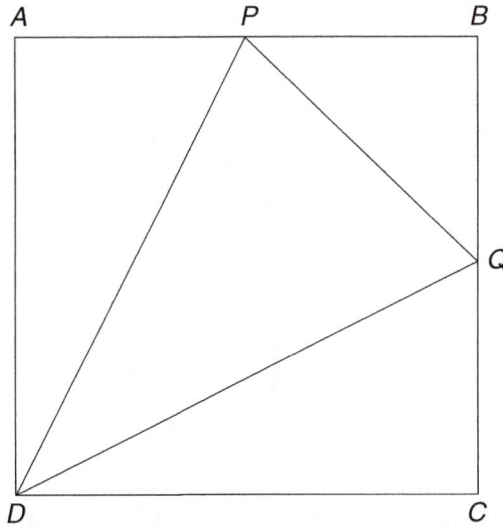

Figure 4.4

Solution

The usual solution to this problem begins by considering a square with side x, finding the areas of each of the three component right triangles whose sides are either x or $\frac{x}{2}$, and then adding them and subtracting their sum from the whole square to get the area of triangle *DPQ*. We then express this area compared with the area of the entire square as a ratio.

We can make our task a bit easier, however, by employing one of our problem-solving strategies, namely, *solve a simpler analogous problem*. We assign a convenient length to the side of the original square, say 10, and proceed in a manner similar to that already described:

Area of square $ABCD = (10)(10) = 100$.

Area of triangle $APD = (\frac{1}{2})(AP)(AD) = (\frac{1}{2})(5)(10) = 25$.

Area of triangle $PBQ = (\frac{1}{2})(PB)(BQ) = (\frac{1}{2})(5)(5) = \frac{25}{2} = 12\frac{1}{2}$.

Area of triangle $QCD = (\frac{1}{2})(CD)(CQ) = (\frac{1}{2})(10)(5) = 25$.

The sum of the areas of the three right triangles is $62\frac{1}{2}$. By subtracting this area sum from the area of the square, we obtain the area of triangle $DPQ = 37\frac{1}{2}$. Thus, our required ratio is $37\frac{1}{2} : 100 = \frac{3}{8}$.

Let's examine this problem from *another point of view*. Select E and F as midpoints of $\overline{CD}$ and $\overline{AD}$, respectively (Figure 4.5).

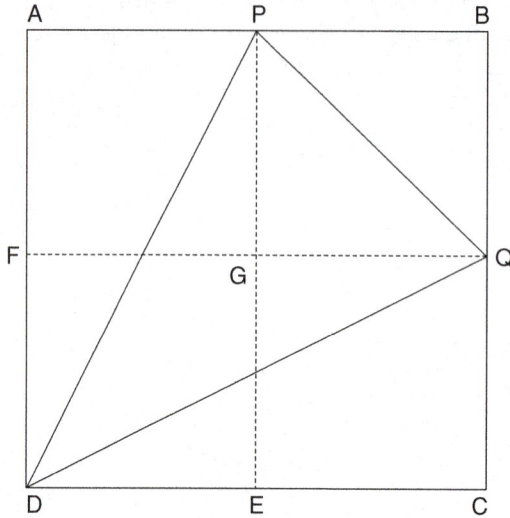

Figure 4.5

Now, because rectangle $APED$ is one half the area of the original square, and diagonal $\overline{DP}$ divides it in half, the area of triangle APD is half the area of the rectangle $APED$ and thus one quarter the area of the original square. Similarly, with F the midpoint of $\overline{AD}$, the area of rectangle $DCQF$ is one half the area of the original square, and triangle DQC is also one quarter the area of the original square. Furthermore, since $\overline{PE}$ and $\overline{QF}$ meet at G, the center of the original square, the area of square $PBQG$ is one quarter that of the original square, and triangle PBQ (which is one half the area of square $PBQG$) is one eighth the area of the original square. We now have the following information:

The area of triangle $APD = \frac{1}{4}$ the area of square $ABCD$.

The area of triangle $QCD = \frac{1}{4}$ the area of square $ABCD$.

The area of triangle $PBQ = \frac{1}{8}$ the area of square $ABCD$.

The sum of the area of the three triangles is $\frac{1}{4} + \frac{1}{4} + \frac{1}{8} = \frac{5}{8}$.

Hence, the area of triangle DPQ is $\frac{3}{8}$ the area of the original square.

Problem 4.7

How many different candy items can a vending machine offer if each item costs a different amount of money and the machine accepts, at most, one coin for each of the slots from among a penny, nickel, dime, or quarter?

Solution

The immediate approach to solving this problem would be to make a list of all possible combinations of the four coins in an organized manner. However, this could prove difficult (and confusing) for students if they are not systematic in the way they create this list. It is also quite easy to miss one or more possible coin combinations.

However, let's look at this problem from *another point of view*. We can solve it by considering each of the coin slots separately. That is, for each item, a decision about inserting or not inserting a coin into each slot has to be made. Thus, one either puts a penny into the penny slot or not—two possibilities. One either puts a nickel into the nickel slot or not (again, two possibilities). One either puts a dime into the dime slot or not. Finally, one either puts a quarter into the quarter slot or not. Then, using the fundamental counting principle, there are $2 \times 2 \times 2 \times 2 = 16$ ways of inserting or not inserting coins into the machine with, at most, one coin per slot. However, one of these 16 options involves not putting any coins into the slots, and because there are no free candy items in the machine, there are $16 - 1$ or 15 ways.

Problem 4.8

River Vale has a population of 6,800, which is decreasing at a rate of 120 people per year. Altaussee has a population of 4,200, which is increasing at a rate of 80 people per year. In how many years will the populations of the two towns be equal?

Solution

Some students may set up an equation where x represents the number of years until the populations are equal:

$$6{,}800 - 120x = 4{,}200 + 80x$$
$$2{,}600 = 200x$$
$$13 = x.$$

The populations will be equal in 13 years.

Other students may create a table and follow the increases/decreases as they take place on a year-by-year basis:

Year	River Vale	Altaussee
	6,800	4,200
1	6,680	4,280
2	6,560	4,360
3	6,440	4,440
4	6,320	4,520
5	6,200	4,600
6	6,080	4,680
7	5,960	4,760
8	5,840	4,840
9	5,720	4,920
10	5,600	5,000
11	5,480	5,080
12	5,360	5,160
13	5,240	5,240

They will be the same after 13 years.

Still other students may wish to use a graphic approach by drawing two line graphs,

$$y = 6,800 - 120x$$
$$y = 4,200 + 80x,$$

and finding their point of intersection.

Although these solutions are all satisfactory, let's examine this problem from *another point of view*. Since one town is losing 120 people per year and the other is gaining 80 people per year, the net result is a change of 200 people per year. Since the towns begin with populations that are 2,600 apart, it will take $2,600 \div 200 = 13$ years.

Problem 4.9

Find the value of $(x + y)$ if

$$123x + 321y = 345$$
$$321x + 123y = 543.$$

Solution

When students are confronted with two equations that contain two variables, they automatically revert to the process that has been taught as *the* method of solution, that is, to solve them simultaneously. Students begin by making the coefficients of either x or y the same:

$$(321)(123)x + (321)(321)y = (321)(345)$$
$$(123)(321)x + (123)(123)y = (543)(123)$$
$$39{,}483x + 103{,}041y = 110{,}745$$
$$39{,}483x + 15{,}129y = 66{,}789$$
$$87{,}912y = 43{,}956$$
$$y = 0.5$$
$$(123)x + (321)(0.5) = 345$$
$$123x + 160.5 = 345$$
$$123x = 184.5$$
$$x = 1.5.$$

Thus,

$$(x+y) = 1.5 + 0.5 = 2.$$

Notice that solving this pair of equations simultaneously leads to a great deal of complicated arithmetic computation. Let's examine this problem from *another point of view*. We are not really interested in the specific values for x and y; rather, we are interested in their sum. If we add the two equations, we obtain

$$444x + 444y = 888$$

or

$$x + y = 2.$$

The problem is quite easily solved.

Students should not think that this is merely a "trick" problem, although it would appear so on the surface. This problem exemplifies the important skill of looking at what is to be found in a given problem rather than beginning in the traditional way, given familiar stimuli. Students should begin to realize that there are problems (in everyday life, as well) the solutions to which can be much simpler with a bit of "foresight."

Problem 4.10

If $x + y = 1$ and $\frac{x}{y} = 1$, what is the value of xy?

Solution

One traditional method for solving two equations with two variables is by the method of substitution:

If $\frac{x}{y} = 1$, then $x = y$.

Whereas $x + y = 1$ and $x = y$, then

$$x + y = 1$$
$$y + y = 1$$
$$2y = 1$$
$$y = \tfrac{1}{2}.$$

Thus, $x = \frac{1}{2}$ and $y = \frac{1}{2}$ and $\frac{1}{2} \cdot \frac{1}{2} = \frac{1}{4}$.

Let's look at this problem from *another point of view*. We see that x must equal y, because their quotient is 1. Furthermore, the only two equal numbers whose sum is 1 are $\frac{1}{2}$ and $\frac{1}{2}$; thus, their product is $\frac{1}{4}$.

Although this solution parallels the foregoing algebraic method, it does require a bit more analysis and thought than the purely mechanical (algebraic) method and, hence, offers another strategy for solution.

Problem 4.11

When a number ends in zeros, the zeros are referred to as terminal zeros. For example, 286,000 has three terminal zeros, whereas 607,400 has only two terminal zeros. Let N equal the product of all the natural numbers from 1 through 20; that is, $N = 1 \times 2 \times 3 \times 4 \times 5 \times \cdots \times 19 \times 20$. How many terminal zeros will N have when it is written in standard form?

Solution

At first, students will attempt to multiply the numbers from 1 through 20 on a calculator. Most calculators do not have a display large enough to accommodate the product. However, even if they have a calculator that will give the product, the process is time-consuming and open to error.

Let's examine this problem from *another point of view*. For each zero in the product, we must have a factor of 10. How many 10s are in the final product? This is equivalent to finding the number of 5s in the product, because there are many more 2s, and each 5×2 will produce a 10. There is a 5 in 5, a 5 in 10, a 5 in 15, and a 5 in 20. There will be four 10s and thus four terminal zeros in the product.

Problem 4.12

In Figure 4.6, *ABCD* is a unit square, and *AFCB* and *AECD* are both quarter circles having *B* and *D* as their respective centers. Find the area of the football-shaped portion, *AECF*.

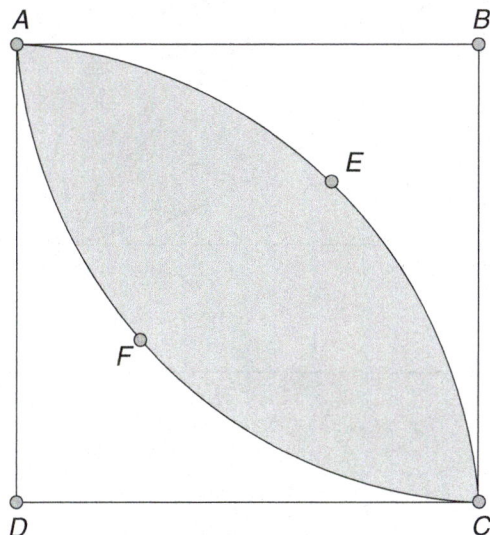

Figure 4.6

Solution

Students have been taught to find the area of unusually shaped figures by dividing the figure into portions, each area of which can be found, and then adding or subtracting as needed. Thus, most students would begin by drawing the diagonal (*AC*), which divides the shaded figure into two: one, a segment of sector *AECD*; the other, a segment of sector *BAFC*. (If we find the area of one segment, we can simply double it to find the required area.) The area of the sector is one quarter of the circle with radius $AD = 1$. Thus, the area of the sector is $\frac{1}{4}\pi R^2 = \frac{1}{4} \times \pi \times 1^2 = \frac{\pi}{4}$. Now we subtract the area of the right triangle *ADC*, which is $\frac{1}{2} \times 1 \times 1 = \frac{1}{2}$. Hence, the area of the segment is $\frac{\pi}{4} - \frac{1}{2}$, and the area of the "football" is twice as much, or $\frac{\pi}{2} - 1$.

Although this is a satisfactory solution, let's examine the problem from *another point of view*. Simply add the areas of the two sectors, *AECD* and *AFCB* (which consist of regions $1 + 2$, and $2 + 3$, respectively). The result is one half the area of the circle, or $\frac{\pi}{2}$. Subtract the area of square *ABCD* (which consists of Regions 1, 2, and 3, respectively). The resulting area is that of *AECF* (Region 2), which was used twice in the addition and only once in the subtraction. Thus, the final area is $\frac{\pi}{2} - 1$.

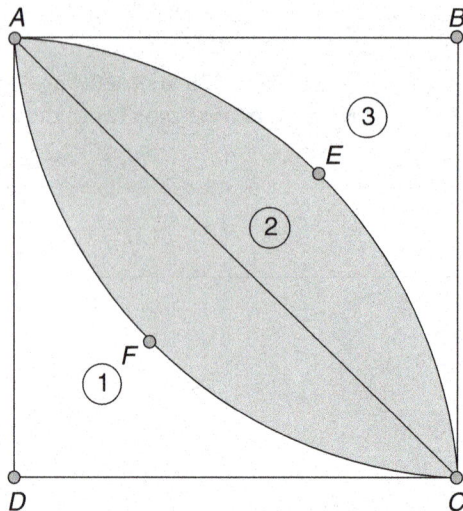

Figure 4.7

Problem 4.13

Solve for x:

$$(x-3)^3 + (x-7)^3 = (2x-10)^3.$$

Solution

The traditional approach to solving this problem is to cube all three of the parenthetical expressions and solve the resulting equation as follows:

$$x^3 - 9x^2 + 27x - 27 + x^3 - 21x^2 + 147x - 343 = 8x^3 - 120x^2 + 600x - 1{,}000$$

$$2x^3 - 30x^2 + 174x - 370 = 8x^3 - 120x^2 + 600x - 1{,}000$$

$$0 = 6x^3 - 90x^2 + 426x - 630$$

$$0 = x^3 - 15x^2 + 71x - 105$$

$$0 = (x-7)(x-5)(x-3)$$

$$x = 3, x = 5, x = 7.$$

Of course, this solution requires a great deal of algebraic manipulation and could easily lead to an error, making the expression unfactorable.

Instead, let's solve this problem by *adopting a different point of view*. Notice that $(x-3) + (x-7) = (2x-10)$. Suppose we let

$$a = x - 3$$
$$b = x - 7.$$

Then,

$$a + b = 2x - 10.$$

Substituting in the original,

$$a^3 + b^3 = (a+b)^3$$
$$a^3 + b^3 = a^3 + 3a^2b + 3ab^2 + b^3$$
$$0 = 3a^2b + 3ab^2 = 3ab(a+b)$$
$$0 = (ab)(a+b).$$

Thus, our solutions are

$$a = 0, b = 0, (a+b) = 0.$$

If $a = 0$, then $x - 3 = 0$, $x = 3$.

If $b = 0$, then $x - 7 = 0$, $x = 7$.

If $a + b = 0$, then $2x - 10 = 0$ and $x = 5$.

Once again, although these steps directly parallel the original algebraic solution, by *adopting the point of view* that we can substitute single variables for the binomials, we are led to a much simpler degree of algebraic manipulation.

Problem 4.14

Find the difference between the areas of the two right triangles *ABC* and *BCD*, where *BC* = 18, *BD* = 30, and *AD* = 9.

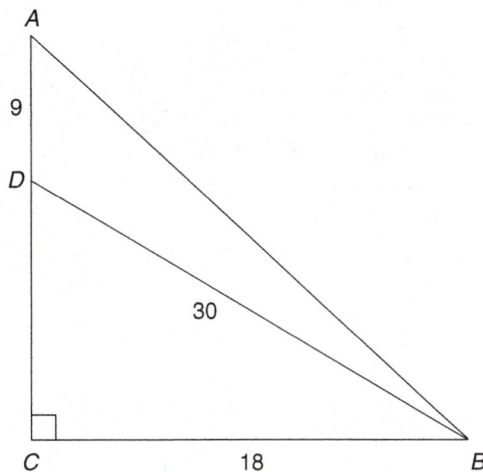

Figure 4.8

Solution

The way the problem is stated leads the problem solver to find the areas of the two right triangles in question, and then take the difference between these areas. This is relatively time-consuming, however, because we first have to use the Pythagorean theorem to find $DC = 24$, recognizing that $\triangle BCD$ is a 9–12–15 Pythagorean triple.

There is another way to solve the problem by *adopting a different point of view*. We revisit the question, which asks for "the difference between the areas"; this is, geometrically speaking, $\triangle ADB$. This obtuse triangle ADB, with base $AD = 9$ and altitude $BC = 18$, has an area that can be computed directly with the popular formula for the area of a triangle,

$$A = \tfrac{1}{2}(\text{base})(\text{height}) = \tfrac{1}{2}(9)(18) = 81.$$

Problem 4.15

If it is now 10:45 a.m., what time will it be in 143,999,999,995 min from now?

Solution

The problem appears to be rather complex. Students who see a large number such as 143,999,999,995 will automatically turn to the calculator to resolve the problem. However, this is a 12-digit number, which is hardly likely to "fit" their calculator displays.

Let's examine this problem from *another point of view*. The number 143,999,999,995 is only 5 min short of 144,000,000,000 min, which is an exact multiple of 60. Thus, $144{,}000{,}000{,}000 \div 60 = 2{,}400{,}000{,}000$ hours, which when divided by 24 yields exactly 100,000,000 days. In this case, the time would once again be 10:45 a.m. Because the number given in our problem was 5 min short of the one we used, the correct time must also be 5 min short, or 10:40 a.m.

Problem 4.16

Fidelio was given four pieces of chain, each consisting of three links (shown in Figure 4.9). Show how these four pieces of chain can be made into a circular chain by opening and closing, *at most*, three links.

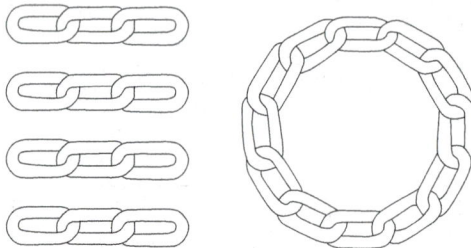

Figure 4.9

Solution

Typically, a first attempt at a solution involves opening the end link of one chain and joining it to the second chain to form a 6-link chain, then opening and closing a link in the third chain and joining it to the 6-link chain to form a 9-link chain. By opening and closing a link in the fourth chain and joining it to the 9-link chain, a 12-link chain, *which is not a circle*, is obtained. Thus, this traditional attempt usually ends unsuccessfully. Students typically try other combinations of opening and closing one link of each of various chain pieces to try to join them together to get the desired result, but this approach will not work.

Here, our strategy of *adopting a different point of view* proves invaluable. Instead of continually trying to open and close *one link of each chain piece*, a different point of view would involve opening *all the links in one chain* and using those links to connect the remaining three chain pieces together and into the required circle chain. This quickly gives the successful conclusion.

Note: A similar version of this problem is Problem 2.13 in Chapter 2.

Problem 4.17

In Figure 4.10, $\overline{AB}$ and $\overline{CD}$ are perpendicular diameters that meet at O. Any point, E, is selected on arc AC, and perpendiculars are drawn to $\overline{AB}$ and $\overline{CD}$, intersecting them at F and G, respectively. If diameter $AB = 16$, find the length of segment FG.

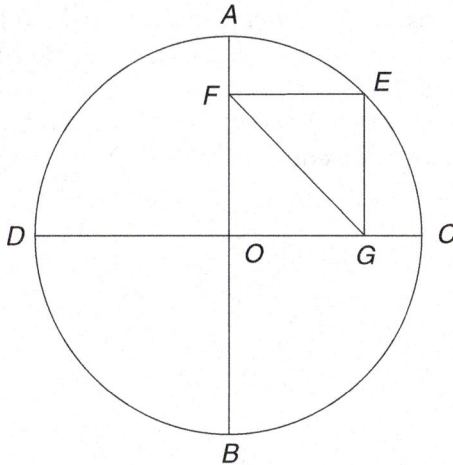

Figure 4.10

Solution

A traditional approach is to draw auxiliary lines and try to place, in a more familiar context, the segment whose length we seek. Thus, we extend $\overline{EF}$ to meet the circle at J, and extend $\overline{EG}$ to meet the circle at H. We now draw

$\overline{JOH}$. Since angle E is a right angle, $\overline{JOH}$ must be a diameter of length 16 (see Figure 4.11).

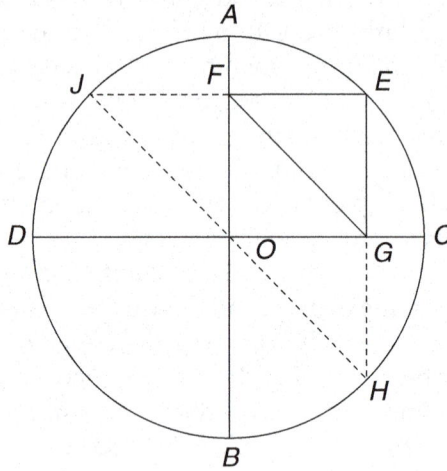

Figure 4.11

Whereas $\overline{JE}$ is a chord of the circle, it is bisected by perpendicular diameter AB. Therefore, $JF = FE$. Similarly, $\overline{EH}$ is a chord of the circle and is bisected by perpendicular diameter CD. Therefore, $EG = GH$. Thus, $JE = 2 \times EF$ and $EH = 2 \times EG$. This makes triangle EFG similar to triangle EJH, and the ratio of similitude is 1:2. Thus, $FG = \frac{1}{2}(16) = 8$.

Although this solution yields the correct answer in a pretty straightforward manner, it may not be easy for students to decide which lines to draw. Let's examine this problem from *another point of view*. Figure $EFOG$ is a rectangle, due to the perpendicular diameters and the perpendiculars dropped from point E to these diameters. We can now draw the other diagonal, OE. Because the diagonals of a rectangle are equal, $FG = OE = 8$ (see Figure 4.12).

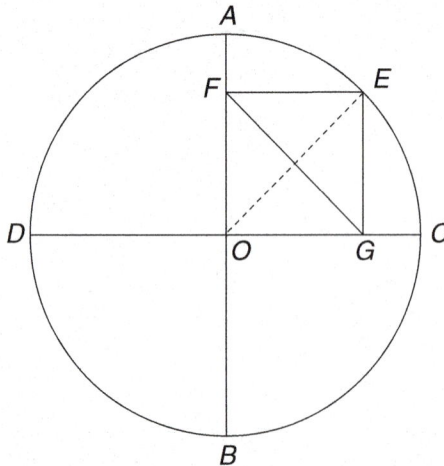

Figure 4.12

Problem 4.18

A box contains four slips of paper. On each slip is written one of the four digits 3, 5, 7, and 9. The slips are drawn from the box one at a time. As they are drawn, they are placed from left to right to form a four-digit number. What is the probability that the number formed is a prime number?

Solution

Students usually begin this problem by writing out the entire sample space:

3579	5379	7953	9753
3597	5397	7935	9735
3759	5739	7395	9573
3795	5793	7359	9537
3975	5973	7539	9357
3957	5937	7593	9375

They then test each of the 24 numbers to determine if it is a prime. This is extremely time-consuming, even with a calculator, due to the size of the numbers involved and the numbers to be tested. It will lead to the correct answer, however, if carried out correctly.

Let's examine this problem from *another point of view*. Whereas the four digits in each number are 3, 5, 7, and 9, the sum of these four digits will always be 24. As this is a multiple of 3, the number formed by these digits must be a multiple of 3 and, therefore, will not be a prime number. We can thus conclude that there will be no prime numbers in this sample space, and the probability requested is thus 0. We looked at this problem from the point of view of divisibility in classes of numbers rather than inspecting each entry separately. This *alternative point of view*, one can clearly see, offers quite an efficient method of solution.

Problem 4.19

A rectangular box has faces that measure 165, 176, and 540 in.^{2} What is the volume of the box?

Solution

Most students might be expected to set up a system of three equations that represent the areas of the three faces, solve them simultaneously to find the three dimensions, and then multiply these dimensions to obtain the volume.

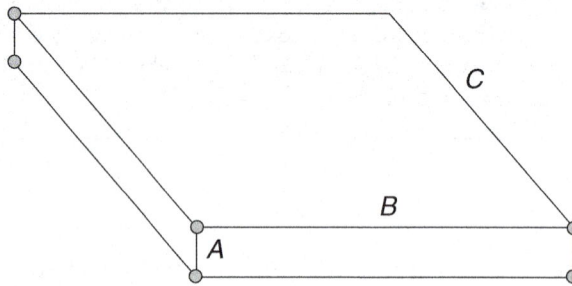

Figure 4.13

We know that

$$a \times b = 165$$
$$a \times c = 176$$
$$b \times c = 540.$$

By solving these equations simultaneously, we obtain $a = \frac{22}{3}$, $b = \frac{45}{2}$, and $c = 24$. Thus, the volume of the box is 3,960 in.^{3}.

As an alternative, we can approach the problem from *another point of view*. We were not asked to find the individual dimensions, a, b, and c. Thus, we proceed as follows:

$$V = a \times b \times c$$
$$V^2 = a \times b \times c \times a \times b \times c$$
$$V^2 = (a \times b) \times (a \times c) \times (b \times c)$$
$$V^2 = 176 \times 165 \times 540$$
$$V = \sqrt{176 \times 165 \times 540}$$
$$= 3,960 \text{ in.}^3$$

Problem 4.20

What is the probability that of five people in a room, at least two will have the same birth date (assuming the exclusion of February 29)?

Solution

The usual approach involves finding the probability that the "first" person matches the birth date of one of the others in the room. Then this sort of reasoning is continued to each of the other people in the room. This, of course, inevitably leads to confusion.

A better way to approach this problem is to look at it from a *different point of view*, namely, to consider the probability of *not* matching birth dates. We begin with the "first" person's birth date.

The probability that the first person's own birth date matches is $\frac{365}{365}$ and that the second person has a different birth date is $\frac{364}{365}$.

The probability that the third person has a birth date different from the previous two persons is $\frac{363}{365}$.

The probability that the fourth person has a birth date different from the previous two persons is $\frac{362}{365}$.

The probability that the fifth person has a birth date different from the previous two persons is $\frac{361}{365}$.

The probability that all five have different birth dates is

$$\frac{365}{365} \cdot \frac{364}{365} \cdot \frac{363}{365} \cdot \frac{362}{365} \cdot \frac{361}{365} = \frac{17{,}267{,}274{,}024}{17{,}748{,}900{,}625} = .9728644263002.$$

Therefore, the probability that they do *not* all have different birth dates or that at least two have the same birth date is $1 - .9728644263002 = .0271355736998$.

Notice that rather than doing directly what the problem asked, we considered the problem from *another point of view*, which made it considerably easier to solve.

Problem 4.21

Prove that the median drawn to the hypotenuse of a right triangle is half the length of the hypotenuse.

Solution

The traditional way to prove this statement is to extend the median $\overline{AM}$ its own length to a point P, and draw $\overline{PB}$ and $\overline{PC}$. The resulting quadrilateral $ABPC$ is a rectangle (because the diagonals bisect each other and it contains one right angle). The diagonals of a rectangle are the same length; therefore, $\overline{AM}$ is half the length of $\overline{BC}$.

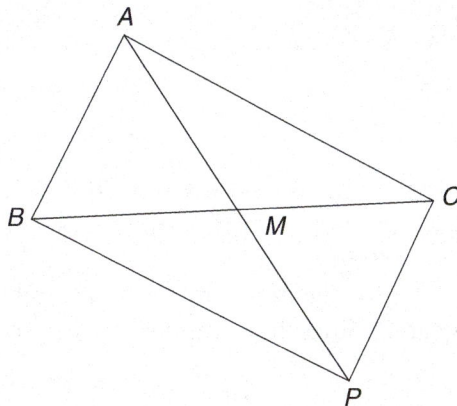

Figure 4.14

We can look at this problem from a *different point of view* by considering the circumcircle of $\triangle ABC$. Since BAC is a right angle, it is inscribed in a semicircle. This makes $\overline{BC}$ the diameter. Since $\overline{BC}$ is the diameter, the center of the circle is at the midpoint, M, of $\overline{BC}$. Therefore, median $\overline{AM}$ of $\triangle ABC$ is also a radius of the circumcircle and therefore half the length of the hypotenuse.

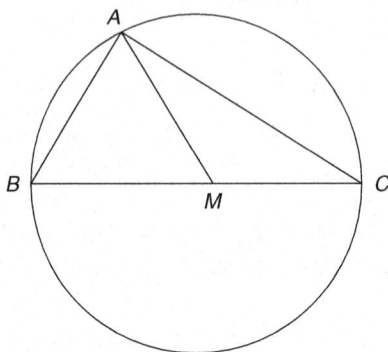

Figure 4.15

Not only have we demonstrated here the value of looking at the problem from a *different point of view* but in this particular case we have shown a very useful (and often neglected) scheme, that of considering the circumcircle of a given figure. The circumcircle, which is a fixed "component" of many geometric figures (all triangles, of course), brings with it many useful properties and helps put other aspects of a given situation into a useful perspective, as the preceding example shows.

Problem 4.22

Express the number 999,973 as the product of primes (not necessarily distinct primes).

Solution

It would be rather difficult, not to mention time-consuming, to try to check for divisibility by the various prime numbers so as to "stumble" on the correct prime factorization.

We can, however, try to get the number into another form—one that may be more manageable. Since the number is close to 1 million, we can write this in the form $1,000,000 - 27 = 999,973$. We now can look at the number from *another point of view*, namely, a difference of two cubes, $100^3 - 3^3$.

By factoring the difference of two cubes, $a^3 - b^3 = (a - b)(a^2 + ab + b^2)$, we get $100^3 - 3^3 = (100 - 3)(100^2 + 300 + 3^2) = 97 \times 10,309$. By *intelligent guessing and testing*, we find that 13 divides 10,309 twice; thus, $10,309 = 13 \times 13 \times 61$. Therefore, $999,973 = 97 \times 61 \times 13 \times 13$.

Problem 4.23

A cat chases a mouse, which has a 160-m head start. For every 7 m the mouse runs, the cat runs 9 m. How far must the cat run to catch the mouse?

Solution

This (almost) typical uniform motion problem has one disconcerting aspect: It doesn't give the speeds in the usual form, as meters per minute or meters per second. Thus, a usual "textbook" solution is not immediately forthcoming. It is hoped that students will see that the relative speeds are, in fact, given: For any time interval (seconds, minutes, or hours), the speed can be called (for example) $9x$ and $7x$ meters per minute (or any other time interval).

Once this complication has been settled, the rest of the problem can be solved in the usual way. That is, if the distance the mouse runs is d, then the distance the cat runs is $d + 160$. Therefore, the time the mouse runs is $\frac{d}{7x}$ and the time the cat runs is $\frac{d+160}{9x}$. Because both times are the same $\left(\frac{d}{7x} = \frac{d+160}{9x}\right)$ and then $d = 560$, the cat runs $560 + 160 = 720$ m.

We can look at this problem from *another point of view*. The cat gains $9 - 7 = 2$ m for each 9-m interval it runs. To make up the mouse's 160-m head start, the cat must run $\frac{160}{2} = 80$ intervals. Because each interval for the cat is 9 m, the cat runs $(80)(9) = 720$ m.

The best method to use to solve a problem is the one that the individual learner feels comfortable with and can genuinely understand. Some students may not be able to exercise a sufficient level of abstraction to understand how to use our strategy of *considering a different point of view*. These students may feel more comfortable using a more "automatic," more "mechanical" procedure. For students who can appreciate the second (perhaps more elegant) method, the teacher has an "obligation" to demonstrate and explain that method. The more solutions teachers show their classes, the more they can appeal to the individual learner and the broader the instructional program will be. This instructional broadening is a desirable form of enrichment.

Problem 4.24

Find the real number values that satisfy the following three equations simultaneously:

$$xyz^3 = 24, xy^3z = 54, x^3yz = 6.$$

Solution

Typically, students are trained to solve equations simultaneously by either substitution or addition. The latter makes no sense here, and the former becomes rather cumbersome because numerous substitutions are required.

We can look at this problem from a *different point of view*. First, let us look at the constants in factored form:

$$xyz^3 = 2^3 \times 3$$
$$xy^3z = 3^3 \times 2$$
$$x^3yz = 2 \times 3.$$

Multiplying these three equations together gives us

$$x^5y^5z^5 = 3^5 \times 2^5$$

or

$$xyz = 3 \times 2 = 6.$$

By dividing each of the original equations by $xyz = 6$, we get

$$z^2 = 4, y^2 = 9, x^2 = 1.$$

All three of the variables can be positive, or two can be negative. So the solutions are

Solution	x	y	z
1	1	3	2
2	−1	3	−2
3	1	−3	−2
4	−1	−3	2

Problem 4.25

Find the value of the following (without a calculator, of course!):

$$\frac{10^2 + 11^2 + 12^2 + 13^2 + 14^2}{365}.$$

Solution

Rather than doing the indicated arithmetic, consider *adopting a different point of view*, that is, rewriting each of the terms as follows:

$$\frac{(12-2)^2 + (12-1)^2 + 12^2 + (12+1)^2 + (12+2)^2}{365}.$$

By expanding each of the binomial squares, we get

$$\frac{(12^2 - 48 + 4) + (12^2 - 24 + 1) + 12^2 + (12^2 + 24 + 1) + (12^2 + 48 + 4)}{365}.$$

This can be simplified by combining terms as follows:

$$\frac{5(12^2) + 4 + 1 + 1 + 4}{(5)(73)}.$$

This gives us

$$\frac{720 + 10}{(5)(73)} = 2.$$

Although a calculator computation would have been just as efficient, this is perhaps more elegant!

Problem 4.26

Find the measure of the angle *ABC* formed by the two diagonals of the given cube.

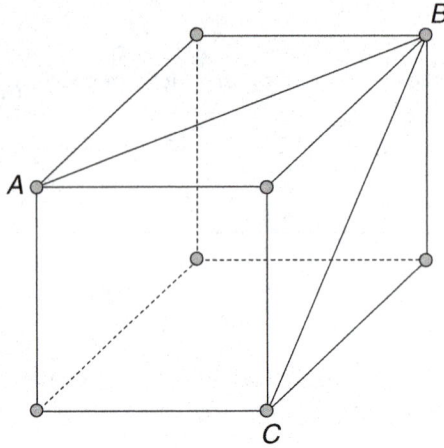

Figure 4.16

Solution

A student's first reaction is to somehow work with the trihedral angle at B. This will lead to a great deal of confusion. If one adopts a different point of view, then one could focus on the plane determined by the points A, B, and C.

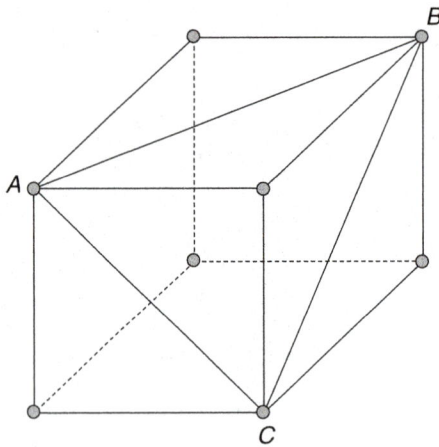

Figure 4.17

By drawing the segment AC, we get an equilateral triangle ABC, where each angle is $60°$. Thus, $\angle ABC = 60°$.

5

Solving a Simpler Analogous Problem

Although by now it should be apparent that there is usually more than one way to solve a problem, the issue at hand is to discover (or determine) the best, most efficient, or most revealing method for solving a particular problem. One method that sometimes turns out to be most revealing is to change the given problem into one that may be easier to solve and, by solving this ancillary problem, gain the insight needed to solve the original problem. In fact, many times younger children will change the numbers in a problem to simpler numbers to avoid the confusion. Thus, when a problem refers to 1,257 and 1,385 to see if the sum is odd or even, young children may resort to using 7 and 5 to attempt to find a method for resolving the problem. They then apply this same method to the larger and more complicated numbers. Although the following example seems to skirt the issue of exactness, it is a practical way to deal with an everyday problem that does not require an absolutely exact answer.

THE *SOLVING A SIMPLER ANALOGOUS PROBLEM* STRATEGY IN EVERYDAY LIFE PROBLEM-SOLVING SITUATIONS

Americans traveling abroad find that daily temperatures are usually given in degrees Celsius. Thus, they usually convert Celsius temperatures to the more common (to them) Fahrenheit scale. Rather than use the formula $F = \frac{9}{5}C + 32$, we can approximate by doubling the Celsius given temperature and adding 30°. Although the Fahrenheit temperature is merely an approximation, it is generally adequate for everyday purposes. We see here, however, that by solving a somewhat simpler problem, we have essentially arrived at a useful answer.

When people purchase a new computer, they rarely try to learn how to use all the capabilities of the machine at one time. Rather, they learn how to use a few of the simple, basic features; that is, they examine a series of simpler problems. These simpler problems are then combined into a variety of sequences. By solving the simpler problem of mastering a few steps at a time, they eventually master the complex whole.

APPLYING THE *SOLVING A SIMPLER ANALOGOUS PROBLEM* STRATEGY TO SOLVE MATHEMATICS PROBLEMS

Consider the following problem from geometry:

> Given that the angle sum of all pentagrams (i.e., a five-pointed star) is constant, determine that angle sum. (One such pentagram is shown in Figure 5.1.)

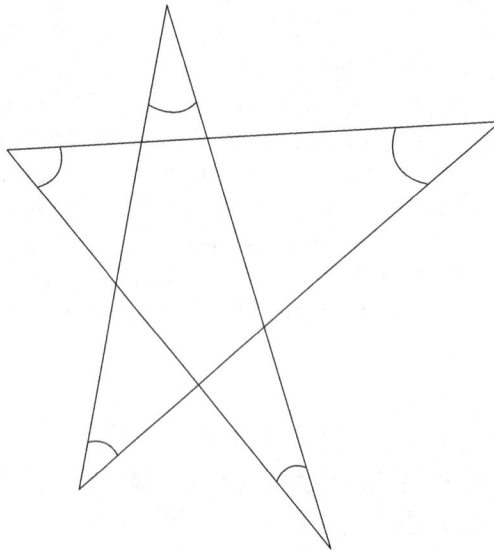

Figure 5.1

This particular strategy, *solving a simpler analogous problem*, can be referred to as specification without loss of generality. That is, if no restrictions are given in the problem, we may select a special case of the given situation to examine. Because, in this problem, the type of pentagram was not specified, we can assume the pentagram to be regular, that is, one that is inscribable in a circle (i.e., all its vertices lie on the circle). In the latter case, we notice that each of the angles is now an inscribed angle of the circle, and so has half the measure of the intercepted arc (see Figure 5.2).

Consequently, we obtain

$$m\angle A = \tfrac{1}{2}m\widehat{CD}, m\angle B = \tfrac{1}{2}m\widehat{ED}, m\angle C = \tfrac{1}{2}m\widehat{AE}, m\angle D = \tfrac{1}{2}m\widehat{AB}, m\angle E = \tfrac{1}{2}m\widehat{BC}.$$

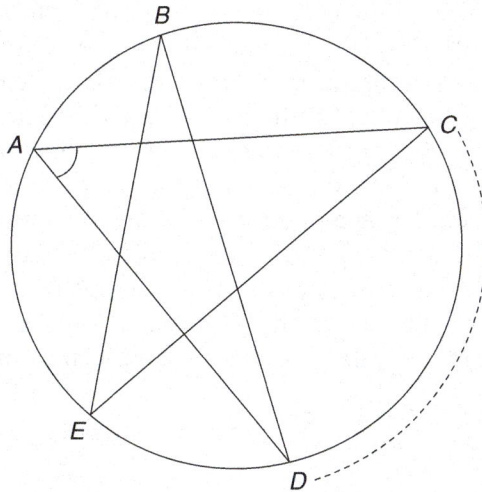

Figure 5.2

If we add these equalities, we obtain

$$m\angle A + m\angle B + m\angle C + m\angle D + m\angle E = \tfrac{1}{2}\left(\widehat{CD} + \widehat{ED} + \widehat{AE} + \widehat{AB} + \widehat{BC}\right)$$
$$= \tfrac{1}{2} \times 360° = 180°.$$

That is, the sum of measures of the angles of the pentagram is one half the degree measure of the circle, or 180°. Again, note that there was no loss of generality by allowing the nonspecified pentagram to assume a more useful configuration. Yet this change made the solution of the problem much more manageable and solvable. By *adopting a different point of view*, we had a simpler yet analogous problem to solve, one that led to the solution of the original problem immediately.

Problems need not always be taken from geometry to make use of this valuable strategy. Consider the following problem that confronts many of us.

A special pack of three CDs is priced at $39.00 at the Village Music Shop. The store manager puts the set on sale for 20% off, and then adds an additional 10% discount for Monday only. Maria comes into the store on Monday and wants to know what discount she is really getting. A sales person tells Maria that she is receiving a total discount of 30% (20% + 10%) and the CDs would sell for $27.30 ($39–11.70). The manager intervenes and tells Maria that the CDs should sell for $28.08, a combined discount of 28%. Which one is correct?

Rather than work with the price of $39, let's *solve a simpler problem* where we assume a base price. Because we are working with percents, let's use a base price of $100. Now, a 30% discount (the first case) reduces the price to $70. In the second case, a discount of 20% reduces the price to $80, and the second discount of 10% on the $80 further reduces the price to $72. Based on a price of $100, the combined discounts result in a single discount equivalent to 28%. We can now simply take 72% of the original price of $39 and solve the problem. Solving a simpler, analogous problem enables us to quickly resolve the problem at hand. The manager was correct; the CDs should sell for $28.08.

Sometimes a problem can appear to be unusually overwhelming. Yet by considering a simpler case of the situation presented, the problem can become much more manageable. Take, for example, the following problem[1]:

$$\text{If } {}_xP_y = \frac{((25!)!)!}{(3!)!}, \text{ what is the value of } x - y?$$

At first glance, the nest of factorials can be a bit upsetting. Considering a *simpler analogous problem* where, say, ${}_7P_3 = \frac{7!}{(7-3)!}$, we notice that only the denominator plays a role in the determination of $x - y$. Thus, we must evaluate only $(3!)! = 720$ to get the answer. The inspection of a simpler analogous problem gave us the necessary key to the solution, namely, the numerator did not play a role in answering the question.

PROBLEMS USING THE *SOLVING A SIMPLER ANALOGOUS PROBLEM* STRATEGY

Problem 5.1

The divisors of 360 add up to 1,170. What is the sum of the reciprocals of the divisors of 360?

---

1. This problem was contributed by Dr. Stephen E. Moresh.

The most obvious solution would be to find all the divisors of 360, take their reciprocals, and then add. The divisors of 360 are 1, 2, 3, 4, 5, 6, 8, 9, ..., 120, 180, 360. The reciprocals are $\frac{1}{1}, \frac{1}{2}, \frac{1}{3}, \frac{1}{4}, \frac{1}{5}, \frac{1}{6}, \frac{1}{8}, \frac{1}{9}, \ldots, \frac{1}{120}, \frac{1}{180}, \frac{1}{360}$. We now find the common denominator (360), convert all the fractions to their equivalents, and then add. It is quite easy to make a mechanical or computational error, as well as possibly miss one or more divisors.

Let's examine a *simpler analogous problem*. Let's find the sum of the *reciprocals* of the divisors of 12 and see if this helps. The divisors of 12 are 1, 2, 3, 4, 6, and 12. Their sum is $1 + 2 + 3 + 4 + 6 + 12 = 28$. Now let's find the sum of the reciprocals of these factors:

$$\frac{1}{1} + \frac{1}{2} + \frac{1}{3} + \frac{1}{4} + \frac{1}{6} + \frac{1}{12} = \frac{28}{12}.$$

Aha! The numerator of the fraction is the sum of the divisors, while the denominator is the number we're working with. Now we can solve our original problem.

The sum of the factors of 360 is 1,170. Thus, the sum of the reciprocals of the factors must be $\frac{1,170}{360}$.

Problem 5.2

At the end of the seventh inning, the score of the baseball game was Thunder, 8, and Rifles, 8. How many different scores were possible at the end of the sixth inning?

Solution

The most usual approach to this problem is to list all the possible scores. Even if this is done systematically, it is a difficult task, and students rarely can be certain that they have listed them all. Let's apply the problem-solving strategy of *solving a simpler problem* and see what happens. We reduce the scores to 0-0, then 1-1, then 2-2, and so on. It is hoped that a pattern will emerge. (Again, notice that we are making use of more than one single strategy in solving the problem.)

Score	How Many	Actual Scores
0-0	1	0-0
1-1	4	0-1,1-0,0-0,1-1
2-2	9	2-0, 0-2, 1-0, 1-1, 2-1, 1-2, 0-1, 0-0, 2-2
3-3	16	3-0, 0-3, 2-0, 0-2,1-0,1-1, 3-1, 1-3, 2-1, 1-2, 0-1, 0-0, 3-2, 2-3, 2-2, 3-3

Aha! The numbers in the "How Many" column are perfect squares. For a score of $n - n$, there must have been $(n + 1)^2$ scores. Thus, for a score of 8-8, there were 9^2 or 81 possible previous scores.

Notice that we can also examine this problem from *another point of view*. There are 9 possible scores for Thunder (namely, 0-8) and 9 possible scores for Rifles (0-8). Thus, there are 9×9 or 81 possible scores.

Problem 5.3

In Figure 5.3, point *E* lies on $\overline{AB}$ and point *C* lies on $\overline{FG}$. The area of parallelogram *ABCD* = 20 square units. Find the area of parallelogram *EFGD*.

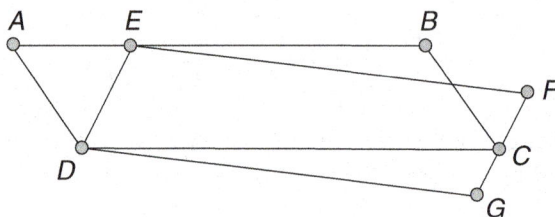

Figure 5.3

Solution

Although the solution would not occur to many people at first thought, the problem can be readily solved using only the tools found in a high school geometry course. Begin by drawing $\overline{EC}$ (see Figure 5.4).

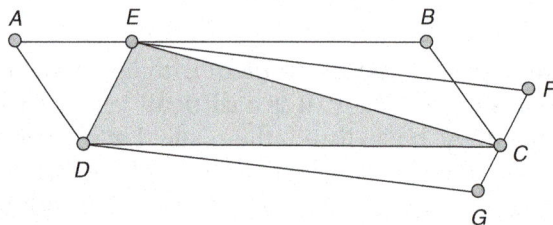

Figure 5.4

Since triangle *EDC* and parallelogram *ABCD* share a common base ($\overline{DC}$) and a common altitude (a perpendicular from *E* to $\overline{DC}$), the area of triangle *EDC* is equal to one half the area of parallelogram *ABCD*.

Similarly, triangle *EDC* and parallelogram *EFGD* share the same base ($\overline{ED}$) and the same altitude to that base (a perpendicular from *C* to $\overline{ED}$); hence, the area of triangle *EDC* equals one half the area of parallelogram *EFGD*.

Now, because the areas of parallelograms *ABCD* and *EFGD* are both equal to the same area (twice the area of triangle *EDC*), the area of the two parallelograms must be equal. Thus, the area of parallelogram *EFGD* = 20 square units.

Although the foregoing solution method is not often used, it is effective and efficient. Nevertheless, this problem can be solved quite elegantly by *solving a simpler analogous problem* (without loss of generality). Recall the original given conditions that the two parallelograms had to have a common vertex (D) and a vertex of one had to be on the side of the other as shown with points E and C. Now, let us suppose that C coincides with G and that E coincides with A. This satisfies the given condition of the original problem and makes the two parallelograms coincide. Thus, the area of parallelogram $EFGD = 20$ square units.

We could also look at this last solution as one of *using extremes*. That is, we could consider point E on $\overline{AB}$, yet placed at an extreme, such as on point A. Similarly, we could place C on G and satisfy all the conditions of the original problem. Thus, the problem is trivial, in that the two parallelograms coincide.

Problem 5.4

What is the product of $0.33\overline{3}$ and $0.66\overline{6}$?

Solution

Students try to punch these two decimals into their calculators and attempt to find the product, but how do you punch a never-ending decimal into a calculator?

Consider a *simpler analogous problem* by changing the given repeating decimals into their equivalent fraction form:

$$0.333\overline{3} = \tfrac{1}{3}, 0.666\overline{6} = \tfrac{2}{3}.$$

Now, simply multiply $\tfrac{1}{3} \times \tfrac{2}{3} = \tfrac{2}{9} = 0.22\overline{2}$.

Problem 5.5

For consecutive, positive, odd integers a, b, and c (where $a < b < c$), is the sign of the expression $(c - a)(b - a)(c - b)(a - c)(a - b)(b - c)$ positive or negative?

Solution

Some students may wish to actually multiply the six factors and obtain the product. They then substitute values for a, b, and c (say 15, 17, and 19) to obtain the sign of the expression.

However, we can solve this problem by solving a *simpler analogous problem*. We start by selecting some conveniently small, consecutive, positive, odd integers to replace a, b, and c. Let's choose the simplest ones: $a = 1$, $b = 3$, and $c = 5$. Then,

$$
\begin{aligned}
(c - a)&(b - a)(c - b)(a - c)(a - b)(b - c) \\
&= (5 - 1)(3 - 1)(5 - 3)(1 - 5)(1 - 3)(3 - 5) \\
&= \ \ (4) \quad (2) \quad \ (2) \ \ (-4) \ \ (-2) \ \ (-2) \\
&= -256.
\end{aligned}
$$

Thus, the sign of the expression is negative.

An alternative solution is to note that $(a - c)$ is the negative of $(c - a)$; also, $(a - b)$ and $(b - a)$ are negatives of one another, as are $(b - c)$ and $(c - b)$. Therefore, there are three negative factors in the product, ensuring that the product will be negative.

Note: This problem also could have been done in the same way if the given numbers were not necessarily consecutive, just all three different.

Problem 5.6

Given the four numbers

   7,895

   13,127

   51,873

   7,356

what percent of their sum is their average?

Solution

The typical student does exactly what the problem calls for. That is, first find the sum of the four numbers; then find their average. Finally, divide and convert to a percent.

We can solve a *simpler analogous problem* by considering the general case. Let the sum of these numbers be represented by S. Then, their average is $S/4$. Now, to find what percentage the average is of the sum, we first divide $\frac{S/4}{S} = \frac{1}{4}$. We now change $\frac{1}{4}$ to a percentage and get 25%.

Problem 5.7

To extend the amount of wine in a 16-oz bottle, Bob decides on the following procedure. On the 1st day, he will only drink 1 oz of the wine and then fill the bottle with water. On the 2nd day, he will drink 2 oz of the mixture and then again fill the bottle with water. On the 3rd day, he will drink 3 oz of the mixture and again fill the bottle with water. He will continue this procedure for succeeding days until he empties the bottle by drinking 16 oz of the mixture on the 16th day. How many ounces of water will Bob drink altogether?

Solution

It is very easy for a student to get bogged down with a problem like this. Many students will make a table showing the amount of wine and water in the bottle on each day and attempt to compute the proportional amounts of each type of liquid Bob drinks on any given day. We can more easily resolve the problem by examining it from *another point of view*, namely, "How much water does Bob add to the mixture each day?" Whereas he eventually empties the bottle (on the 16th day) and it held no water to begin with, he must have consumed all the water that was put into the bottle. On the 1st day, Bob added 1 oz of water. On the 2nd day, he added 2 oz of water. On the 3rd day, he added 3 oz of water. On the 15th day, he added 15 oz of water. (You should ask your students why no water was added on the 16th day.) Therefore, the number of ounces of water Bob consumed was

$$1+2+3+4+5+6+7+8+9+10+11+12+13+14+15=120 \text{ oz.}$$

Although this solution is indeed valid, a slightly *simpler analogous problem* to consider would be to find out how much liquid Bob drank altogether and then simply deduct the amount of wine, namely, 16 oz. Thus,

$$1+2+3+4+5+6+7+8+9+10$$
$$+11+12+13+14+15+16-16=120.$$

Bob consumed 136 oz of liquid, of which 120 oz was water.

Problem 5.8

In Figure 5.5, the two unequal circles intersect at *P* and *Q*, and $\overline{APB}$ is parallel to $\overline{DQC}$. Show that *ABCD* is a parallelogram.

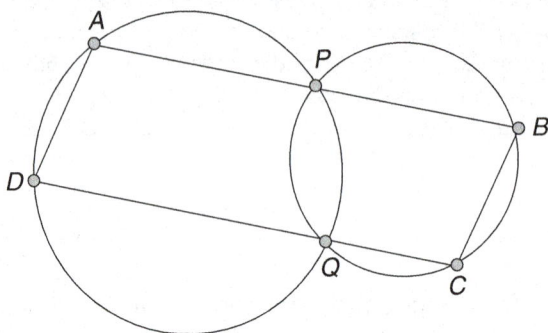

Figure 5.5

Solution

The usual initial approach by students is to examine the chord lengths in an attempt to show that $\overline{AP} + \overline{PB} = \overline{DQ} + \overline{QC}$. When this fails, the students examine the inscribed angles and their intercepted arcs. Again, this procedure is usually doomed to failure.

The demonstration that follows depends on making a *simpler analogous problem* out of this puzzling situation. One often-used technique is to draw an auxiliary line, which reduces the problem to a much simpler one.

We draw $\overline{PQ}$ (see Figure 5.6) and then proceed as follows:

1. ∠*A* is supplementary to ∠*PQD*, and ∠*C* is supplementary to ∠*BPQ*, because the opposite angles of an inscribed quadrilateral are supplementary.

2. We were given that $\overline{APB}$ is parallel to $\overline{DQC}$. Thus, $m\angle BPQ = m\angle PQD$, because the alternate interior angles of parallel lines have equal measure.

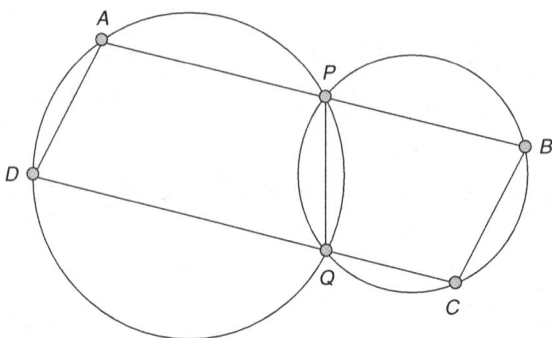

Figure 5.6

3. This means that $m\angle A = m\angle C$, because they are each supplementary to angles with equal measure.

4. In a similar manner, we can show that $m\angle B = m\angle D$.

5. Therefore, $ABCD$ is a parallelogram because its opposite angles are congruent.

The auxiliary line segment $\overline{PQ}$ allowed us to simplify the problem, which made it solvable.

Another solution can be found using the strategy of *adopting a different point of view*. Using the relationship that the base angles of an isosceles trapezoid are congruent, we can get from isosceles trapezoids $APQD$ and $CQPB$ that $m\angle DAP = m\angle APQ = m\angle PQC = m\angle QCB$. Since $\angle C$ is supplementary to $\angle B$, by substitution, $\angle A$ is supplementary to $\angle B$, and hence $\overline{AD}$ is parallel to $\overline{BC}$, and $ABCD$ is a parallelogram.

Problem 5.9

Find the sum of the coefficients in the binomial expansion of $(x + y)^8$.

Solution

The traditional solution to this problem involves finding the coefficients of the nine terms in the expansion. Some students will expand the binomial and obtain

$$(x+y)^8 = x^8 + 8x^7y + 28x^6y^2 + 56x^5y^3 + 70x^4y^4 + 56x^3y^5 + 28x^2y^6 + 8xy^7 + y^8.$$

By adding the coefficients,

$$1 + 8 + 28 + 56 + 70 + 56 + 28 + 8 + 1 = 256.$$

Another somewhat traditional solution is to express the nine coefficients in combinatorial form and then add them:

$_8C_0 = 1$	$_8C_3 = 56$	$_8C_6 = 28$
$_8C_1 = 8$	$_8C_4 = 70$	$_8C_7 = 8$
$_8C_2 = 28$	$_8C_5 = 56$	$_8C_8 = 1$

Again we obtain the sum of 256.

However, a more elegant approach, one that greatly diminishes the amount of work needed, can be found by *solving a simpler problem*. No values for x and y were specified, so we let $x = y = 1$ in the original expression. Notice that, in the original expansion with $x = y = 1$, the only thing remaining is the sum of the coefficients on the right-hand side of the equation. Thus, $(x + y)^8 = (1 + 1)^8 = (2)^8 = 256$.

Problem 5.10

Find the value of

$$\frac{2+4+6+8+\cdots+34+36+38}{3+6+9+12+\cdots+51+54+57}.$$

Solution

The traditional approach, and one that many students will use, is to add the 19 numbers in the numerator and the 19 numbers in the denominator (using a calculator), and then divide the two sums to find the value of the fraction (again using a calculator). This solution is valid and should yield the correct answer. However, it requires a great deal of effort, and it is easy to make a mistake.

Instead, let's *solve a simpler problem* and see if it leads us to the answer to the original problem. We'll begin with one term in the numerator and denominator, then expand to two terms in each, then three, and so on:

$$\frac{2}{3}=\frac{2}{3},\quad \frac{2+4}{3+6}=\frac{6}{9}=\frac{2}{3},\quad \frac{2+4+6}{3+6+9}=\frac{12}{18}=\frac{2}{3},\quad \frac{2+4+6+8}{3+6+9+12}=\frac{20}{30}=\frac{2}{3}.$$

The answer is $\frac{2}{3}$.

An alternate solution also requires *solving a simpler problem* by getting the problem into a factored form:

$$\frac{2(1+2+3+\cdots+17+18+19)}{3(1+2+3+\cdots+17+18+19)}=\frac{2}{3}.$$

Problem 5.11

In Figure 5.7, the ratio of the diameters of the three circles is 2:3:5. Find the ratio of the area of the shaded region to the area of the larger circle.

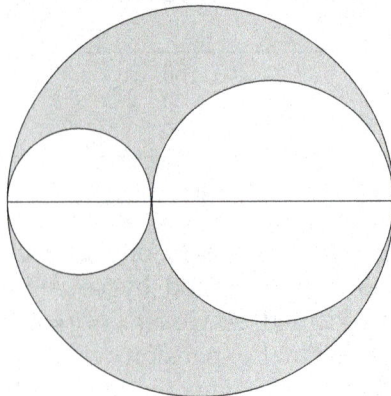

Figure 5.7

Solution

Students may begin by trying to find the areas of each of the three circles and then determining the required ratios. This is impossible in this problem because the sizes of the circles are not given. We could use the strategy of *solving a simpler analogous problem* or imposing a specification without loss of generality. This involves assigning convenient lengths to the three diameters, yet keeping them in the required ratio of 2:3:5, say 2, 3, and 5 in., then finding each of the areas of the three circles, and forming the required ratio.

However, even this is not the most efficient way to a solution. Another of our strategies, namely, *logical reasoning*, generates a simple solution. Whereas the ratio of the linear parts (the diameters) of these similar figures (circles) is given as 2:3:5, the respective areas must be in the ratios of $2^2 : 3^2 : 5^2 = 4 : 9 : 25$. Let's assume that the area of the largest circle is 25 (a specification without loss of generality). Then, the areas of the other two circles would be 4 and 9 for a sum of 13. The area of the shaded region would be $25 - 13 = 12$. The required ratio is 12:25.

Problem 5.12

Find all the integral values of x that satisfy

$$(3x + 7)^{(x^2 - 9)} = 1.$$

Solution

The sight of a linear expression raised to a quadratic exponent appears to require a rather lengthy and complex solution. The traditional algebraic solution requires advanced algebraic facility.

However, let's examine a *simpler analogous version of the problem* to find out what is really taking place here. For example, let's look at $a^b = 1$. This problem is a bit less frightening and somewhat easier to examine and discuss. The expression has a value of 1 when the base, a, is 1, because $(1)^b = 1$ for any value of b. Similarly, the expression also has the value 1 when the exponent is 0, because $(a)^0 = 1$ for any nonzero value of a. Now we have a method for attacking the original problem. Have the students go back to the original problem and apply what they found in their examination of the simpler version.

Case 1

Whereas 1 raised to any power equals 1, set the base equal to 1:

$$3x + 7 = 1$$
$$3x = -6$$
$$x = -2.$$

Case 2

Whereas any nonzero expression raised to the 0 power equals 1, set the exponent equal to 0:

$$x^2 - 9 = 0$$
$$(x - 3)(x + 3) = 0$$
$$x = 3, \; x = -3$$

Case 3

When -1 is raised to an even power, it also has a value of $+1$. Consider $3x + 7 = -1$. Then, $x = -\frac{8}{3}$, which is nonintegral.

Thus, there are three integral values of x for which the equation is correct, namely, $+3$, -3, and -2.

Problem 5.13

Given 19 consecutive integers that sum to 95, what is the 10th of these numbers?

Solution

Many students will write out the 19 consecutive numbers in algebraic form as $x, (x+1), (x+2), (x+3), \ldots, (x+17), (x+18)$ and then use these to give a sum of 95.

Sometimes merely recognizing that a simpler version of a particular problem will give us what we are looking for is a difficult process in itself. This problem is an excellent illustration of this. There is a *simpler, yet analogous way* to proceed. By recognizing that the 10th integer of 19 integers is the "middle" one, we may represent this as x, the rest as $(x-9), (x-8), (x-7), \ldots, (x-1), (x), (x+1), \ldots, (x+8), (x+9)$, and sum these to 95. Notice that by pairing the first and last terms $(x-9) + (x+9)$, the second and next to last, $(x-8) + (x+8)$, and so forth, we arrive at $19x = 95$, and the 10th integer, $x = 5$.

We can also approach the problem in a still simpler manner. The "middle" term is the average (or arithmetic mean) of the given 19 integers. Thus, we simply take the sum, 95, and divide it by the numbers of integers, 19. The 10th integer is 5.

Problem 5.14

From any point in or on an equilateral triangle, the sum of the distances to the three sides is the same as for any other such point. What is the sum of these distances if an equilateral triangle has a side length of 4?

Solution

There are several ways to solve this problem. One of the easiest to understand is to select any point in the equilateral triangle (something expected of the typical student) and draw the three perpendiculars to the sides.

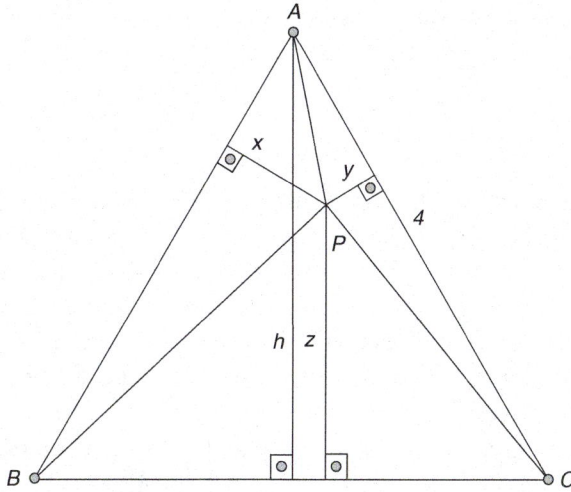

Figure 5.8

By equating the area of $\triangle ABC$ with the sum of the areas of triangles APB, BPC, and CPA using the three altitudes x, y, z and the base 4, we get the area

$$\triangle ABC = \tfrac{1}{2}(4)(h) = \tfrac{1}{2}(4)(x) + \tfrac{1}{2}(4)(y) + \tfrac{1}{2}(4)(z) = \tfrac{1}{2}(4)(x+y+z).$$

Therefore, $h = x + y + z$. In this case, we find the altitude of the equilateral triangle is $2\sqrt{3}$. Thus, $x + y + z = 2\sqrt{3}$.

Without loss of generality, we will consider *a simpler analogous problem*. Because we can choose to place the point P anywhere in or on the equilateral triangle (as the problem states), suppose we place P on A. Then the solution becomes trivial. The perpendiculars to $\overline{AB}$ and $\overline{AC}$ both have length 0, and the perpendicular to $\overline{BC}$ is simply the altitude of the triangle, or $2\sqrt{3}$.

Note that this solution strategy also fits our strategy description for *considering extreme cases*. What we have done is consider the extreme case, where the point assumes the position of the extreme of a triangle, the vertex.[2] This shows that the selection of a strategy is flexible.

---

2. This is discussed as an extreme case in the introduction to Chapter 6.

Problem 5.15

The basketball squad is taking part in a free-throw contest. The 1st player scored x free throws. The 2nd shooter scored y free throws. The 3rd shooter made the same number of free throws as the arithmetic mean of the number of free throws made by the first two shooters. Each subsequent shooter in the contest scored the arithmetic mean of the number of free throws made by all the preceding shooters. How many free throws did the 12th player make?

Solution

Some students may try to solve this problem by finding the arithmetic mean for each of the 12 players in turn. This requires a great deal of time and effort, and it is easy to make an error in the algebraic manipulation.

Instead, let's examine a *simpler analogous problem*. We will replace x and y with simple numbers and see what happens. Suppose the first player made 8 free throws (x) and the second made 12 free throws (y). Then the third player had a score equal to their arithmetic mean, or $\frac{8+12}{2} = \frac{20}{2} = 10$. Now, the fourth player had a score equal to the arithmetic mean of the first three players, namely, $\frac{8+12+10}{3} = \frac{30}{3} = 10$. Similarly, the score made by the fifth player is the arithmetic mean of the scores of the first four players, $\frac{8+12+10+10}{4} = \frac{40}{4} = 10$. Aha! The score made by any player after the first two will always be the arithmetic mean of the scores of the first two players. The correct answer to the problem is the arithmetic mean of the scores of the first two players, namely, $\frac{x+y}{2}$. The *simpler analogous problem* enabled us to determine the method to use to solve the original problem quite quickly.

Problem 5.16

How many subsets of the set $\{m, a, t, h\}$ do not contain the letter m?

Solution

Students' first reaction to solving this problem would be to list the entire sample space, that is, all possible combinations of these letters, and then count those that do not contain the element m. It is hoped that this would be done in a well-organized fashion.

The problem can be very neatly solved by restating the problem as a *simpler analogous problem*. That is, look at the problem as if it did not even contain the letter m. In other words, we are asked to find the number of subsets of the set $\{a, t, h\}$, which is clearly 2^3, which equals 8.

Problem 5.17

Assume that the shuttle trains traveling between New York and Washington leave each city every hour on the hour. On its trip from Washington to New York, a shuttle train will meet x shuttle trains going in the opposite direction. If the one-way trip in either direction requires exactly 4 hr, what is the value of x?

Solution

To determine the speed of the trains and simulate the situation to enable counting the number of passings would be time-consuming and could easily lead to a miscount. We can, however, solve this problem by changing it to *a simpler analogous problem*. Consider the following: At the moment train *A* leaves Washington, say at 2 p.m., the train that left New York at 10 a.m. is just pulling into the Washington station. When train *A* arrives in New York at 6 p.m., a train is leaving New York heading for Washington. Thus, train *A* meets all trains from New York leaving at 10 a.m., 11 a.m., 12 noon, 1 p.m., 2 p.m., 3 p.m., 4 p.m., 5 p.m., and 6 p.m., nine trains in all.

Problem 5.18

Two trains serving the Chicago to New York route, a distance of 800 miles, start toward each other at the same time (along the same tracks). One train is traveling uniformly at 60 mph and the other at 40 mph. At the same time, a bee begins to fly from the front of one of the trains, at a speed of 80 mph, toward the oncoming train. After touching the front of this second train, the bee reverses direction and flies toward the first train (still at the same speed of 80 mph). The bee continues this back-and-forth flying until the two trains collide, crushing the bee. How many miles did the bee fly?

Solution

One is naturally drawn to find the individual distances that the bee traveled. An immediate reaction is to set up an equation based on the relationship rate $\times$ time = distance. However, this back-and-forth path is rather difficult to determine, because it requires considerable calculation. Even then, it is very difficult to solve the problem in this way.

A much more elegant approach would be to *solve a simpler analogous problem* (we could also say we are looking at the problem from *a different point of view*). We seek the distance the bee traveled. If we knew the time the bee traveled, we could determine the bee's distance because we already know the bee's speed.

The time the bee traveled can be easily calculated, because it traveled the entire time the two trains traveled (until they collided). To determine the time, t, the trains traveled, we set up an equation as follows: The distance of the first train is $60t$ and the distance of the second train is $40t$. The total distance the two trains traveled is 800 miles. Therefore, $60t + 40t = 800$ and $t = 8$, which is also the time the bee traveled. We can now find the distance the bee traveled, which is $(8)(80) = 640$ miles.

Problem 5.19

In Figure 5.9, $\overline{CD}$ and $\overline{EF}$ are, respectively, the north and south banks of a river with a uniform width of 1 mile. Town A is 3 miles north of $\overline{CD}$; town B is 5 miles south of $\overline{EF}$ and 15 miles east of town A. If crossing at the riverbanks can be only at right angles to the banks, find the length of the shortest path from town A to town B.

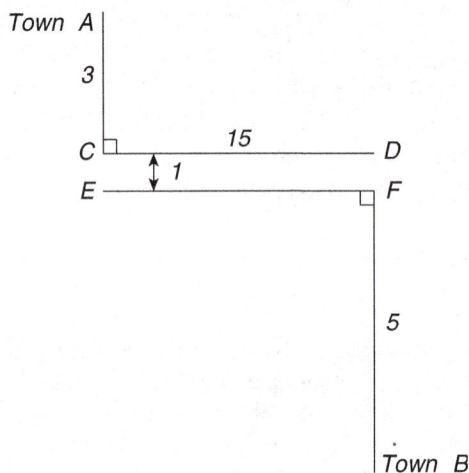

Figure 5.9

Solution

There are a number of ways in which this problem can be solved. The most expedient way is to use our strategy of *solving a simpler analogous problem*—one that modifies the problem without any loss of generality. This entails considering the banks as merged. Then, obviously, the shortest path is the segment $\overline{AB}$ (see Figure 5.10).

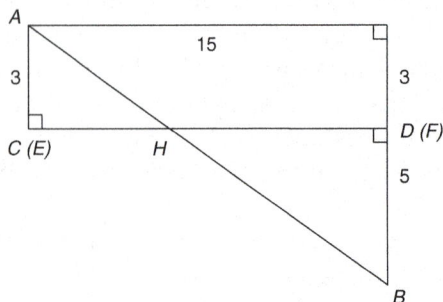

Figure 5.10

$AB^2 = 15^2 + 8^2$, $AB = 17$. Because there is a displacement of 1 mile at the crossing point H, the shortest path is $17 + 1 = 18$ miles.

Note: From the proportionality of the sides of similar triangles, we find that the crossing point is $5\frac{5}{8}$ miles east of C along $\overline{CD}$.

Problem 5.20

For circle O, $\overline{AB} \perp \overline{CD}$; find the diameter of the circle in terms of a, b, c, and d.

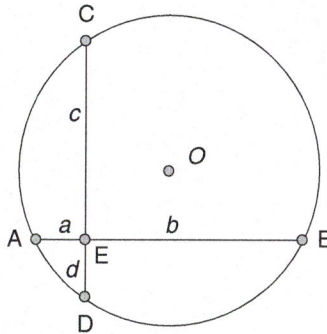

Figure 5.11

Solution

It is natural to seek to use the Pythagorean theorem since perpendicularity was given. Similarity may also come into play. However, these approaches usually leave the diameter out of discussion. This can lead to frustration.

Here, the relationship between $\angle CEB$ and arcs $\widehat{CB}$ and $\widehat{AD}$ ought to be considered. Once the relationship that $m\angle CEB = \frac{1}{2}(m\widehat{CB} + m\widehat{AD})$ is established, it is clear that $m\widehat{CB} + m\widehat{AD} = 180°$.

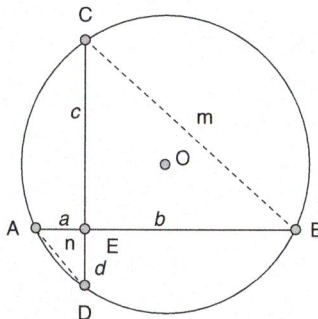

Figure 5.12

Consider the two right triangles $\triangle CEB$ and $\triangle AED$ and apply the Pythagorean theorem to each one.

Then, $m^2 = c^2 + b^2$ or $m = \sqrt{c^2 + b^2}$, and $n^2 = a^2 + d^2$ or $n = \sqrt{a^2 + d^2}$.

Let us do something a bit unusual now and use the strategy of solving a simpler analogous problem (without loss of generality). We will move arcs CB and AD along the circle so that they share a common endpoint, A and C.

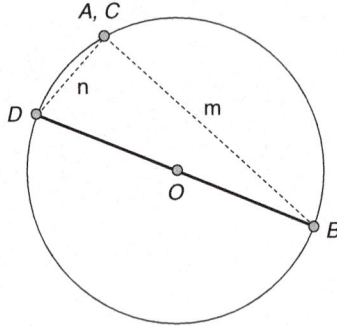

Figure 5.13

Since $m\widehat{CB} + m\widehat{AD} = 180°$, $\overline{DB}$ must be a diameter of circle O, and since $\angle DAB$ is inscribed in a semicircle, $\angle DAB$ is a right angle. Therefore, diameter $BD = \sqrt{m^2 + n^2}$, which from the above equals $\sqrt{(c^2 + b^2) + (a^2 + d^2)} = \sqrt{a^2 + b^2 + c^2 + d^2}$.

Therefore, a simply stated problem has a surprise solution, critically dependent on angle measurement with a circle, specifically, of the angle formed by two chords intersecting in a circle. It is also important to see that we were able to move the chords to a more desirable position without any loss of generality and we then created a more easily solved problem.

6

Considering Extreme Cases

To analyze some situations, whether in a mathematical setting or not, it can be helpful to look at extreme cases. Holding some variables constant while others vary to extremes sometimes yields useful insights into a given situation. Some problems can often be solved much more easily by considering extreme cases of the given situation. By considering extremes, we may be changing variables in the problem, but only those that do not affect the actual problem situation. Here, we must be careful to consider only extremes that do not change the nature of the crucial variables of the problem. In addition, we must be careful that changing a variable does not affect other variables as well.

Used properly, this can be one of the most useful strategies for solving mathematical problems as well as problems in everyday life. We frequently use this sort of reasoning when we confront someone in a negotiation situation. Suppose you feel that your position is right. You are concerned that pushing your point too far with your colleague could cause other problems. Often, we pose this situation in the context of a "worst-case scenario." That is, what is the worst that can happen if our argument goes awry? Then we proceed. This worst-case scenario anticipation is a form of *extreme-case consideration*.

THE *CONSIDERING EXTREME CASES* STRATEGY IN EVERYDAY LIFE PROBLEM-SOLVING SITUATIONS

On observing that the windshield of your car appears to get wetter the faster the car is moving in a rainstorm, you might be inclined to conclude that the car would not get as wet if it were to move slower. This leads to the next natural question, namely, "Is it better to walk slowly or to run in a rainstorm to minimize your wetness?" Setting aside the amount of wetness that the front of your body might get from the storm, let us consider two extreme cases for the top of the head: first, going extremely fast, and second, going so slowly as to be practically stationary. In the first case, there will be a certain amount of wetness on the top of your head, but if you proceed at practically a 0-mph speed, you would get drenched! Therefore, we conclude that the faster you move, the dryer you stay.

The previous illustration of this rather useful problem-solving technique, *using extreme cases*, demonstrates how we use this strategy to cleanly sort out an otherwise cumbersome problem situation. We also use this same strategy of considering extremes in more everyday situations. People who plan to buy an item for which bargaining plays a part, such as buying a house or an item at a garage sale, must determine a strategy to make the seller an offer. They must decide what the lowest (extreme) price ought to be and what the highest (extreme) price might be and then orient themselves from there. In general, we often consider the extreme values of anything we plan to purchase and then make our decision about which item to settle on based on the extreme situations.

When budgeting time, we must *consider extreme cases* to be sure that time allocations are adequate. For example, allowing the maximum amount of time for each of a series of tasks assures when the series of tasks will certainly be completed.

Extreme cases are also used when we seek to test a product, say stereo speakers. We want to test them at extremely low volume and at extremely high volume. We then take for granted (with a modicum of justification) that because the speakers pass the extreme conditions test they will also function properly between these extreme situations.

APPLYING THE *CONSIDERING EXTREME CASES* STRATEGY TO SOLVE MATHEMATICS PROBLEMS

Here is an interesting mathematical problem that will shed some more light on using this method of extreme cases:

Two concentric circles are 10 units apart (as shown in Figure 6.1). What is the difference between the circumferences of the circles?

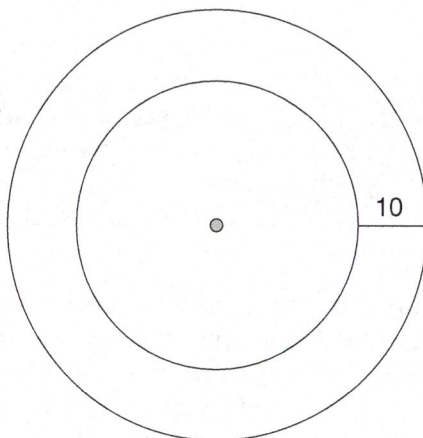

Figure 6.1

The traditional straightforward method for solving this problem is to find the diameters of the two circles, find the circumference of each circle, and then find their difference. Because the lengths of the diameters are not given, the problem is a bit more complicated than usual. Let d represent the diameter of the smaller circle. Then $d + 20$ is the diameter of the larger circle. The circumferences of the two circles will then be πd and $\pi(d + 20)$, respectively. Their difference is $\pi(d + 20) - \pi d = 20\pi$.

A more elegant procedure is to *use an extreme case*. Let the smaller of the two circles become smaller and smaller until it reaches an "extreme" and becomes a "point circle." In this case, it becomes the center of the larger circle. The distance between the two circles now becomes the radius of the larger circle. The difference between the lengths of the circumferences of the two circles at the start is now merely the circumference of the larger circle, or 20π.

Although both procedures yield the same answer, notice how much more work is required for the traditional solution of actually taking the difference of the lengths of the circumferences of the two circles.

Let's consider another situation. Teachers are often interested in finding different ways to demonstrate that the area of a circle equals πr^2. Here is one way in which the *extreme case* strategy can be used.

Consider the circle as the *extreme case* of a regular polygon of n sides, where n approaches infinity. Then, we can make use of the formula for the area of the regular polygon, $A = \frac{1}{2}(aP)$, where a is the apothem (the perpendicular distance from the center of the polygon to one of its sides) and

P is the perimeter. In the *extreme case* we are considering, the apothem equals the radius, r, and the perimeter equals the circumference, $2\pi r$. Thus, the area $= \frac{1}{2}(a)(P) = \frac{1}{2}(r)(2\pi r) = \pi r^2$.

Here is another problem that lends itself to the use of the *extreme cases* strategy:

In a drawer, there are 8 blue socks, 6 green socks, and 12 black socks. What is the smallest number of socks that must be taken from the drawer without looking at them to be certain of having 2 black socks?

This problem requires a form of *extreme case* reasoning, which again calls for setting up the "worst-case scenario." This would have us pick the 8 blue socks and the 6 green socks before a single black sock is selected. The next two picks would have to be black socks. In this situation, it took 16 picks before we were *certain* of getting 2 black socks. Naturally, we might have achieved our goal of getting 2 black socks on our first two tries, but it was not assured, and it would have been highly unusual. Even if we picked 10 socks at random, we could not be certain that we had 2 black ones among them.

A simple extension of this problem is illuminating. Now that we know it would take 16 picks to be certain of getting 2 black socks, how many picks would be necessary to be certain of getting 4 black socks? If you know the answer immediately, you are a logical reasoning whiz! Yes, you only need two more picks, for a total of 18. You've already accounted for the worst case—picking all the socks of the other colors plus 2 black socks with your first 16 picks—so the next two picks can only provide you with 2 black socks. Using the *extreme case* technique can also help define a given problem and then facilitate a solution. Consider the problem of proving the following theorem[1]:

From a point in an equilateral triangle, the sum of the distances to the three sides of the triangle is a constant.

---

1. For a few proofs of this theorem as well as some interesting applications of the theorem, see Posamentier, Alfred S. (2002). *Advanced Euclidean geometry: Excursions for secondary teachers and students*. Emeryville, CA: Key College Publishing.

There are several ways to prove this theorem. However, before embarking on a proof, it would be desirable to know what this "constant" is. We can inspect this question by considering extreme positions for this randomly placed point. Suppose we place this point on a side of the triangle (despite its violation of the given condition, namely, being *in* the triangle). This would have the effect of reducing the distance to this side to 0. How could we reduce the distances to two of the sides of the triangle to 0? By placing the point so that it lies on two sides at the same time, that is, at a vertex. Now a revisit to the original question becomes trivial. The sum of the distances to the three sides is now simply the altitude of the equilateral triangle. And so we have found out what this constant probably is—the altitude of the triangle. Therefore, examining an extreme case was an important aid in the pursuit of a solution. Once we know more precisely what we have to prove, the more easily we should be able to accomplish the task. (See Problem 5.14 for another approach to this problem.)

PROBLEMS USING THE *CONSIDERING EXTREME CASES* STRATEGY

Problem 6.1

In a drawer, there are 8 blue socks, 6 green socks, and 12 black socks. What is the smallest number of socks that must be taken from the drawer without looking at the socks to be certain of having 2 socks of the same color?

Solution

At first glance this problem appears to be similar to the model problem discussed previously. However, there is a slight difference. In this case, we are looking for a matching pair of socks of *any* color. We now apply *extreme case* reasoning, similar to that which we used previously. The worst-case scenario has us picking 1 blue sock, 1 green sock, and 1 black sock in our first three picks. Thus, the fourth sock must provide us with a matching pair, regardless of what color it is. The smallest number of socks to guarantee a matching pair is 4.

Problem 6.2

In circle O, chord $\overline{ED}$ is perpendicular to diameter $\overline{AB}$ at G. Point P is any point on arc AD, and $\overline{PB}$ intersects $\overline{ED}$ at N. $\overline{PG}$ intersects arc EB at F. Show that $BN \geq FG$.

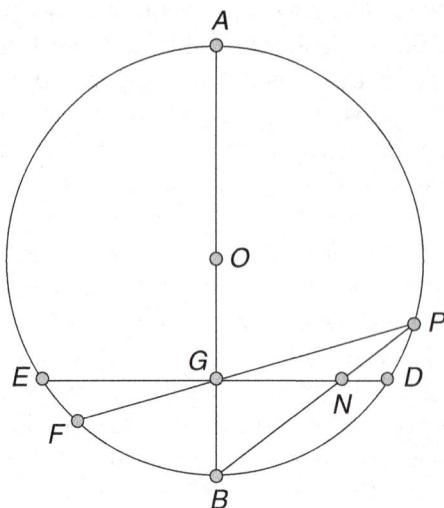

Figure 6.2

Solution

The traditional method for resolving this problem involves drawing auxiliary lines, and turns out to be quite complicated. If we use our strategy of *considering extreme cases*, the problem becomes fairly easy to resolve.

We are told that point P must be on arc AD, but its exact location on the arc is not specified. Therefore, we can place point P at either extreme and make the assumption that the lines will behave as though they move from one extreme to the other as P moves from A to D.

Let's first consider what happens if point P coincides with point A. In this case, $\overline{BN}$ will coincide with $\overline{BG}$, and $\overline{FG}$ becomes coincident with $\overline{BG}$. Consequently, $BN = FG$ at this extreme (where P coincides with A).

Now, let's consider what happens if point P coincides with point D. In this case, $\overline{BN}$ is now coincident with $\overline{BD}$, and $\overline{FG}$ becomes $\overline{EG}$. However, because $\overline{EG}$ is of the same length as $\overline{DG}$, we can simply compare $\overline{BD}$ with $\overline{DG}$. Because triangle BDG is a right triangle, its hypotenuse ($\overline{BD}$, which equals $\overline{BN}$) must be the longest side. We now have $BN > DG$ at this extreme (where P coincides with D). Thus, $BN > FG$, which solves the problem.

Although this procedure may sound complicated, it's actually quite simple, especially compared with the more traditional solution, which is far too complicated to warrant wasting precious space here.

Problem 6.3

There is only one four-digit perfect square that is formed by a pair of different two-digit perfect squares placed side by side. Find it.

Solution

Many students begin this problem by forming all possible four-digit numbers composed of two two-digit perfect squares and then trying to find which of these is itself a perfect square. This takes a great deal of time and depends on the students obtaining all the perfect four-digit squares made from two-digit squares. It's obviously rather complex.

Let's consider the extreme cases for the four-digit squares. The only possible two-digit perfect squares are 16, 25, 36, 49, 64, and 81. The answer must lie between 1,625 (the *smallest* possible four-digit number from the given options) and 8,164 (the *largest* possible from the given options). The square root of 1,625 is 40.31, whereas the square root of 8,164 is 90.35. Thus, the square root must lie between 40 and 90. Using our calculator, $40 \times 40 = 1,600$ and $41 \times 41 = 1,681$. Aha, 16 and 81 are both two-digit perfect squares! Because the problem stated that there is only one four-digit number satisfying the given conditions, we need look no further; the answer is 1,681.

Problem 6.4

In Figure 6.3, $\overline{AB}$ is a chord of the larger of the two concentric circles and is tangent to the smaller circle at T. Find the area of the shaded region between the two circles if $AB = 8$.

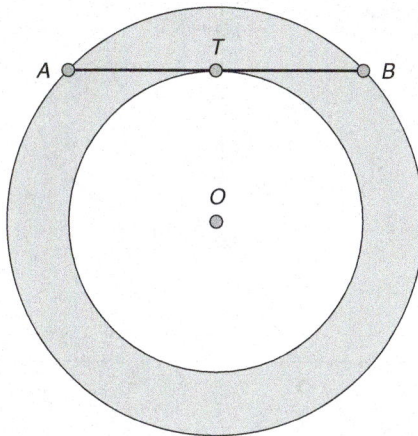

Figure 6.3

Solution

We know that a radius is perpendicular to a tangent at the point of contact (T). Furthermore, a radius perpendicular to a chord divides the chord into two equal segments. Thus, $AT = BT = 4$. We know that the area of the region between the two circles (the doughnut shape) can be found by obtaining the difference between the areas of the two circles. Thus, the area of this region between the two circles equals $\pi R^2 - \pi r^2 = \pi(R^2 - r^2)$. Now, whereas $OC = R$ and $OT = r$, $CT = (R - r)$ and $DT = (R + r)$ (Figure 6.4).

Using the "product of the segments of the chords" theorem, we obtain

$$(R - r)(R + r) = 4 \times 4$$
$$R^2 - r^2 = 16.$$

Therefore, the area of the region between the two circles equals 16π square units.

We can also solve this problem by drawing line segment $\overline{OA}$. We now create a right triangle ATO, in which $(OA)^2 = (OT)^2 + 4^2$, or $R^2 - r^2 = 16$.

We can also look at this problem by *considering an extreme case*. Let's assume that the smaller circle gets smaller and smaller, until it becomes a point that coincides with point O. Then, $\overline{AB}$ becomes a diameter of the larger circle, and the area of the region between the two circles becomes the area of the larger circle, which equals $\pi R^2 = 16\pi$.

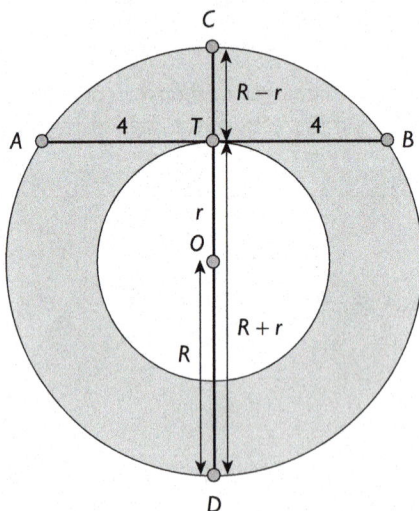

Figure 6.4

Problem 6.5

Imagine a metal hoop fitted tightly around the Earth at the equator. We now cut the hoop and insert a piece exactly 10 ft long. Now we hold the hoop in a position so that it is exactly concentric with the equator. How far above the surface will the hoop now be?

Solution

Students usually begin by drawing the situation (Figure 6.5). In this figure, C is the original circumference of the hoop and r is the radius; C' is the circumference of the hoop with the 10 ft added, R is the new radius, and x is the distance (in feet) of the new hoop above the Earth's surface:

(original circle) $C = 2\pi r$

(new circle) $C' = 2\pi R = C + 10$

$$C + 10 = 2\pi(r + x)$$
$$C + 10 = 2\pi r + 2\pi x$$
$$10 = 2\pi x$$
$$\frac{5}{\pi} = x$$
$$1.6 = x.$$

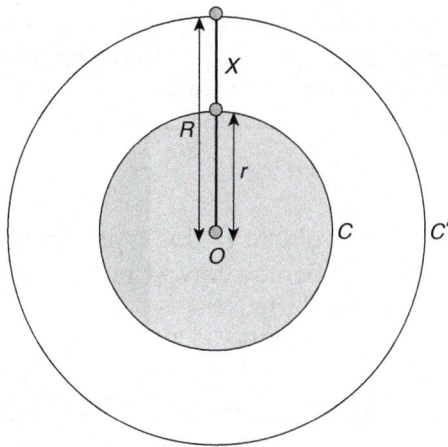

Figure 6.5

Let's solve this problem by *considering the extreme case*. Let the original circle shrink until r equals 0 (Figure 6.6). Now, the original "hoop" has become point O, with $C = 0$.

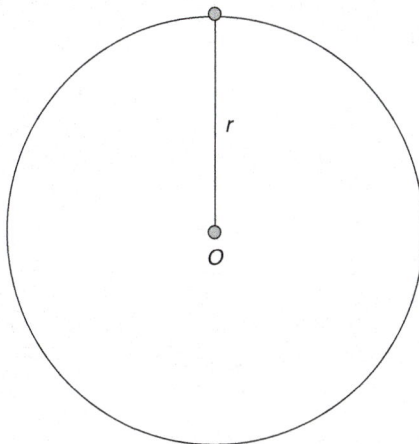

Figure 6.6

The distance we seek is the length of the radius of a circle with a circumference of 10 ft. Thus,

$$10 = 2\pi r$$
$$\frac{5}{\pi} = r$$
$$1.6 = r.$$

The distance above the surface is 1.6 ft.

Problem 6.6

Senta's mathematics teacher has given the class five tests this semester, each scored from 0 to 100 inclusive. Senta had an average of 90 for the five tests. What was the lowest possible score Senta could have earned on any one test?

Solution

Students usually begin a problem of this type by using a trial-and-error method in an attempt to find Senta's lowest possible score. However, this procedure does not guarantee finding it.

Let's *consider the extreme case*. If Senta had an overall average of 90 for the five tests, the total of her scores must be $5 \times 90 = 450$. Now, consider the extreme (highest) possible score for each of the first four tests, namely, 100 for each. This is a total of 400. Thus, the lowest possible score on one test for Senta would have been 50, so as to achieve the total of 450.

Problem 6.7

Two squares, each with sides measuring 8 units, are placed such that a vertex of one lies at the center of the other. Find the area of quadrilateral *ENCL*.

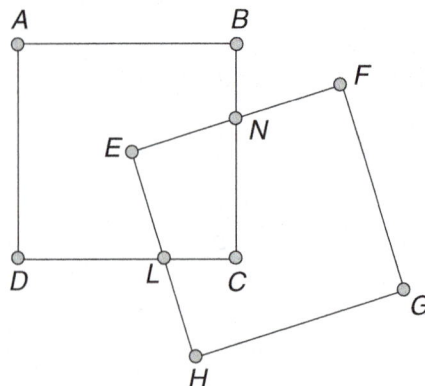

Figure 6.7

Solution

The traditional solution starts by drawing $\overline{EB}$ and $\overline{EC}$.

Then, $\triangle ENB \cong \triangle ELC$ because $EB = EC$, $m \angle BEN = m \angle CEL$ (both are complements of $\angle NEC$), and $m \angle EBN = m \angle ECL$. Thus, the area of $ENCL =$ area of $\triangle BEN +$ area of $\triangle ENC = \frac{1}{4}$ the area of the original square $= 16$ square units.

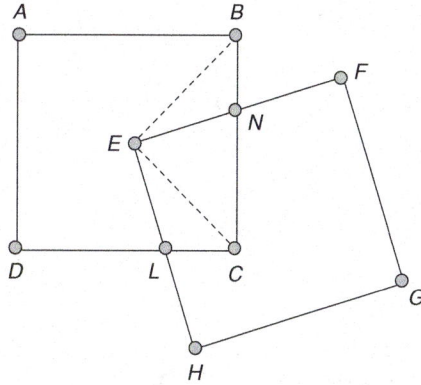

Figure 6.8

We can, however, make the problem much simpler by *considering an extreme case*, namely, to situate the squares so that E is at the requisite center of $ABCD$, but $\overline{EF}$ and $\overline{EH}$ contain the vertices B and C, respectively. In this extreme case, quadrilateral $ENCL$ reduces to $\triangle EBC$, which is $\frac{1}{4}$ the area of $ABCD$ or $\frac{1}{4}(64) = 16$ square units.

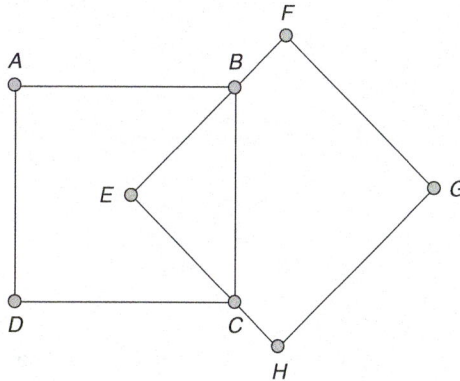

Figure 6.9

Problem 6.8

In Figure 6.10, $m \angle ABC = 120°$, and $\triangle PQR$ is equilateral and has vertices Q and R on $\overline{AB}$ and $\overline{BC}$, respectively. As equilateral triangle PQR changes size and moves, with Q and R remaining on the rays of $\angle ABC$, what is the path taken by point P?

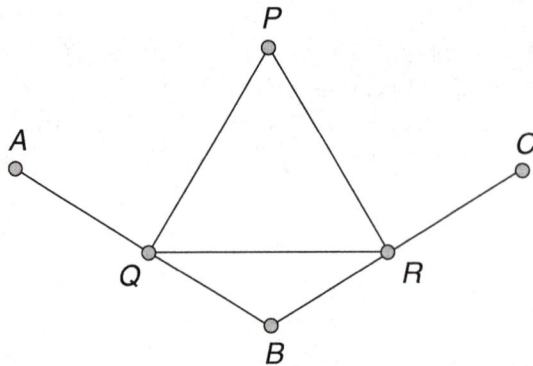

Figure 6.10

Solution

The traditional solution considers one position for $\triangle PQR$ and draws the auxiliary line segment PB (Figure 6.11). Quadrilateral $QPRB$ is cyclic (and can, therefore, be inscribed in a circle) because $m\angle QPR = 60°$, making the opposite angles supplementary.

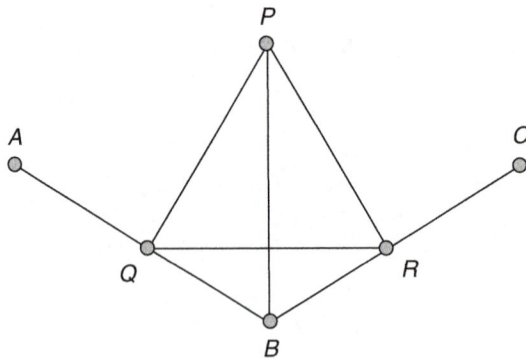

Figure 6.11

Because $m\angle PBR = m\angle RQP$ (both intercept the "arc"—not drawn—for which $\overline{PR}$ would be a chord) and $m\angle PBQ = m\angle QRP$ (both intercept the "arc"—again, not drawn—for which $\overline{PQ}$ would be the chord), $\angle QBP \cong \angle RBP$. This implies that P is on the angle bisector of $\angle ABC$.

Now, let's attack this problem by *considering the extreme case*, where point Q falls directly on point B (Figure 6.12).

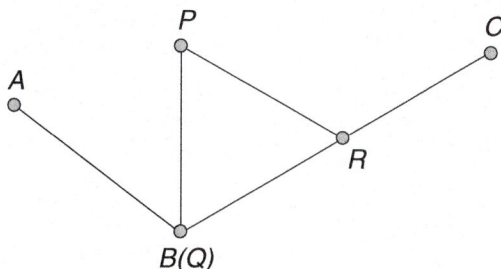

Figure 6.12

Now $m\angle PB(Q)R = 60°$ and P is on the angle bisector of $\angle ABC$. Similarly, if R falls onto B, we obtain the same result, but on the other side. With both of these extremes showing that P lies on the angle bisector, we should consider that this would be true for all positions of point P.

Problem 6.9

Find the missing digits in the seven-digit number

$$1, 2, \_, \_, \_, \_, 6$$

so that the number itself is equal to the product of three consecutive numbers. What are those three numbers?

Solution

Students may begin by simply guessing and testing various numbers in the hope that they might get lucky and guess the digits. This is highly unlikely. Instead, let's use the strategy of *considering extreme cases*. The smallest possible number would be 1,200,006, whereas the largest possible number is 1,299,996. Because we are looking for our answer to be the product of three consecutive numbers, let's examine the cube root of each of these extremes to determine the approximate magnitude of the three numbers.

The cube root of 1,200,006 is approximately 106, whereas the cube root of 1,299,996 is approximately 109. This limits our choices a great deal. Furthermore, the given number has a units digit of 6. Thus, our three consecutive numbers must end with either 1, 2, and 3 or 6, 7, and 8 since these are the products whose units digit ends in 6. With these two clues, our numbers are easily found as 106, 107, and 108. Their product is 1,224,936, and the problem is solved.

Problem 6.10

A rectangle has adjacent sides of 10 units and 8 units, respectively. A second rectangle with adjacent sides of 6 units and 4 units overlaps the first rectangle as shown in Figure 6.13. What is the difference between the two nonoverlapping regions of the two rectangles?

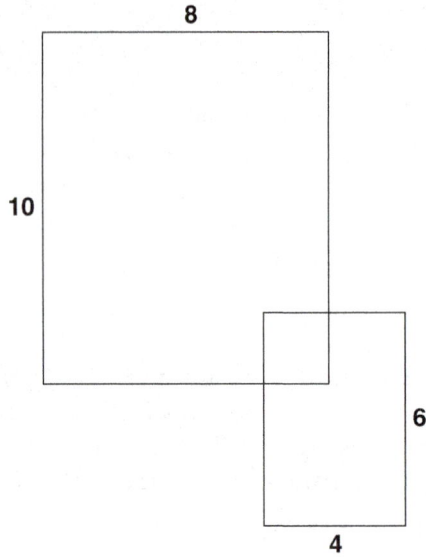

Figure 6.13

Solution

Students may try to solve this problem directly by trying to find the area of each rectangle and then trying to somehow find the area of the common region. They will quickly find themselves at a loss. Let's consider the *extreme case* of this situation. Whereas the area and placement of the region of overlap were not specified, we can assume an overlap of 0.

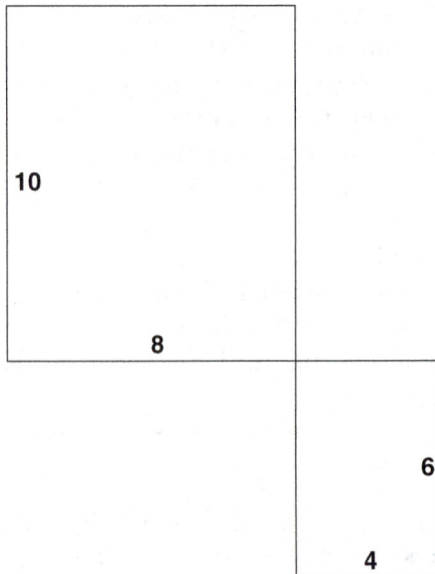

Figure 6.14

Now we see that the difference is 80 square units − 24 square units = 56 square units. To reinforce our answer, let us consider several other *extreme cases*. Consider rectangles that have a single unit of overlap.

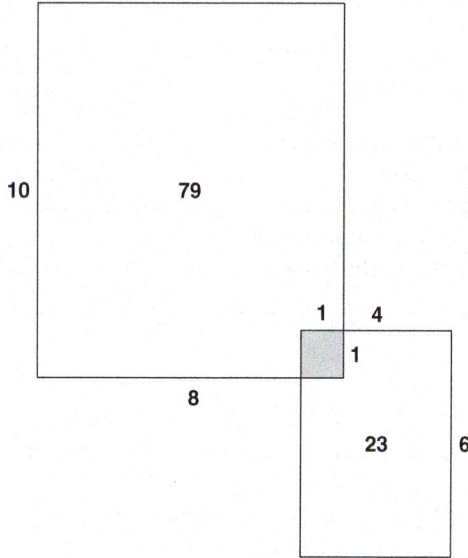

Figure 6.15

The nonoverlapping difference is 79 square units − 23 square units = 56 square units. Finally, let's consider the *extreme case*, where the smaller rectangle is entirely enclosed within the larger.

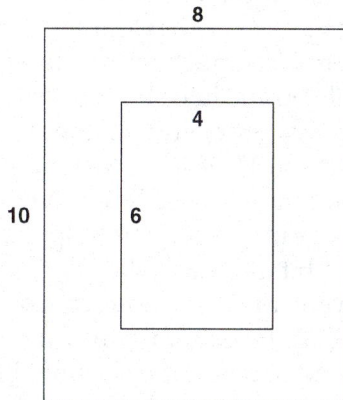

Figure 6.16

Again, the nonoverlapping region is 56 square units. Once again, emphasize to your students the value of considering the *extreme situations* of a problem. We might also consider having looked at this problem from a *different point of view*.

Notice that you need not consider each of the foregoing situations as described. For some students, the initial idea that the rectangles merely share a common point might be sufficient. For others, however, considering the other situations might be necessary for them to conclude the correct answer.

Problem 6.11

We have two 1-gal bottles. One contains 1 qt of grape juice and the other contains 1 qt of apple juice. We take 1 T (tablespoon) of grape juice and pour it into the apple juice. Then, we take 1 T of this new mixture (apple juice and grape juice) and pour it into the bottle of grape juice. Is there more grape juice in the apple juice bottle or more apple juice in the grape juice bottle?

Solution

We can figure this out in any of the usual ways—often referred to as mixture problems—or we can be "clever" and use the strategy of *using extremes*.

To do this, we will consider the tablespoon quantity to be a bit larger. We will use an extremely large quantity. We'll let this quantity actually be the entire 1 qt. That is, following the instruction given in the problem statement, we will take the entire amount (1 qt of grape juice) and pour it into the apple juice bottle. This mixture is now 50% apple juice and 50% grape juice. We then pour 1 qt of this mixture back into the grape juice bottle. The mixture is now the same in both bottles. Therefore, there is as much apple juice in the grape juice bottle as there is grape juice in the apple juice bottle!

We can consider another form of an extreme case, where the spoon doing the juice transporting has a zero quantity. In this case the conclusion follows immediately: There is as much grape juice in the apple juice bottle as there is apple juice in the grape juice bottle, that is, zero.

Yet another solution to this problem uses the strategy we call *logical reasoning*. With the first "transport" of juice there is only grape juice on the tablespoon. On the second "transport" of juice, there is as much apple juice on the spoon as there is grape juice in the apple juice bottle. This may require students to think a bit, but most should "get it" soon.

Some students may want to see a more concrete solution or may feel (with some justification) that the extremes may not hold throughout. Have them consider two containers, one with 12 white beans (called the white-bean container) and the other with 12 red beans (called the red-bean container). We will use the strategy of *considering a simpler analogous problem*. Suppose we move 6 white beans from the white-bean container to the red-bean container. This red-bean container will now have 12 red beans and

6 white beans, or 18 beans in total. From this red-bean container, we will remove 6 beans in the proportion of the contents (i.e., red:white $= 2{:}1$) back to the white-bean container. So we will now move 4 red beans and 2 white beans, bringing the contents to white-bean container to 8 white beans $(6+2)$ and 4 red beans, while the red-bean container now remains with 4 white beans and 8 red beans. In other words, there are as many red beans (4) in the white-bean container as there are white beans (4) in the red-bean container.

Problem 6.12

A car is driving along a highway at a constant speed of 55 mph. The driver notices a second car, exactly $\frac{1}{2}$ mile behind. The second car passes the first, exactly 1 min later. How fast was the second car traveling, assuming its speed was constant?

Solution

The traditional solution is to set up a series of rate $\times$ time $=$ distance boxes, which many textbooks guide students to use for this sort of problem. This would be done as follows:

Rate	$\times$	Time	$=$	Distance
55		$\dfrac{1}{60}$		$\dfrac{55}{60}$
x		$\dfrac{1}{60}$		$\dfrac{x}{60}$

$$\frac{55}{60} + \frac{1}{2} = \frac{x}{60}$$
$$55 + 30 = x$$
$$x = 85.$$

The second car was traveling at a rate of 85 mph.

An alternate approach is to *consider extremes*. We assume that the first car is going *extremely* slowly, that is, at 0 mph. Under these conditions, the second car travels $\frac{1}{2}$ mile in 1 min to catch the first car. Thus, the second car would have to travel 30 mph. When the first car is moving at 0 mph, then the second car is traveling 30 mph faster. If, on the other hand, the first car is traveling at 55 mph, then the second car must be traveling at 85 mph (within the legal limit, of course!).

Problem 6.13

Figure 6.17 depicts three congruent circles with radius length 1, two of which are tangent externally and a third that is drawn through the point of tangency, T, of the first two, cutting the first two circles at points A and B. What is the length of arc $ADT +$ arc BET?

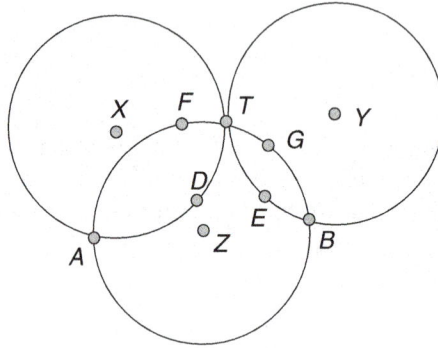

Figure 6.17

Solution

Typically, students begin this problem with no idea about the length of the arc sum. Although a clever student can probably "stumble" onto a correct answer, students would be well advised to analyze the problem situation first. Here, the strategy of *considering extremes* is very helpful.

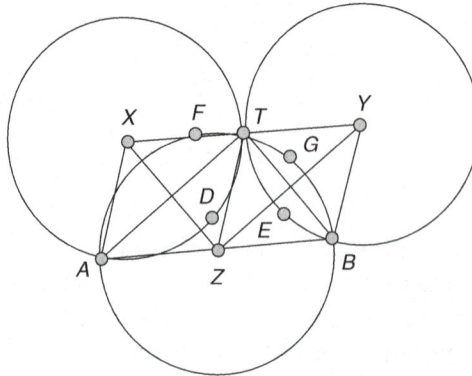

Figure 6.18

Whereas the exact position of the third circle, Z, is not determined, except that it must contain tangency point T, we have the flexibility to move it to an extreme position, say to overlap circle Z on circle X. Notice as you "mentally" rotate circle Z toward the overlap position with circle X that arc BET

gets smaller as arc *ADT* gets larger. In its final position, arc *ADT* will assume the arc of the semicircle of circle *X*. Again, using the *extreme case situation*, we now have strong evidence that the sum of the two arcs *ADT* and *BET* will have a length equal to the semicircular arc of one of the circles.

We can easily prove this by showing that triangle *ATB* is a right triangle.[2] Therefore, $\overline{AZB}$ is the diameter of circle *Z* (see Figure 6.18).

Whereas arc *ADT* is equal in length to arc *AFT*, arc *BET* is equal in length to arc *BGT*. The sum of lengths of arcs *ADT* and *BET* equals arc length sum *AFT* + *BGT*, which equals the semicircle (because the right triangle is inscribed in arc *ATB*). Therefore, the length sought is π.

Problem 6.14

P is any point on side $\overline{AB}$ of $\triangle ABC$, where *M* is the midpoint of $\overline{AC}$ and *N* is the midpoint of $\overline{BC}$. What is the ratio of the area of quadrilateral *MPNC* to the area of $\triangle ABC$? (See Figure 6.19.)

Solution

The expected solution entails the student drawing $\overline{BM}$ and then recognizing that $\triangle BMC$ has half the area of $\triangle ABC$ (because the median of a triangle partitions it into two equal areas). Also, since $\overline{MN}$ is parallel to $\overline{AB}$, $\triangle MBN$ has the same area as $\triangle MPN$. The area of $\triangle BMN$ + area $\triangle NMC = \frac{1}{2}$ area $\triangle ABC$.

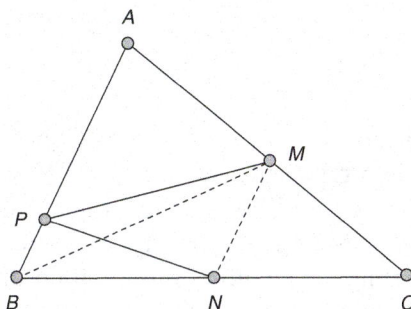

Figure 6.19

Now, by substitution, we have area $\triangle MPN$ + area $\triangle MCN = \frac{1}{2}$ area $\triangle ABC$. This is to say that the area of quadrilateral *MPNC* is $\frac{1}{2}$ area $\triangle ABC$.

We could make this problem (practically) trivial by choosing a convenient point, *P*, on $\overline{AB}$. By using our strategy of *considering extremes*, suppose *P* was

---

2. To prove triangle *ATB* is a right triangle, consider the rhombuses *AXTZ* and *BYTZ* (all sides are radii), where diagonals $\overline{AT}$ and $\overline{BT}$ bisect their respective angles of the rhombuses. Whereas *X*, *T*, and *Y* are collinear ($\overline{AB}$ and $\overline{YT}$ are each perpendicular to the common tangent line at *T*), $m \angle ATZ + m \angle BTZ = 90°$.

at one extreme end of $\overline{AB}$, say at point B. In that case, the quadrilateral $MPNC$ reduces to MBC, because the length of $\overline{BP}$ is 0. As we mentioned previously, $\triangle MBC$ results from a median partitioning a triangle; hence, the area of $\triangle MBC$ is one half the area of $\triangle ABC$.

Problem 6.15

Point M is the midpoint of side $\overline{AB}$ of $\triangle ABC$. P is any point on $\overline{AM}$. A line parallel to $\overline{PC}$, through point M, meets $\overline{BC}$ at D. What part of the area of $\triangle ABC$ is the area of $\triangle BDP$?

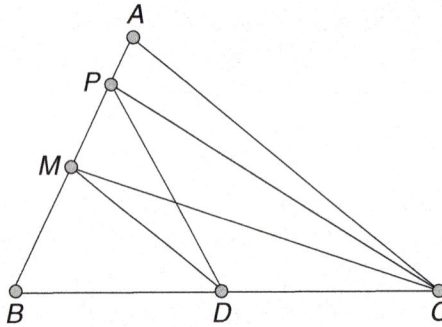

Figure 6.20

Solution

The area of $\triangle BMC$ is one half the area of $\triangle ABC$ (because the median partitions a triangle into two equal areas). Area $\triangle BMC =$ area $\triangle BMD +$ area $\triangle CMD =$ area $\triangle BMD +$ area $\triangle PMD$, which equals area $\triangle BPD = \frac{1}{2}$ area $\triangle ABC$. This conclusion rests on the property that when the vertices of two triangles lie on a line parallel to a common base, their areas are equal.

The foregoing solution might be expected from a reasonably good student. However, the problem can be considerably simplified by very carefully using our strategy of *considering extreme cases*. Let us select point P at an extreme position, either at point M or at point A. Suppose P is selected at point A. Notice that as P moves along $\overline{BA}$ toward A, $\overline{MD}$, which must stay parallel to $\overline{PC}$, moves toward a position whereby D approaches the midpoint of $\overline{BC}$. That final position for D then has $\overline{AD}$ as a median of $\triangle ABC$. Thus the area of $\triangle PBD$ is one half the area $\triangle ABC$.

Problem 6.16

There are 50 teachers' mailboxes in George Washington High School's general office. One day, the letter carrier delivers 151 pieces of mail for the teachers. After all the letters have been distributed, one mailbox has more letters than any other mailbox. What is the smallest number of letters it can have?

This solution, by *considering extreme cases*, provides an interesting example where we must watch all movements when we move a point to an extreme position. In itself, it is a very useful example and contrasts nicely to the previous problem's solution.

Solution

Students have a tendency to "fumble around" aimlessly with this sort of problem, usually not knowing where to start. Sometimes, guessing and testing may work here. The advisable approach for a problem of this sort is to consider extremes. Naturally, it is possible for one teacher to get all the delivered mail, but this is not guaranteed. To best assess this situation, we *consider the extreme case* where the mail is as evenly distributed as possible. Thus, each teacher would receive 3 pieces of mail with the exception of one teacher, who would have to receive the 151st piece of mail. Therefore, 4 pieces of mail is the most that any one teacher is *guaranteed* to receive.

Problem 6.17

Let's Make a Deal was a long-running television game show that featured a problematic situation. A randomly selected audience member would come on stage and be presented with three doors, behind one of which was a car, and behind the other two, donkeys. She was asked to select one. If she selected the door with the car, she would be the car's new owner. There was only one wrinkle in this: After the contestant made her selection, the host, Monty Hall, knowing where the car was located, exposed one of the two donkeys behind a not-selected door (leaving two doors still unopened) and the audience participant was asked if she wanted to stay with her original selection (not yet revealed) or switch to the other unopened door. At this point, to heighten the suspense, the rest of the audience would shout out "stay" or "switch" with seemingly equal frequency. The question is, what to do? Does it make a difference? If so, which is the better strategy (i.e., with the greater probability of winning) to use here?

Solution

You might have students speculate about what they think intuitively is the best strategy. Most will probably say that there is no difference, since at the end you have a one out of two chance of getting the car. Tell them they are wrong, and then you will have a very curious audience in front of you.

Let us look at this now step by step. The result gradually will become clear.

There are *two donkeys* and *one car* behind these doors.

You must try to get the car. You select Door #3.

Monty Hall opens one of the doors that you *did not* select and exposes a donkey.

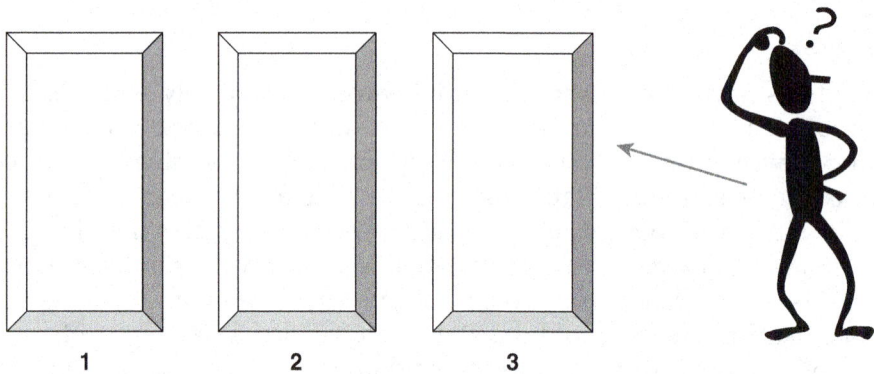

Figure 6.21

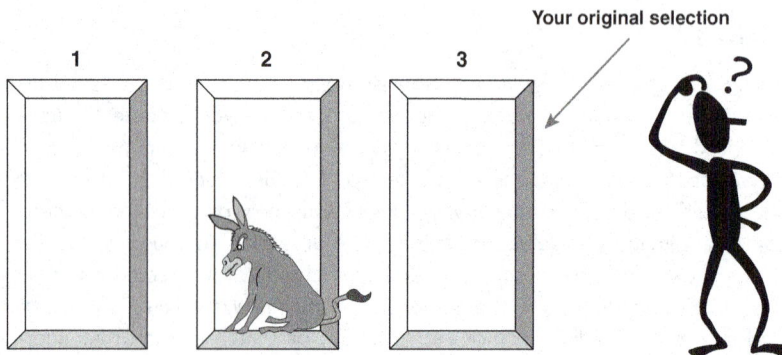

Figure 6.22

He asks, "Do you still want your first choice door, or do you want to switch to the other closed door?"

To help make a decision, we will use the problem-solving strategy of *considering an extreme case*.

Suppose there were 1,000 doors instead of just three doors.

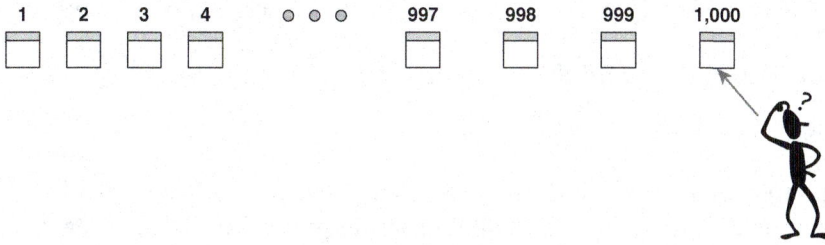

Figure 6.23

You choose Door 1,000. How likely is it that you chose the right door?

Very unlikely, since the probability of getting the right door is $\dfrac{1}{1,000}$.

How likely is it that the car is behind one of the other doors?

Very unlikely, $\dfrac{999}{1,000}$.

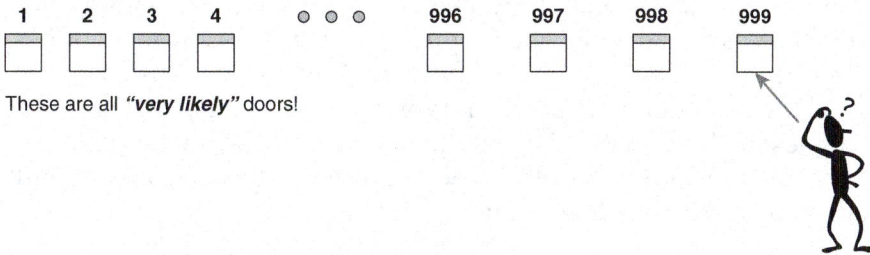

These are all *"very likely"* doors!

Figure 6.24

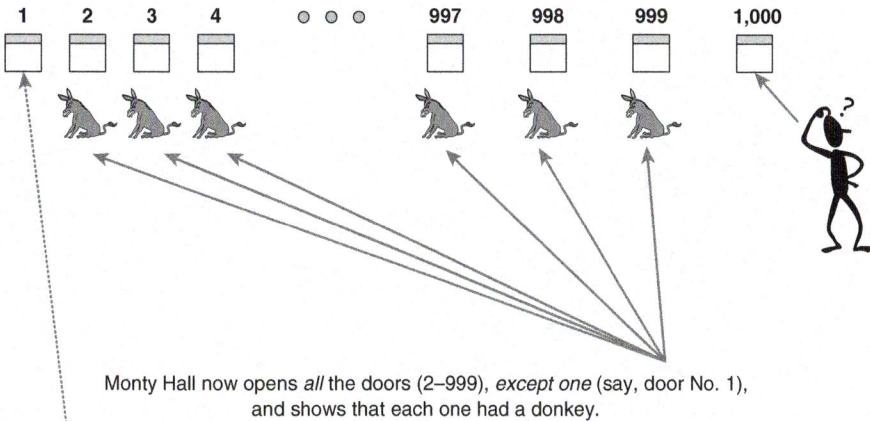

Monty Hall now opens *all* the doors (2–999), *except one* (say, door No. 1), and shows that each one had a donkey.

A *"very likely"* door is left: Door 1.

Figure 6.25

We are now ready to answer the question. Which is a better choice?

Door 1,000 (*Very unlikely* door), or

Door 1 (*Very likely* door)?

The answer is now obvious. We ought to select the "very likely" door, which means "switching" is the better strategy for the audience participant to follow.

In the extreme case, it is much easier to see the best strategy than had we tried to analyze the situation with the three doors in the original problem. The principle is the same in either situation.

You might want to mention to students that this problem has caused many an argument in academic circles and was also a topic of discussion in the *New York Times* and other popular publications as well. John Tierney wrote in the *New York Times* (Sunday, July 21, 1991),

> Perhaps it was only an illusion, but for a moment here it seemed that an end might be in sight to the debate raging among mathematicians, readers of *Parade* magazine, and fans of the television game show *Let's Make a Deal*. They began arguing last September after Marilyn vos Savant published a puzzle in *Parade*. As readers of her "Ask Marilyn" column are reminded each week, Ms. vos Savant is listed in the Guinness Book of World Records Hall of Fame for "Highest IQ," but that credential did not impress the public when she answered this question from a reader. She gave the right answer, but still many mathematicians argued.

7

Making a Drawing (Visual Representation)

To make a drawing to solve a geometric problem is expected; not to do so is foolhardy! In this section, we consider the use of a drawing to solve a problem where a visual representation is not the usual approach based on the nature of the problem. You should realize that some people are visual learners; they learn best when they can see what is taking place. Often, a nonvisual approach will stymie their efforts to solve the problem. In real life, there are many decisions that are based on the visual presentation of data and relationships, wherein a visual representation acts more as a facilitator than as an expected element of the situation. In sociology, for example, there are sociograms, which show visually the interrelationships of a group. Graph theory enables the inspection of geometric relationships, which depend on location and interdependence rather than on size or shape. The famous "Bridges of Königsberg" problem can easily be resolved or explained by setting up a network diagram as a visual representation of the situation.

THE *MAKING A DRAWING* (VISUAL REPRESENTATION) STRATEGY IN EVERYDAY LIFE PROBLEM-SOLVING SITUATIONS

We use diagrams or drawings quite a bit in everyday life. We use a map to determine how to reach a specific destination. We sometimes sketch our own maps to explain a route to another person, when we could explain the travel instructions verbally. Drawing a picture makes the description clearer and easier to follow. After all, it has been said many times that one picture is worth 1,000 words.

Companies that manufacture technical instruments typically provide users with a picture of the device to better explain how to use the instrument. Certainly they could give instructions in written form, but additional clarity is gained by referring to a picture of the item being described. We take such pictorial renditions for granted. A person taking personal notes of a lecture or simply writing down personal reminders will often revert to drawing symbols or even pictures to make note taking more efficient.

An inspection of the daily newspaper reveals numerous situations in which visual rather than verbal descriptions are offered. This can be seen in the use of descriptive graphs to represent data and in diagrams that explain geographic stories or automobile accidents.

When we move or begin to furnish an apartment, it is usually advantageous to make a scale drawing or sketch on graph paper of the floor plan, and then sketch in the furniture and where it will be placed. In many cases, there is too much furniture involved or it will not fit where you intend to place it. By rearranging the furniture on your drawing or visual representation, you can save a great deal of time and expense when you finally buy or place the furniture.

In basketball and football, just to name a few sports, the coach often resorts to making a diagram to better explain a strategy to the players. This is another example of using a diagram to solve the problem of explaining an idea to others.

APPLYING THE *MAKING A DRAWING* (VISUAL REPRESENTATION) STRATEGY TO SOLVE MATHEMATICS PROBLEMS

Consider the following problem, one in which a diagram is not expected.

> At 5:00, a clock strikes 5 chimes in 5 sec. How long will it take the same clock at the same rate to strike 10 chimes at 10:00? (Assume that the chime itself takes no time.)

The answer is *not* 10 sec. The nature of this problem does not lead us to anticipate the need for a drawing. However, let us use a drawing of the situation to see exactly what is taking place. In the drawing in Figure 7.1, each dot represents a chime. Thus, the total time is 5 sec, and there are four intervals between chimes. Therefore, each interval must take $\frac{5}{4}$ sec.

Figure 7.1

Now let's examine the second case. Here, we can see from the diagram that the 10 chimes give us 9 intervals.

Figure 7.2

Because each interval takes $\frac{5}{4}$ sec, the entire clock striking at 10:00 will take $9 \times \frac{5}{4}$ or $11\frac{1}{4}$ sec.

PROBLEMS USING THE *MAKING A DRAWING* (VISUAL REPRESENTATION) STRATEGY

Problem 7.1

Among 40 Girl Scouts in one troop at Camp Ellwood, 14 fell into the lake, 13 came down with poison ivy, and 16 were lost on the orientation hike. Three girls had poison ivy and fell into the lake. Five girls fell into the lake and got lost. Eight came down with poison ivy and were also lost. Two girls experienced all three mishaps. How many of the Girl Scouts in this troop escaped with none of these mishaps?

Solution

Traditionally, students begin to solve this problem by adding all the cases given and then subtracting duplicate things that happened to people. Rarely is this procedure effective.

Let's examine the problem with a *visual representation*. We'll make a drawing to show the data with a set of Euler circles (a Venn diagram):

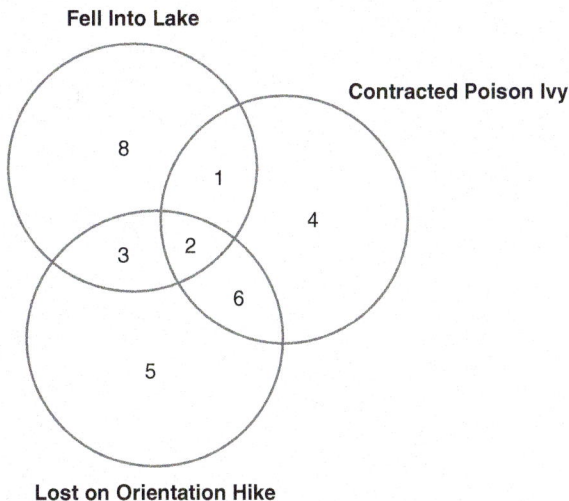

Figure 7.3

The area of overlap for all three circles contains the two Girl Scouts who were lost, fell into the lake, and contracted poison ivy. The circles reveal:

Total in Lake = 14	Poison ivy + lost = 8
Lake + poison ivy = 3	Total Poison ivy = 13
Lake + lost = 5	Total Lost = 16
Total = 8 + 3 + 2 + 1 + 4 + 6 + 5 = 29	

There were $40 - 29 = 11$ who suffered none of these mishaps.

Problem 7.2

Emily has her model trains set up on a circular track. There are six telephone poles, evenly spaced around the track. It takes the engine of the train 12 sec to go from the first to the third pole. At this same rate, how long will it take the engine to go completely around the track?

Solution

Many students attempt to solve this problem by setting up a proportion:

$$\frac{3 \text{ poles}}{12 \text{ s}} = \frac{6 \text{ poles}}{x \text{ s}}.$$

Unfortunately, this method yields 24 sec, which is not the correct answer. Let's use our visual representation strategy and make a drawing.

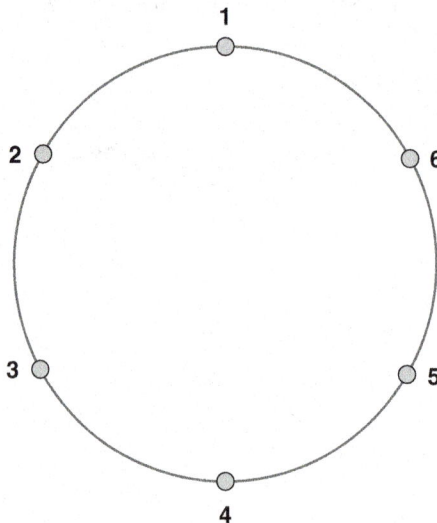

Figure 7.4

As the drawing reveals, it is the spaces we are interested in and not the poles themselves. To go from Pole 1 to Pole 3 is two spaces. Thus, it takes 6 sec to go from one pole to the next pole. Since there are six spaces to go completely around the circle, it will take 6×6 or 36 sec.

Notice that from Pole 1 to Pole 3 is one third of the way, not one half. Hence, it will take three times as long to go all the way around the circle. Thus, it takes 3×12 or 36 sec.

Problem 7.3

Al is holding four cards in his hand: the ace of spades, the ace of hearts, the ace of clubs, and the ace of diamonds. Steve pulls two of the cards from Al's hand without looking. What is the probability that Steve has pulled at least one black ace?

Solution

The students will probably make an initial guess of 2 out of 4 or $\frac{1}{2}$. However, if we *make a drawing* of the possible outcomes, we find that this is not correct:

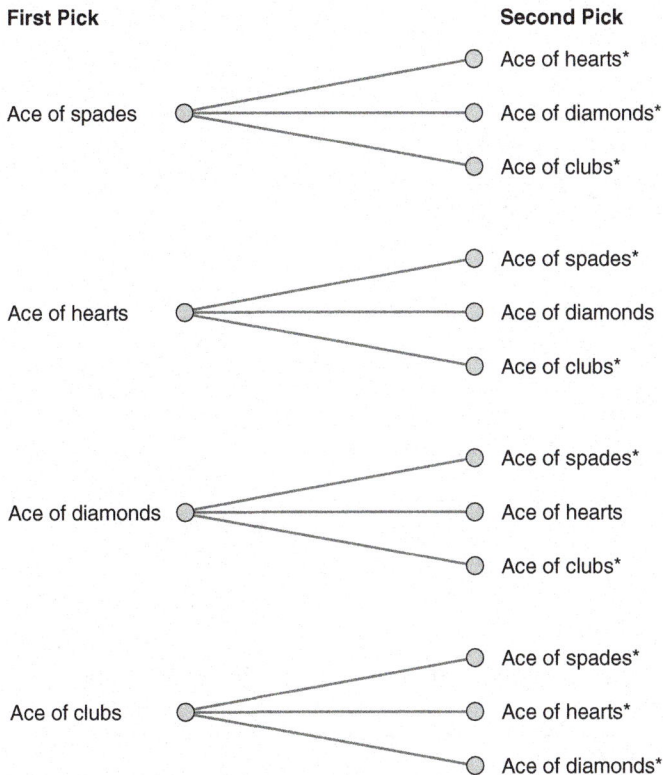

First Pick

Ace of spades
- Ace of hearts*
- Ace of diamonds*
- Ace of clubs*

Ace of hearts
- Ace of spades*
- Ace of diamonds
- Ace of clubs*

Ace of diamonds
- Ace of spades*
- Ace of hearts
- Ace of clubs*

Ace of clubs
- Ace of spades*
- Ace of hearts*
- Ace of diamonds*

Second Pick

(Where* refers to a success: At least one black ace)

Figure 7.5

Our drawing quickly reveals that there are 12 possible occurrences, of which 10 are successful (i.e., at least one ace drawn is black). The correct answer is $\frac{10}{12}$ or $\frac{5}{6}$, not the $\frac{1}{2}$ initially guessed. Making a careful drawing of the situation quickly reveals the correct answer.

Problem 7.4

Given that $\frac{1}{8}$ of a number is $\frac{1}{5}$, what is $\frac{5}{8}$ of that number?

Solution

The traditional approach to this problem is to solve it using algebra. We let x represent the number. Then,

$$\frac{1}{8}(x) = \frac{1}{5}$$

$$\frac{x}{8} = \frac{1}{5}$$

$$5x = 8$$

$$x = \frac{8}{5}$$

$$\left(\frac{5}{8}\right)\left(\frac{8}{5}\right) = 1.$$

We can use our *visual representation* strategy by *making a drawing*. Divide a whole unit into eight equal pieces:

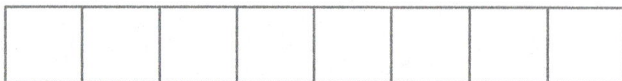

Figure 7.6

Now, each of these eighths must be $\frac{1}{5}$:

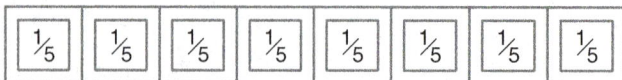

Figure 7.7

Since each of these eighths equals $\frac{1}{5}$, $\frac{5}{8}$ would be five of them, or $5\left(\frac{1}{5}\right) = 1$.

Problem 7.5

Alex has a beaker that contains 9 liters of a mixture that is 50% alcohol and 50% water. His science experiment requires him to reduce the alcohol concentration to 30%. How many liters of pure water must he add?

Solution

Typically, students will use a chart to organize the given data (albeit in a rather mechanical way) and then use one of the columns to obtain an equation (or a set of equations) that they solve to get the desired answer. This is often difficult to do, especially when the problem differs from others preceding it, because this is done in a purely mechanical way, with no understanding of what is taking place.

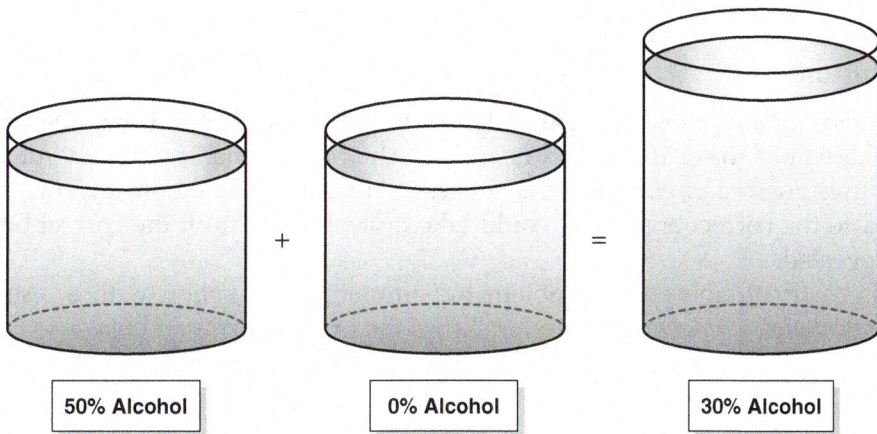

Figure 7.8

We will use a *visual representation* (*drawing*) to better "see" what's going on. The situation is shown in Figure 7.8.

The numbers in each beaker represent the amount of liquid they contain, and the numbers below each beaker (the "label") represent the percent of alcohol in each. That is, the first beaker contains 9 liters, of which 50% is alcohol; the second beaker contains x liters, of which 0% is alcohol; the final beaker contains $(9+x)$ liters, of which 30% will be alcohol. We can now write a single equation to represent the *amount* of alcohol present in the beakers:

(Beaker 1)		(Beaker 2)		(Beaker 3)
0.50(9)	+	0.0x	=	0.30(9 + x)
450			=	270 + 30x
		180	=	30x
		6	=	x

Alex must add 6 liters of pure water to reduce the alcohol content to the required 30%.

Problem 7.6

Steve is the jackpot contestant on a local quiz show and is going to try to win a new car. The host places eight boxes, numbered 1 to 8 clockwise, in a circular arrangement. Starting with any box, Steve is to count three boxes (clockwise) and push the third box out of the circle. Continuing where he left off (with the fourth box), he resumes counting around the circle and pushes away every third box until only one box is left. If that box contains the key to the car, Steve will win the car. Which box should Steve begin with to win the car, if the key is in box number 8?

Solution

Traditionally, most students attempt to guess which box holds the key and then test to see if that box is, indeed, the correct one. If not, they make another guess and continue the process. Although this should eventually lead to the correct answer, it could take quite a while until the correct box is revealed.

Let's try to solve this problem by simulating the action with a *visual representation* (*drawing*). Figure 7.9 shows the original array of boxes.

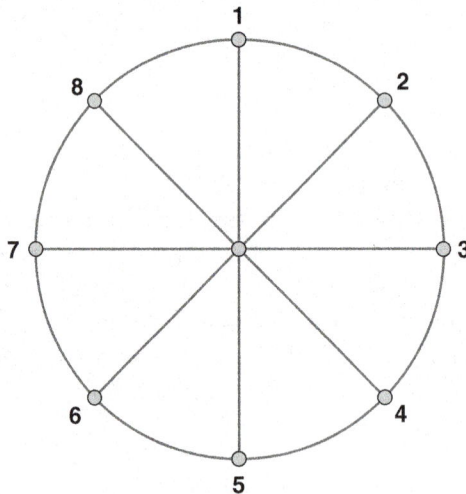

Figure 7.9

Steve "removes" every third box—numbers 3 and 6 (see Figure 7.10).

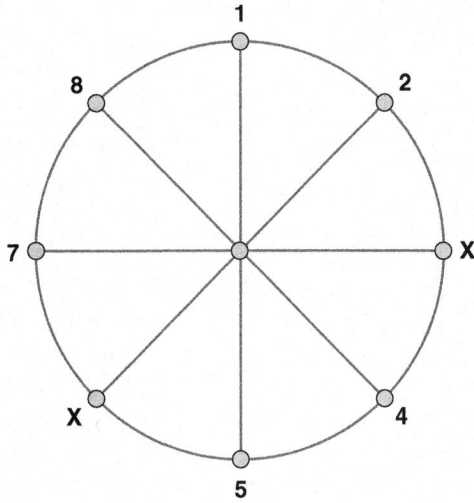

Figure 7.10

He continues removing every third box. (This time, number 1 is the third box—he counts 7, 8, 1; see Figure 7.11.)

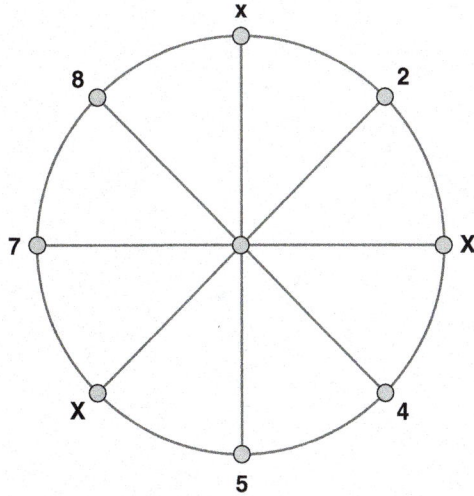

Figure 7.11

He continues, this time removing boxes numbered 5 and 2 (counting 2, 4, 5—7, 8, 2; see Figure 7.12).

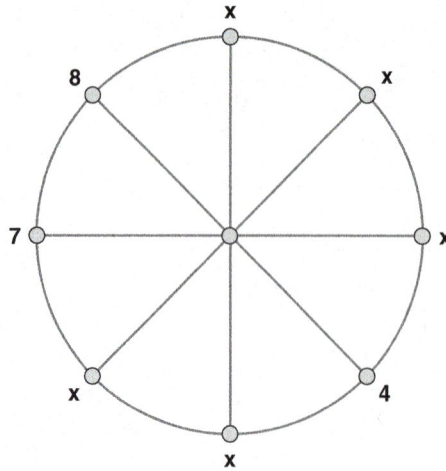

Figure 7.12

He now removes number 8 (counting 4, 7, 8) and then number 4 (counting 4, 7, 4). This leaves only number 7, which is the box he would have been left with if he started his counting scheme with box number 1 (Figure 7.13). Since the key is in box number 8, the "correct" starting box is number 2 (the one after number 1).

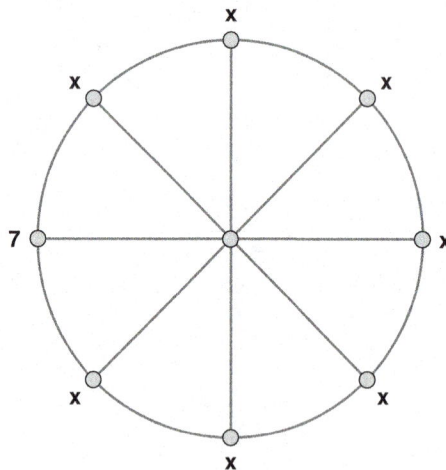

Figure 7.13

Problem 7.7

Douglas and Seth are both part-time workers in the local pizza shop. The shop is open 7 days a week. Douglas works 1 day and then has 2 days off before he works again. Seth works 1 day and then has 3 days off before he works again. Douglas and Seth both worked on Tuesday, March 1. On which other days in March do Douglas and Seth work together?

Solution

Many students will make a pair of lists, one for each boy, showing all the dates in March on which each works. They then compare the dates on these lists to determine those on which both boys work. This is a perfectly valid method of solution and eventually yields the correct answer.

However, let's examine this problem with a *visual representation*. We'll make a drawing of a calendar and then simply place initials on those dates on which each boy works.

S	M	T	W	TH	F	S
		D 1 S	2	3	D 4	5 S
6	D 7	8	9 S	D 10	11	12
D 13 S	14	15	D 16	17 S	18	D 19
20	21 S	D 22	23	24	D 25 S	26
27	D 28	29 S	30	D 31		

Figure 7.14

Those dates that contain two sets of initials are the dates on which the two boys work together. The figure readily shows these dates to be March 13 and March 25.

Some students may attack this problem from *another point of view*. Because 4 and 3 are relatively prime (the number of days in the work cycle of each of the boys, respectively), their common multiple, 12, provides the days between those on which they work together. Thus, day $1 + 12 = 13$, is a day on which they work together after the first day, and day $13 + 12 = 25$ is the day on which they next work together.

Problem 7.8

If, on the average, a hen and a half can lay an egg and a half in a day and a half, how many eggs should 6 hens lay in 8 days?

Solution

This is an old problem, one that most students have encountered at one time or another. Traditionally, the problem is solved as follows. Whereas $\frac{3}{2}$ hens work for $\frac{3}{2}$ days, we may speak of the job of laying an egg and a half ($\frac{3}{2}$ eggs) as taking $(\frac{3}{2})(\frac{3}{2})$ or $(\frac{9}{4})$ "hen-days." Similarly, the second job takes $(6) \times (8)$ or 48 "hen-days." Thus, we form the following proportion: Let x equal the number of eggs laid by 6 hens in 8 days. Then,

$$\frac{\frac{9}{4}\text{hen-days}}{48 \text{ hen-days}} = \frac{\frac{3}{2}\text{eggs}}{x \text{ eggs}}.$$

Multiply the product of the means and extremes:

$$\left(\frac{9}{4}\right)(x) = (48)\left(\frac{3}{2}\right)$$

$$\frac{9x}{4} = 72$$

$$x = 32.$$

As an alternative solution, we may set up the following *visual representation* (here in the form of a tabular layout) of the situation:

	$\frac{3}{2}$ hens lay $\frac{3}{2}$ eggs in $\frac{3}{2}$ days	
(double hens and eggs from previous line)	3 hens lay 3 eggs in $\frac{3}{2}$ days	
	3 hens lay 6 eggs in 3 days	(double eggs and days from previous line)
	3 hens lay 2 eggs in 1 day	($\frac{1}{3}$ eggs and days from previous line)
(double hens and eggs from previous line)	6 hens lay 4 eggs in 1 day	
	6 hens lay 32 eggs in 8 days	(8 times eggs and days from previous line).

The 6 hens should lay 32 eggs in 8 days.

Problem 7.9

Each corner of a rectangular prism has a triangular pyramid cut off, and no two cut-off pyramids can intersect. (One of the cut corners is labeled in Figure 7.15.) How many edges does the new figure have after all the corners have been cut?

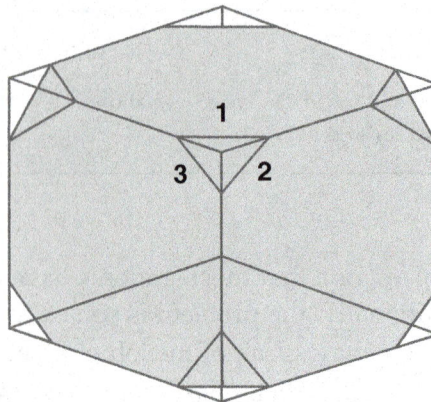

Figure 7.15

Solution

A typical solution attempted by many students is to apply Euler's formula, $F + V = E + 2$. However, this will not be too helpful, because all parts of the relationship are difficult to find. Instead, let's make a drawing of the "before and after" situation using one corner of the prism. We'll then multiply the result by 8 to obtain the final total.

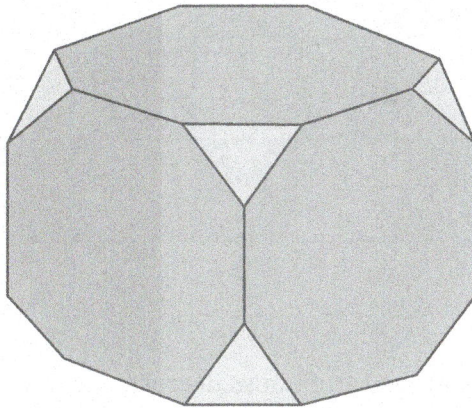

Figure 7.16

The original rectangular prism had 12 edges. Cutting off a triangular pyramid at each corner introduces 3 additional segments. Generating 3 additional line segments at each corner means we have generated 24 new line segments. Thus, the new figure has $12 + 24$ or 36 line segments that form the edges.

Problem 7.10

In Mr. Strauss's classroom, there are 25 seats arranged in a square array, consisting of 5 rows with 5 seats in each row. Mr. Strauss wants the students to change their seats by moving to either the seat immediately in back, immediately in front, or immediately to the right or left. Can his instructions be carried out? Why or why not?

Solution

A typical approach is to use 25 markers to represent the seats, arrange them in a square array, and then move them about as explained in the problem to find out if it can or cannot be done. This procedure is difficult, awkward, and probably will not produce the correct answer.

Let's approach this problem by making a *visual representation* of the situation. We can regard the room as a square "checkerboard" arrangement of 5 rows and 5 seats as shown in Figure 7.17.

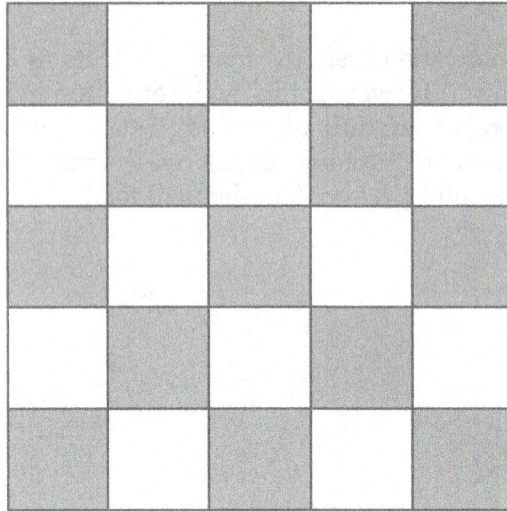

Figure 7.17

Now, to change seats as Mr. Strauss instructed, each student must move from a black square (or "seat") into a white square. Because there are 13 black squares and only 12 white squares, the students cannot follow Mr. Strauss's directions.

Problem 7.11

A jeweler makes silver earrings from silver blanks. Each blank makes 1 earring. The shavings left over from 6 blanks are then melted down and recast to form another blank. The jeweler orders 36 blanks to fill an order. How many earrings can be made from the 36 blanks?

Solution

Students usually assume that 36 blanks will yield 36 earrings. They are quite surprised when they find that this is not the correct answer. Some astute students may recognize that the leftover silver can form 6 additional blanks, thus yielding 42 earrings. This, too, is incorrect.

Let's use the *visual representation* (*make a drawing*) strategy to see what happens as the jeweler works. From the original 36 blanks, we do obtain 36 earrings. However, notice that the shavings left over from these 36 blanks are melted down and form 6 new blanks, yielding 6 additional earrings. However, we don't stop here—the shavings from these 6 blanks are then melted down and recast to form 1 new blank from which we obtain 1 additional earring. Thus, 43 earrings are possible (Figure 7.18).

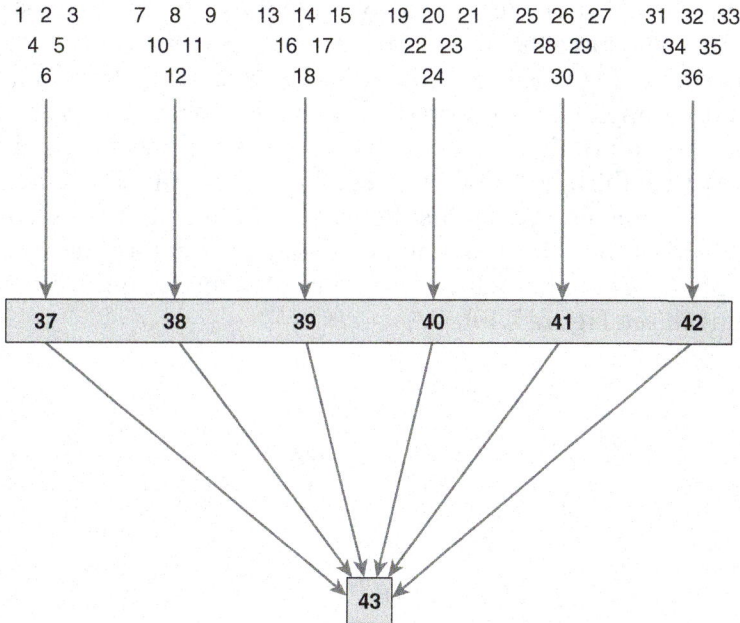

Figure 7.18

Problem 7.12

Magdalene leaves home on a business trip, traveling at 50 mph. One hour after she leaves, her son finds a briefcase with all her notes at home. He jumps onto the family Harley and takes off after her at 70 mph. How long will it take him to catch up to her?

Solution

The traditional, algebraic solution is as follows: Let t represent the time traveled by the woman until the son reaches her, and let $(t-1)$ represent the time traveled by the son until he catches up to her. Then, we obtain the equation

$$50t = 70(t-1)$$
$$50t = 70t - 70$$
$$70 = 20t$$
$$3\frac{1}{2} = t.$$

At this point, many students will stop and give $3\frac{1}{2}$ as their answer, but this is not what we were asked to find. We want the time the *son* traveled until he caught up. The correct answer is $3\frac{1}{2} - 1 = 2\frac{1}{2}$ hr, and, of course, this solution method is only open to students who can understand the problem and who have the necessary algebra background.

Let's examine this problem with a *visual representation* (*make a drawing*). We draw two lines, one to represent each trip. Magdalene has traveled 50 miles at the end of the first hour, 100 at the end of the second hour, 150 at the end of the third, and 200 by the end of the fourth. The son has traveled 70 miles at the end of the first hour, 140 at the end of the second, and 210 at the end of the third (passing her somewhere before she reaches the 200-mile point). Thus, he will overtake her at some time during *his* third hour of travel (see Figure 7.19).

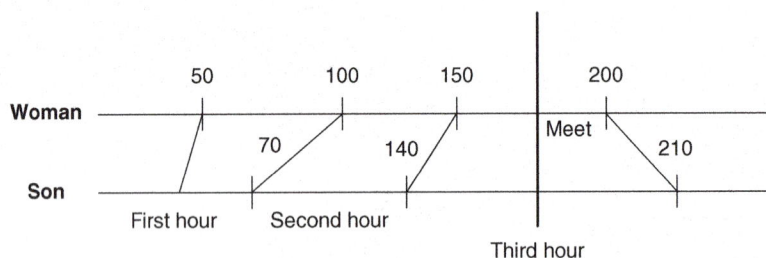

Figure 7.19

At this point, we can simply use our *intelligent guessing and testing* strategy and try various values between 2 and 3 hr. If we guess $2\frac{1}{4}$ hr of travel for the son and $3\frac{1}{4}$ hr for the woman, we find that the woman has traveled 162.5 miles and the son only 157.5 miles—not a long enough travel time for the son to overtake the mother.

Let's try $2\frac{1}{2}$ hr of travel. The son has traveled $2.5 \times 70 = 175$ miles. The woman has traveled $3.5 \times 50 = 175$ miles. Aha! They meet after the son has traveled $2\frac{1}{2}$ hr.

Notice that, once again, we made use of more than one single strategy. As we have said several times before, problem-solving strategies are not always used singly but are most likely to be used in conjunction with one another.

Problem 7.13

Two tests each contain 25 different questions. If the first 5 questions on Test I are added to the end of Test II, and the first 5 questions from Test II are added to the end of Test I, each test now has 30 questions. How many questions will be the same on both tests, assuming they began with no questions in common?

Solution

The traditional solution is to simulate the situation presented in the problem. This can be quite confusing.

Let's make a chart of the "before and after" situation, showing what has taken place in this problem:

Before Test I	A	B	C	D	$\cdots$	W	X	Y					
Test II	1	2	3	4	$\cdots$	23	24	25					
After Test I	A	B	C	D	E	$\cdots$	W	X	Y	1	2	3	4	5
Test II	1	2	3	4	5	$\cdots$	23	24	25	A	B	C	D	E

The tests now contain 10 questions in common (i.e., 1, 2, 3, 4, 5 and A, B, C, D, E).

Using a *drawing* we can also see this solution directly. The arrows in Figure 7.20 indicate the copying of questions.

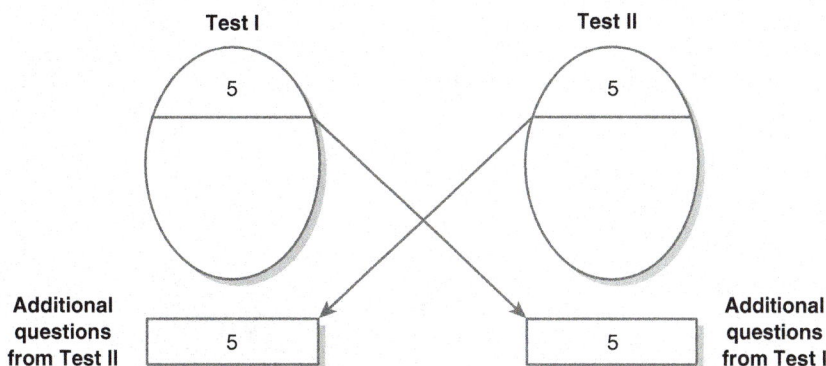

Figure 7.20

We can clearly see that both tests have $5 + 5 = 10$ questions in common.

Problem 7.14

Fly-by-Night Airlines has a flight from New Orleans to New York at 6:16 p.m. each day. On last Tuesday's flight, 480 passengers were aboard. Of these, one eighth flew in first class and the rest in coach class. Two thirds of those in coach were members of the CCNY Alumni Association on the way to a reunion. One fourth of the Alumni Association members on board and flying in coach were female. How many female passengers were in the Alumni Association?

Solution

There is a great deal of information given in this problem. The traditional approach is to set up algebraic expressions that summarize the given information. Such an approach should lead to an answer. However, to better comprehend what is going on, students may feel it necessary *to make a visual representation* of the situation. Let's represent the entire population on board with a large rectangle.

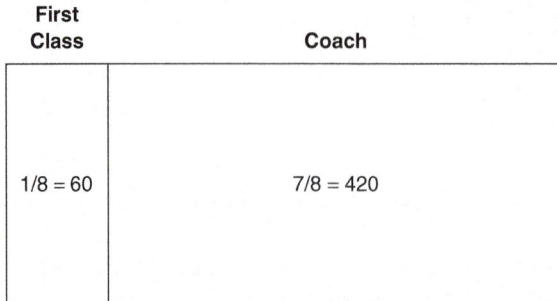

First Class   **Coach**

1/8 = 60   7/8 = 420

Figure 7.21

Now we can divide the coach portion into thirds, and take two of them:

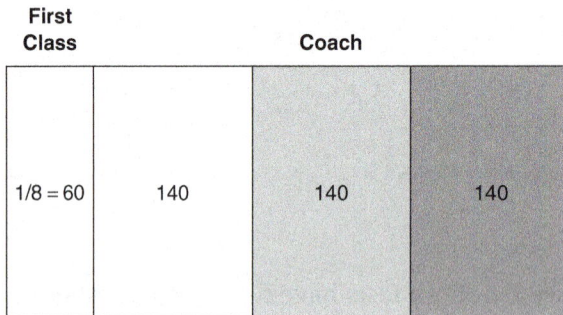

First Class   **Coach**

1/8 = 60   140   140   140

Figure 7.22

We finally take one quarter of these two thirds:

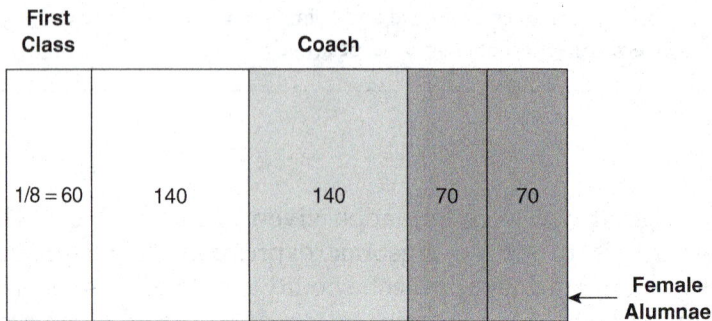

First Class   **Coach**

1/8 = 60   140   140   70   70

← **Female Alumnae**

Figure 7.23

At this point, the answer is easily found to be one half of 140, or 70.

Problem 7.15

Eva left her house to drive to city hall in Boise. Her car's odometer read 32,518 miles. She drove 5 miles but realized that she had left her briefcase at home. So she returned home, picked up her briefcase, and drove to city hall. After her meeting, she turned around and drove directly home. Her odometer now read 32,966. How far is Eva's home from the Boise city hall?

Solution

This is obviously not the typical (or expected) "uniform motion" problem. In fact, if students attempt to solve it by drawing the typical $R \times T = D$ chart, they may become quite confused. To better visualize the given information in the problem, encourage students *to make a visual representation* of the situation and see exactly what is taking place.

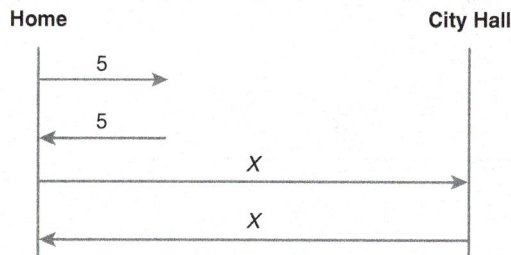

Figure 7.24

If we let the distance from Eva's house to city hall in Boise be represented by x, we obtain the simple equation:

$$2x + 10 = 32{,}966 - 32{,}518$$
$$2x + 10 = 448$$
$$2x = 438$$
$$x = 219.$$

Problem 7.16

At the county fair, there are several employees assigned the task of tracking the number of people who participate in specific activities each day. Rosalinde's notes showed that from Monday through Saturday there were 510 people at the games of chance booth. Gabriel recorded that from Monday through Wednesday there were 392 players at the booth. Frank found that on Tuesday and Friday there were 220 players. Adele found that on Wednesday, Thursday, and Saturday there were a total of 208 players. Finally, Alfred found that from Thursday through Saturday there were 118 players at the booth. Assuming that all the figures were correct, how many players were at the games of chance booth on Monday?

Solution

The usual approach is to set up a series of equations using variables to represent the different days of the week. This will result in a set of five linear equations with six variables as follows (of course, not every variable will occur in every equation):

$$M+T+W+H+F+S=510, \qquad [7.1]$$
$$M+T+W=392, \qquad [7.2]$$
$$T+F=220, \qquad [7.3]$$
$$W+H+S=208, \qquad [7.4]$$
$$H+F+S=118, \qquad [7.5]$$

Now, by solving the set simultaneously, students attempt to obtain the answer. Once again, the process is rather complicated and beyond their ability. (Few of them realize that by subtracting Equations 7.3 and 7.4 from 7.1, they obtain $M=82$.)

Let's make a *visual representation* (*drawing*) of the attendance figures as they were reported:

	Monday	Tuesday	Wednesday	Thursday	Friday	Saturday	Total
Rosalinde	×	×	×	×	×	×	510
Gabriel	×	×	×				392
Frank		×			×		220
Adele			×	×		×	208
Alfred				×	×	×	118

Notice that, except for Monday, every day is mentioned three times. This results in twice the attendance being accounted for by the last four people, except for the "missing" Monday. This yields the single equation

$$2(510) - (392 + 220 + 208 + 118) = \text{Monday's attendance}$$
$$1,020 - 938 = 82.$$

There were 82 people at the booth on Monday.

Problem 7.17

A local pet shop owner just bought her holiday supply of baby chickens and baby rabbits. She doesn't really remember how many of each she bought, but she has a system. She knows that she bought a total of 22 animals, a number exactly equal to her age. Furthermore, she also recalls that the animals had a total of 56 legs, her mother's age. How many chickens and how many rabbits did she buy?

Solution

The standard approach is to set up a system of two equations in two variables as follows:

Let r represent the number of rabbits she bought.

Let c represent the number of chickens she bought.

Then,

$$r + c = 22$$

$4r + 2c = 56$ (rabbits have four legs each; chickens have two legs each).

Solving these equations simultaneously yields

$$4r + 4c = 88$$
$$4r + 2c = 56$$
$$2c = 32$$
$$c = 16$$
$$r = 6.$$

The pet shop owner bought 16 chickens and 6 rabbits.

Of course, this method of solution depends on the students' ability to set up a system of equations and to solve them simultaneously. Not all students are equipped with this algebraic skill. However, we can solve this problem by *making a visual representation* (*drawing a picture*) of the situation.

We can first reduce the number of animals to 11 and the number of legs to 28, reminding ourselves to multiply the answers we obtain by 2. Now, we draw 11 circles to represent the 11 animals:

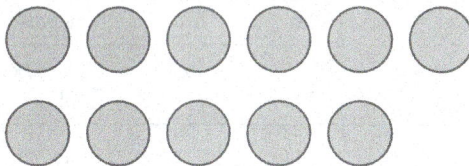

Figure 7.25

Now, whether the animals are chickens or rabbits, they must have at least 2 legs. We now place 2 legs on each circle:

Figure 7.26

This leaves us with 6 additional legs, which we place on the "rabbits" in pairs, to give them a total of 4 legs each:

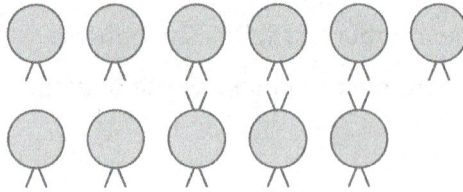

Figure 7.27

Thus, the drawing shows us a total of 3 rabbits and 8 chickens. Remembering to double our answers, we obtain 6 rabbits and 16 chickens as before.

Problem 7.18

It is 1,000 miles from New York to St. Louis. A train leaves New York for St. Louis at 9:00 a.m. and travels at a constant rate of 80 mph. Two hours later, a second train leaves St. Louis for New York on a parallel track and travels at a constant rate of 65 mph. Which train will be closer to New York when the two trains pass each other?

Solution

Many students will develop a table showing the relationship between rate, time, and distance for the two trains:

	Rate	Time	Distance
Train 1	80	x	$80x$
Train 2	65	$x-2$	$65(x-2)$

They then form an equation from the "distance box":

$$80x + 65(x - 2) = 1,000$$
$$80x + 65x - 130 = 1,000$$
$$145x = 1,130$$
$$x = \frac{1,130}{145} = \frac{226}{29}.$$

This raises the question, "Where should we go from here?" The student may then find the required distance, only to find a surprising result, which could have been directly addressed with the following strategy.

Let's examine this problem by *drawing a picture* (*making a visual representation*) of the situation. One train leaves New York for St. Louis; the other leaves St. Louis headed for New York. If we are interested in which train is closer to New York when they meet, let's examine our drawing:

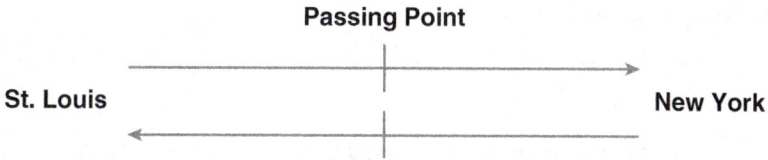

Figure 7.28

Aha! When the two trains meet (wherever it may be) they will be exactly the same distance from New York. The problem is easily solved with a drawing.

Problem 7.19

There is a frog at the bottom of a well that is 100-ft deep. The frog laboriously climbs upward 5 ft during the daytime. However, at night, he falls asleep and slips back 4 ft. At this rate, how many days will it take for the frog to get out of the well?

Solution

In the traditional approach, recognizing that the frog has a net gain of 1 ft per 24-hr day, students assume that it will take the frog 100 days to get out of the well. This is not so. The clever student, realizing that this is an incorrect answer, will eventually "see the light" and obtain the right answer. Let's examine this by *making a drawing* of the situation.

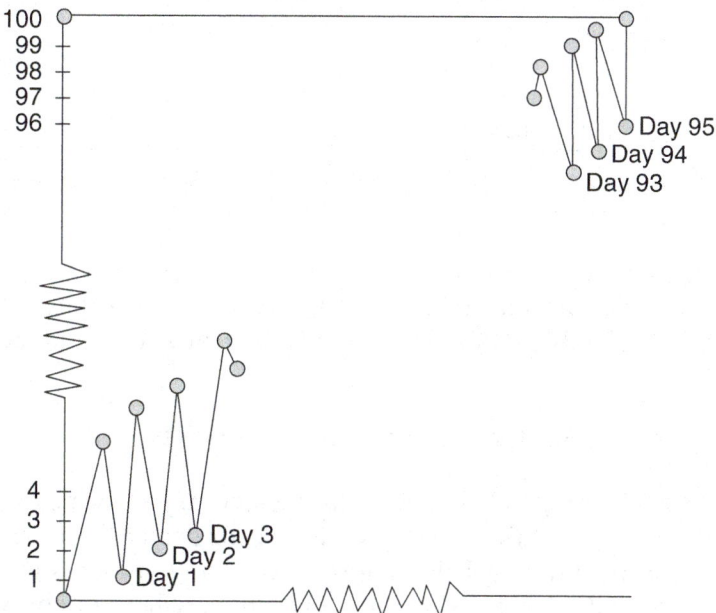

Figure 7.29

It is true that the frog shows a net gain of 1 ft per day, so the frog has reached a height of 95 ft at the end of day 95—a point 5 ft from the top of the well. However, during the 96th day, he climbs 5 ft more and is out of the well, so he doesn't slip back that night.

Problem 7.20

Two trains, one 350 ft long and the other 450 ft long, pass each other completely in 8 sec moving in opposite directions. Moving in the same direction, they pass each other completely in 16 sec. Find the speed of the slower train (in feet per second).

Solution

We begin by letting x equal the speed of the faster train and y equal the speed of the slower train. *Making a drawing* of what is occurring here would be helpful.

When the trains are moving in opposite directions:

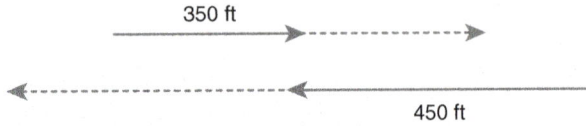

350 ft

450 ft

Figure 7.30

We can see from the diagram that the relative speed with which they pass each other is $x + y$.

When the trains are moving in the same direction:

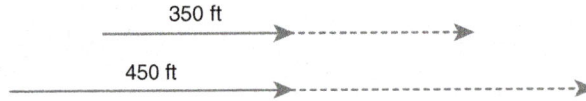

350 ft

450 ft

Figure 7.31

Here, the relative speed at which they pass each other is $x - y$.

In each case, the distance required to pass each other is the sum of their lengths: $350 + 450 = 800$ ft. Because the product of speed and time gives the distance,

$$8(x + y) = 800 \text{ and } 16(x - y) = 800.$$

Therefore, $x = 75$ and $y = 25$, which is the speed of the slower train.

It should be stressed that it is very difficult to depict the motion of the trains through diagrams, yet the diagrams do assist students to visualize this rather difficult concept of relative motion. Teachers ought to stretch the abstraction ability of their students, which is what this sort of problem provides.

Problem 7.21

Mr. Lohengrin saw a row of swans on a lake. In front of two swans, there were two swans. Behind two swans there were two swans, and between two swans there were exactly two swans. What is the minimum number of swans Mr. Lohengrin could have seen?

Solution

We can try to use reasoning to solve this problem. In fact, that may well be the first approach that a student would take. In so doing, students may have some difficulty understanding what the problem states, or they may automatically guess that there were six swans.

It would be advisable to use our strategy of *making a drawing* of the described situation. If we begin with two swans situated in front of another two swans, we get a row of four swans:

Figure 7.32

This also represents the second situation: exactly two swans behind two swans. What remains is to depict exactly two swans between two other swans (using the least number of swans). This can be achieved by considering the following drawing:

Figure 7.33

Therefore, the minimum number of swans Mr. Lohengrin could have seen is a row of four.

8

Intelligent Guessing and Testing (Including Approximation)

This technique is often referred to as the method of trial and error. This is an oversimplification, because this problem-solving strategy is, in its own right, quite sophisticated. It is particularly useful when it is necessary to limit the values for a variable to make the solution more manageable. It is also helpful when the general case is far more complicated than a specific case, with which you can narrow down the options in an effort to focus on the correct answer. In using this strategy, we make a guess and then test it against the conditions of the problem. Each succeeding guess is based on information we obtain from testing the previous guess. Keep in mind that there is a great deal of difference between a "guess" and an "intelligent guess."

It is interesting to note that solving an equation is really only a variation of intelligent guessing and testing. In the "solve" part we put forth a guess, arrived at intelligently by some careful mathematical manipulations. In the "check" or verification part, we test our guess to show that it is indeed correct. An interesting fact is that any problem that can be solved with a pair of equations in two variables solved simultaneously can always be solved by using the *intelligent guessing and testing* strategy along with a table to record the guesses, tests, and new guesses.

THE *INTELLIGENT GUESSING AND TESTING* (INCLUDING APPROXIMATION) STRATEGY IN EVERYDAY LIFE PROBLEM-SOLVING SITUATIONS

A common use for this procedure is the test "poke" that we make in cooking a roast to determine if it is ready to be served. We poke a thermometer into the center of the meat rather than cut the roast prematurely. We can read the temperature inside the meat to verify our guess, enabling us to more accurately determine its state of readiness. We are guessing and testing. If our initial guess that the roast is done proves incorrect when we test the guess with the thermometer, we continue cooking the meat for another few minutes until we are ready to guess again.

This same procedure is also used by a carpenter who cannot get the precise measurements of an odd-shaped piece of wood to fit a specific place. The carpenter, too, estimates the size and shape of the piece of wood and then, by continuously testing its fit and modifying it, solves the construction problem.

A lawyer wanting to determine the possible guilt or innocence of a potential client might intelligently select a key question and test the client candidate with it. The type of response to such an unexpected and cleverly phrased key question could prove quite effective in "guessing" about innocence or guilt in a preliminary (of course, not a legal) sense. This would possibly be enough to guide the lawyer in deciding whether or not to represent the potential client.

APPLYING THE *INTELLIGENT GUESSING AND TESTING* (INCLUDING APPROXIMATION) STRATEGY TO SOLVE MATHEMATICS PROBLEMS

Consider the following problem:

> Barbara took a 20-question multiple-choice test. The test was scored +5 for each correct answer, −2 for each wrong answer, and 0 if the question was omitted. Barbara scored a 44, even though she omitted some questions. How many questions did Barbara omit?

Let us attempt to solve this problem algebraically.

Let $x=$ the number of questions answered correctly.

Let $y=$ the number of questions answered incorrectly.

Let $z=$ the number of questions omitted.

Then,

$$x + y + z = 20$$
$$5x - 2y + 0z = 44.$$

Effectively, we now have only two equations containing three variables. Students would expect to find another equation if they are to solve the system and arrive at a unique set of answers. Furthermore, we know that there must be some nonzero value for z, because the problem stated that Barbara omitted some questions.

If we now continue with the solution process, we obtain the equation

$$7x + 2z = 84.$$

Solving for z,

$$z = \frac{84 - 7x}{2}.$$

Because z is a positive integer, x must be even and at least 10 if we are to get a score of 44. (Because the denominator of the fraction is 2, x must be even for the numerator to be divisible by 2. Furthermore, if x has any value less than 10, we would not be able to find a y that would yield a score of 44.) This leads to the following table, arrived at by solving this equation as a Diophantine equation (an equation in two or more variables with integer coefficients and whose roots are positive integers):

x	10	12	14
y	3	8	13
z	7	0	−7

The conditions of the problem now lead us to the single answer that Barbara omitted 7 questions, because we know she did not omit 0 nor could she omit a negative number of questions.

Now let's solve the problem using *intelligent guessing and testing*. Examine the number of questions Barbara had correct. It must be at least 10, because if she had answered only 9 correctly, she would have received a score of $9 \times 5 = 45$, and by subtracting an even number, she could never end up with 44. With 10 correct, Barbara would have had 3 wrong for a score of 44. Thus, she would have omitted 7 questions. This is *a* correct answer, but is it the only answer? Suppose Barbara had answered 11 questions correctly. There is no way she could arrive at 44 by subtracting an even number from 55. Therefore, 11 is impossible. Suppose we guess 12 correct. Then, $12 \times 5 = 60$ and $60 - 16 = 44$, which means she had 12 correct, 8 wrong, and none omitted. However, this contradicts the statement of the original problem. Therefore, the "omitted 7" option is the only one. By guessing and testing, we arrived at the answer in a more efficient manner and have confidence that our answer is unique.

PROBLEMS USING THE *INTELLIGENT GUESSING AND TESTING* (INCLUDING APPROXIMATION) STRATEGY

Problem 8.1

Evelyn has five boxes of apples. When she weighs them two at a time, she obtains the following weights (in pounds [lb]):

110 112 113 114 115 116 117 118 120 121.

What are the weights of the individual boxes of apples?

Solution

Students can begin by setting up a series of equations. Let the five weights be, in ascending order, a, b, c, d, and e (where e is the sole odd weight).[1] Then, we obtain the following 10 equations:

$$a+e=113 \quad a+c=112 \quad c+d=120$$
$$b+e=115 \quad a+d=114 \quad d+e=121.$$
$$c+e=117 \quad b+c=116$$
$$a+b=110 \quad b+d=118$$

Subtracting the first two equations yields $b-a=2$, but the fourth equation tells us that $b+a=110$. Thus, $b=56$ and $a=54$. Now, because $a+c=112$, $c=58$. Finally, because $a+e=133$, $e=59$. Therefore, because $d+e=121$, $d=62$. This is a good method if we cleverly select the correct equations to combine. Furthermore, 10 equations in 5 variables suggest that the answers may not be unique.

We can solve this problem in a much easier manner by using our strategy of *intelligent guessing and testing*. We begin by guessing one half of 110, or 55 and 55, as two of the box weights. However, this makes no sense, because there are no duplications in weight. So, we make a new guess of 56 and 54. (This accounts for the 110.) Now we try 58. This permits us to account for the 110 $(54+56)$, 112 $(54+58)$, and 114 $(56+58)$. Now, how can we obtain the first odd number, 113? We can try 57. Now we test our guess. This is not correct, because $54+57=111$, a weight not given. Let's try 59. We obtain $54+59=113, 56+59=115, 58+59=117$, and, finally, $62+59=121$. Thus, the five weights are 54, 56, 58, 59, and 62 lb. To test the uniqueness of our answers, we can try weights smaller than 54 and larger

---

1. Since each box is weighted with each of the others, a box is weighted four times. It takes an odd number plus an even number to give an odd sum. There are four odd sums (113, 115, 117, 121); thus, there can be only one odd weight or only one even weight.

than 62. In each case, we arrive at duplicate weights, or at weights larger or smaller than those given. Thus, our original set of five weights was unique.

Problem 8.2

Find the value of x and the value of y, if x and y are positive integers and

$$\frac{x}{4} + \frac{y}{5} = \frac{19}{20}.$$

Solution

It is uncommon for students to work with one equation in two variables. In most cases, they simply guess wildly at integers until they find some that satisfy the equation. Obviously, this is not the most ideal method for solving the problem. There are systematic ways to solve this equation in positive integers—an application of a linear Diophantine equation. The procedures are often cumbersome and not worthy of the space it would take.

Instead, let's take another look at this equation and use our *intelligent guessing and testing* strategy. We begin by solving the equation for x:

$$x = \frac{19 - 4y}{5}.$$

We know that $x > 0$. Using the *intelligent guessing and testing* strategy, we find that the only possible integral values for y are 1, 2, 3, and 4. (Any positive integral value of y greater than 4 will make x negative.) Substituting these values in turn, we find that only $y = 1$ will give an integral value for x, namely, $x = 3$. Therefore, $x = 3$ and $y = 1$ are the values we seek.

Problem 8.3

A piece of wire 52 in. long is cut into two parts. Each part is bent to form a square. The total area of the two squares is 97 $in.^2$ How much larger is a side of the larger square than a side of the smaller square? (Consider only integral lengths for the sides.)

Solution

Most students would solve this problem algebraically as follows. Let x represent a side of the larger square and y represent a side of the smaller square. Then we obtain the following two equations:

$$x^2 + y^2 = 97$$
$$4x + 4y = 52.$$

Dividing the second equation through by 4 and solving for y, we obtain

$$y = 13 - x.$$

Substituting in the first equation yields

$$x^2 + (13 - x)^2 = 97$$
$$x^2 + 169 - 26x + x^2 = 97$$
$$2x^2 - 26x + 72 = 0$$
$$x^2 - 13x + 36 = 0$$
$$(x - 9)(x - 4) = 0,$$

$$x = 9 \quad x = 4$$
$$y = 4 \quad y = 9.$$

The sides of the squares are 9 in. and 4 in.; their difference is 5 in.

Although this method is relatively straightforward, it does require a knowledge of and the ability to solve quadratic equations. Let's look at this problem using our strategy of *intelligent guessing and testing*. We prepare a table of areas whose sum is 97 and test for those areas that are perfect squares as follows:

Smaller Area Square	Larger Area Square	Total Area
1	96	97
4	93	97
9	88	97
16	81	97*
25	72	97
36	61	97

Note: The asterisk (*) indicates the only set of areas whose sum is 97 and where each area is a perfect square. The two squares have areas 16 and 81 and their sides are 4 and 9, respectively. The difference between the sides is 5 in.

If we were to continue the table, the next row entries would be 49 – 48 – 97, and the areas in the first column would no longer be smaller than the areas in the second column. The table ensures that we have a unique set of answers to the problem.

Problem 8.4

Heckle and Jeckle make bracelets from beads and sell them at local crafts shows. Yesterday, they sold some of the bracelets for $1.00 each and half as many for $1.50 each. Altogether they took in $87.50. How many of each type did they sell?

Solution

The traditional approach for most students with an algebra background would be as follows:

Let x represents the number of bracelets sold at $1.50 each.

Let $2x$ represents the number of bracelets sold at $1.00 each.

Hence,

$$1.00(2x) + 1.50(x) = 87.50$$
$$2x + 1.5x = 87.50$$
$$3.5x = 87.50$$
$$x = 25.$$

They sold 25 bracelets at $1.50 each and 50 bracelets at $1.00 each.

For students without an algebra background, this problem can be solved by using our *intelligent guessing and testing* strategy. We know that the number of bracelets sold at $1.00 each must be even, because the number of bracelets sold for $1.50 each is one half this number. Because $87.50 is the amount of money they earned, we can begin our guessing at $80.

Number	Income at $1	Number	Income at $1.50	Total Income	Conclusion
80	$80	40	$60	$140	Too much
60	$60	30	$45	$105	Too much
40	$40	20	$30	$70	Too little
50	$50	25	$37.50	$87.50	Right

They sold 50 at $1.00 each and 25 at $1.50 each. The table reveals that there will be no other set of answers, because any smaller number for the $1.50 bracelets would yield a final sum less than $87.50. Thus, our answers are unique.

Problem 8.5

Nancy loaned three friends a total of $54. She loaned Phoebe $10 more than she loaned Miriam and loaned Susan twice as much as she loaned Phoebe. How much money did Nancy loan to each friend?

Solution

The usual approach to this problem is to generate an equation as follows:

Let x denote the amount of money Nancy loaned to Miriam.

Let $x + 10$ denote the amount of money Nancy loaned to Phoebe.

Let $2(x + 10)$ denote the amount of money Nancy loaned to Susan.

Then,

$$x + (x + 10) + 2(x + 10) = 54$$
$$2x + 10 + 2x + 20 = 54$$
$$4x + 30 = 54$$
$$4x = 24$$
$$x = 6.$$

Nancy loaned $6 to Miriam, $16 to Phoebe, and $32 to Susan.

Let's see how we can solve this problem using our *intelligent guessing and testing* strategy. We'll make a table to keep track of our guesses.

Guess	Test
Miriam $10	Then Phoebe = $20, Susan = $40. Total = $70 (too much)
Miriam $2	Then Phoebe = $12, Susan = $24. Total = $38 (too little)
Miriam $4	Then Phoebe = $14, Susan = $28. Total = $46 (too little)
Miriam $6	Then Phoebe = $16, Susan = $32. Total = $54 (right)

Nancy loaned $6 to Miriam, $16 to Phoebe, and $32 to Susan.

Problem 8.6

Solve the following system of equations for w, x, y, and z where w, x, y, and z are positive integers:

$$w + x + y + z = 10$$
$$w^2 + x^2 + y^2 + z^2 = 30$$
$$w^3 + x^3 + y^3 + z^3 = 100$$
$$wxyz = 24.$$

Solution

Although this is not a topic that appears in the traditional high school curriculum, students are familiar with systems of three linear equations in three variables and should be able to "handle" these. Most students who see a system of four equations in four variables would solve the linear equation for one variable in terms of the others and then substitute elsewhere into the system in hopes of solving by the method of addition and subtraction. Because of the degrees of these equations, this method is probably doomed to failure.

Instead, let's use the problem-solving strategy of *intelligent guessing and testing*. Because of the small sum (10) in the first equation, we can focus on small values for the variables. We might guess 2, 2, 3, 3 as possible values whose sum is 10. However, testing these values in the fourth equation yields a product of 36, not 24. We need smaller numbers whose sum is 10. Let's guess at 1, 2, 3, and 4 as the possible values for w, x, y, and z, respectively. We test these in the fourth equation. They give the correct product, but do they satisfy the other two equations? They do! We now have one set of values for w, x, y, and z. However, because of the symmetric nature of the variables in the equations, all permutations of these four numbers will also satisfy the system. Thus, we have 4! or 24 possible sets of answers, namely, all the arrangements of 1, 2, 3, and 4. Furthermore, because the product of the degrees of the equations is 24, there are exactly 24 sets of answers. We have them all!

Another solution also uses our *intelligent guessing and testing* strategy in reverse order. We begin with $wxyz = 24$. Consider the factors 6, 4, 1, and 1, whose product is 24, but whose sum is 12, where we needed a sum of 10. Consider the factors 6, 2, 2, and 1, whose product is 24, but whose sum is 11, and not 10 as needed. We now consider factors 4, 3, 2, and 1, whose product is 24 and whose sum is 10. This works! We must now test these values in the remaining two equations to see if they fit there as well. They do, and we have a solution.

Problem 8.7

In Roman numerals, the following two "equations" are correct:

$$\begin{array}{ccc} L & I & X \\ +L & V & I \\ \hline C & X & V \end{array} \qquad X \cdot X = C.$$

Now consider the preceding as letters of the alphabet as representative of Arabic numerals. If we substitute the proper Arabic numerals, the "equations" are also correct. Each letter denotes the same and unique numeral throughout the problem. What are the two "equations" in Arabic numerals?

Solution

Students normally guess numerical values for the letters and keep on trying different combinations until they arrive at a set that satisfies both "equations." This procedure, although it should yield the correct answer, is time-consuming at best.

If we apply the *intelligent guessing and testing* strategy (with the emphasis on the word "intelligent"), we can shorten our labors somewhat.

We know that only the digits 1 through 9 can be used. From the second "equation," C must be a perfect square, namely, 1, 4, or 9. If $C = 1$, then

$X=1$, which contradicts the given conditions. Similarly, if $C=4$, then $X=2$ and $L=2$ (from the leftmost column of the addition). Again, a contradiction, because the letters have unique assignments. Therefore, $C=9$ and $X=3$ is the only possibility remaining. However, for C to equal 9, $L=4$ (with 1 to be "carried" from the preceding column). We now use some logical reasoning. Currently, we have $\Diamond$ and $\heartsuit$

$$
\begin{array}{ccc}
4 & \Diamond & 3 \\
+4 & \heartsuit & \Diamond \\
\hline
9 & 3 & \heartsuit \\
\end{array}
$$

where $\Diamond$ represents a unique digit and $\heartsuit$ represents another unique digit. From the middle column, we see that $\Diamond+\heartsuit$ must equal 13. The only remaining candidates for the sum of 13 are 1, 2, 5, 6, 7, and 8. The possible sums of 13 are found by either $6+7$ or $5+8$. The first pair, 6 and 7, does not fit the first column, whereas 5 and 8 do fit properly. This leads to $I=5$ and $V=8$. The original equations were

$$
\begin{array}{ccc}
4 & 5 & 3 \\
+4 & 8 & 5 \qquad 3\times3=9. \\
\hline
9 & 3 & 8 \\
\end{array}
$$

Problem 8.8

The 1-mile relay team consists of four runners: Gustav, Johann, Richard, and Wolfgang. Coincidentally, the order in which they run their quarter-mile lap is the same as the alphabetical order of their names. Each runner runs his quarter-mile lap 2 sec faster than the previous runner. The team finished the race in exactly 3 min 40 sec. How fast did each runner run his lap?

Solution

Students with a background in algebra would solve the problem as follows:

x equals the time it takes Gustav to run his lap.

$x-2$ equals the time it takes Johann to run his lap.

$x-4$ equals the time it takes Richard to run his lap.

$x-6$ equals the time it takes Wolfgang to run his lap.

Hence,

$$x+(x-2)+(x-4)+(x-6)=220 \text{ (3 min 40 sec} =220 \text{ sec)}$$

$$4x - 12 = 220$$
$$4x = 232$$
$$x = 58.$$

It takes Gustav 58 sec to run his lap, Johann takes 56 sec, Richard takes 54 sec, and Wolfgang takes 52 sec.

Of course, this solution depends on the students having a knowledge of equations and a basic background in algebra. Students who lack this background in algebra can still solve the problem by making use of the *intelligent guessing and testing* strategy. We assume that the runners run at approximately the same speed; thus, we can divide 220 by 4, and obtain 55 as our first guess.

	Gustav	Johann	Richard	Wolfgang	Total Time
Guess 1	55	53	51	49	208 (too little)
Guess 2	60	58	56	54	228 (too much)
Guess 3	59	57	55	53	224 (too much)
Guess 4	58	56	54	52	220 (correct)

Thus, Gustav took 58 sec, Johann 56 sec, Richard took 54 sec, and Wolfgang took 52 sec.

Problem 8.9

At a recent banquet, every two guests shared a dish of chicken, every three guests shared a dish of rice, and every four guests shared a dish of vegetables. If there was a total of 65 dishes in all, how many guests were at the banquet?

Solution

Students who wish to use a typical algebraic solution could proceed as follows:

Let x represent the number of guests at the banquet.

$\frac{x}{2}$ equals the number of dishes of chicken.

$\frac{x}{3}$ equals the number of dishes of rice.

$\frac{x}{4}$ equals the number of dishes of vegetables.

Then,

$$\frac{x}{2} + \frac{x}{3} + \frac{x}{4} = 65$$
$$6x + 4x + 3x = 780$$

$$13x = 780$$
$$x = 60.$$

There were 60 guests at the banquet.

This solution involves interpreting the problem to obtain the various representations needed to write the equation. This interpretation may not be obvious to some students. Some students, especially younger ones, may not have the algebra background that the problem requires. For these students, we can solve the problem by using the *intelligent guessing and testing* strategy. If the dishes were shared by two, three, and four people, respectively (and we assume that there was nothing left over in each dish), then the total number of guests must be a multiple of 2, 3, and 4, or a multiple of 12. We create a table and make a guess, which we will then test before making a second guess.

Number of Guests	Number of Chicken Dishes	Number of Rice Dishes	Number of Vegetable Dishes	Total Number of Dishes
12	6	4	3	13 (too small)
24	12	8	6	26 (still too small)
48	24	16	12	52 (better)
60	30	20	15	65 (right)

There were 60 guests at the banquet.

Problem 8.10

Two children were taking their tropical fish to a school pet show. Emily said to Sarah, "Give me one of your fish and I'll have exactly as many as you have." They walked a little bit further and Sarah said to Emily, "Give me one of your fish and I'll have twice as many as you have." How many fish does each child have?

Solution

The traditional approach to this problem involves the use of two equations in two variables.

Let x denote the number of tropical fish Emily has.

Let y denote the number of tropical fish Sarah has.

Then,

$$y - 1 = x + 1$$
$$y + 1 = 2(x - 1).$$

From the first equation, we obtain

$$y = x + 2$$

Substituting into the second equation yields

$$(x + 2) + 1 = 2(x - 1)$$
$$x + 3 = 2x - 2$$
$$5 = x$$
$$7 = y.$$

Sarah has 7 fish; Emily has 5 fish.

This solution involves students working with two equations in two variables. Because some students may not have this skill, let's solve the problem using the *intelligent guessing and testing* strategy. We can tell, from the difference that 1 fish makes, that the numbers must be small. Hence, we make our first guess as 3 and 5. Then, if Sarah gives 1 fish to Emily, they would each have 4. However, if Emily gives 1 fish to Sarah, she has 6 and Emily has 2, which is three times as many. Let's increase our guess to 4 and 7. Then, if Sarah gives 1 fish to Emily, she has 5 and Sarah has 6. Again, no good. We realize at this point that the difference between the two sought-after numbers must be 2. Let's try 5 and 7. If Sarah gives 1 fish to Emily, they each have 6. If Emily gives 1 fish to Sarah, she has 8 and Emily has 4, exactly twice as many. Thus, the answers are Sarah has 7 fish and Emily has 5 fish.

Problem 8.11

Mrs. Schubert gave her son $4.05 in dimes and quarters. She gave him five more quarters than dimes. How many dimes did Mrs. Schubert give her son?

Solution

To solve this problem, we could create a complete table of all the possible combinations of dimes and quarters and then look for the correct combination. This would be rather tedious. The more frequently used solution probably would be to set up a system of two equations in two variables and solve them simultaneously:

$$Q = D + 5$$
$$25Q + 10D = 405.$$

However, both of these processes are rather time-consuming, even assuming that your students can set up the equations. Let's use the strategy of *intelligent guessing and testing*. Pick a number of dimes, say 5. Then, this would give us 10 quarters because there must be 5 more quarters than dimes. The value of this combination of coins is

$$5(0.10) + 10(0.25) = 3.00.$$

The amount 3.00 is too small.

Let's increase the number of dimes. Let's try 8. We then have $8 \div 5 = 13$ quarters:

$$8(0.10) + 13(0.25) = 4.05.$$

We have the correct answer, 8 dimes.

It is a good idea to have students practice more than one procedure in solving a problem. Thus, even if your students can use the algebraic solution, have them practice the *intelligent guessing and testing* strategy as well, because both can be advantageous in different situations.

Problem 8.12

Jeannette and Jesse bought a rectangular rug in Turkey last summer. The rug has an area of 40.5 ft^2. The length of the rug is twice the width. What is the width of the rug?

Solution

Although students may be able to solve this problem algebraically, the solution will involve a quadratic and a linear equation:

$$LW = 40.5$$
$$L = 2W.$$

An alternative and effective approach would be to use *intelligent guessing and testing*. Make a series of guesses for the width of the rug, double it for the length, and then check the resulting area.

Width(W)	×	Length(L)	=	Area
10		20		200 (too large)
5		10		50 (still too large)
4		8		32 (too small)

The width of the rug must lie somewhere between 4 and 5 ft. Since the area of the rug ends in a "5," this suggests that one of the dimensions must also end with a "5." Let's try 4.5 for our width: $4.5 \times 9 = 40.5$. The width of the rug is 4.5 ft.

Problem 8.13

Hans makes furniture as a hobby. Last year he made 4-legged tables and 3-legged stools as gifts for family and friends. When he finished, he had used up 37 legs. How many stools might he have made?

Solution

The first attempt by students is usually algebraic. They begin by forming an equation. If x represents the number of (4-legged) tables and y represents the number of (3-legged) stools, they get the equation $4x + 3y = 37$. However, this is the only equation they can form.

Algebra students may recognize that this is a Diophantine equation, an equation solved in integers. We can solve this algebraically as follows:

$$3y = 37 - 4x$$
$$y = 12 - x + \frac{1-x}{3}$$

(where $\frac{1-x}{3}$ must be an integer).

If $x = 1$, then $y = 12 - 1 + \frac{1-1}{3} = 11$.

If $x = 4$, then $y = 12 - 4 + \frac{1-4}{3} = 7$.

If $x = 7$, then $y = 12 - 7 + \frac{1-7}{3} = 3$.

If $x = 10$, then $y = 12 - 10 + \frac{1-10}{3} = -1$, which is not possible.

We can solve the problem by using the *intelligent guessing and testing* strategy. Let's make a table to keep track of our guesses and the test results.

	Guesses									
Number of tables	1	2	3	4	5	6	7	8	9	10
Number of legs	4	8	12	16	20	24	28	32	36	40
Number of legs left for stools	33	29	25	21	17	13	9	5	1	0
Number of 3-legged stools	11			7			3			

He might have made 3, 7, or 11 stools.

Problem 8.14

The sum of an integer, its square, and its square root is 276. What is the integer?

Solution

The "properly trained" student will easily set up the equation

$$x + x^2 + \sqrt{x} = 276.$$

The solution of this equation can be found in a number of ways. One involves isolating the $\sqrt{x}$ on one side of the equation to get $\sqrt{x} = 276 - x - x^2$. Squaring both sides leads to a rather cumbersome quartic equation, which is not easily solved by a secondary school student: $x^4 + 2x^3 - 551x^2 - 553x + (276)^2 = 0$.

We could, however, approach this problem with our *intelligent guessing and testing* strategy. We try to use the largest perfect square less than 276. This would be 256. If this is the "square" of the problem statement, then the "number" is 16, and its square root is 4. Now we must test to see if $x + x^2 + \sqrt{x} = 276$. Yes, $16 + 256 + 4 = 276$.

There is no question that the procedure used here is far simpler than solving the quartic equation. Such is not always the case. There may be times when our elegant strategies cannot be used, but we must at least try to see if they can be applied.

Problem 8.15

The sum of five consecutive terms of an arithmetic sequence is 30, and the sum of the squares of these terms is 220. Find the largest of these terms.

Solution

Typically, a student of algebra who has had some experience with arithmetic progressions (or series) will set up the following equations:

$$x + (x+d) + (x+2d) + (x+3d) + (x+4d) = 30$$

and

$$x^2 + (x+d)^2 + (x+2d)^2 + (x+3d)^2 + (x+4d)^2 = 220.$$

Solving these two equations simultaneously is no easy task. Therefore, we would be wise to seek another problem-solving strategy.[2]

Let us use the *intelligent guessing and testing* strategy. Because the sum of the consecutive terms must be 30, their average, $\frac{30}{5} = 6$, will be the middle term. One intelligent guess is for the series to be $4 + 5 + 6 + 7 + 8 = 30$.

---

2. We can also look at this representation from a *different point of view* and perhaps establish a *pattern* (i.e., use two of our other strategies). Such an approach requires a bit of experience, which comes precisely from an application such as this problem offers. We write the algebraic representation of the series as $(a - 2d) + (a - d) + a + (a + d) + (a + 2d) = 30$, which gives us $a = 6$. The second equation may be written as $(6 - 2d)^2 + (6 - d)^2 + 6^2 + (6 + d)^2 + (6 + 2d)^2 = 220$, which gives us $10d^2 = 40$, $d = \pm 2$. Therefore, the largest term is $6 + (2)(2) = 10$.

We must now test these terms for the second equation: $4^2 + 5^2 + 6^2 + 7^2 + 8^2 = 16 + 25 + 36 + 49 + 64 = 190$, which is not the 220 we seek. Therefore, our guess of 4, 5, 6, 7, 8 was incorrect.

Let us consider a second sequence whose middle term is the average of a sequence whose sum is 30: $2 + 4 + 6 + 8 + 10 = 30$. Now we must check to see if the sum of the squares of this conjecture is 220: $2^2 + 4^2 + 6^2 + 8^2 + 10^2 = 220$. Through *intelligent guessing and testing*, we have arrived at the solution to the problem.

Problem 8.16

Find all real values of x that satisfy the equations

$$x^2|x| = 8 \text{ and } x|x^2| = 8.$$

Solution

Typically, students are trained to translate absolute value expressions into pairs of equivalent equations that stem from their definition. This traditional method of solution will suffice but is not the most efficient method for this problem.

Using the *intelligent guessing and testing* strategy, we try $x = 2$ and $x = -2$ in both equations. We find that the solution for the first equation is $x = 2$, and $x = -2$, whereas in the second equation the solution is $x = 2$. Therefore, the solution to the problem is $x = 2$, because it is the only value of x that satisfies both equations.

Problem 8.17

Find the least integer n such that the sum of the first n positive integers exceeds 1,000.

Solution

The sum of the first n integers is obtained by the formula $\frac{n(n+1)}{2}$. From this we can represent the problem as requiring a solution to the equation $\frac{n(n+1)}{2} > 1,000$. This implies $n(n+1) > 2,000$. At this point, we can either solve the ensuing quadratic equation (which is the expected next step) or we can revert to the problem-solving strategy of *intelligent guessing and testing* to solve our problem. Whereas $44 < \sqrt{2,000} < 45$, we can try to take the two consecutive integers as our "guess": $n = 45$ and $(45)(46) = 2,070$.

Therefore, $n = 45$ satisfies the inequality. We used the *intelligent guessing and testing* strategy only as a part of our solution, yet by employing this procedure we simplified our work.

Problem 8.18

Two positive integers differ by 5. If their square roots are added, the sum is also 5. What are the two integers?

Solution

The traditional approach is to set up a system of equations as follows:

Let x denote the first integer.

Let y denote the second integer.

Then,

$$y = x + 5$$
$$\sqrt{x} + \sqrt{y} = 5$$
$$\sqrt{x} + \sqrt{x+5} = 5.$$

Squaring both sides yields

$$x + x + 5 + 2\sqrt{x(x+5)} = 25.$$

By simplifying,

$$2\sqrt{x(x+5)} = -2x + 20.$$

Squaring again, we obtain

$$4x^2 + 20x = 4x^2 - 80x + 400$$
$$100x = 400$$
$$x = 4$$
$$y = 9.$$

The two integers are 4 and 9.

Obviously, this procedure requires a knowledge of equations with radicals and a great deal of careful algebraic manipulation. As an alternative, let us make use of our *intelligent guessing and testing* strategy to solve this problem. Whereas the sum of the square roots of the two integers is 5, the individual square roots must be 4 and 1 or 3 and 2. Thus, the integers must be 16 and 1 or 9 and 4. However, only 9 and 4 have a difference of 5 and must, therefore, be the correct answer.

Problem 8.19

Each a_i of the arithmetic sequence a_0, a_1, 25, a_3, a_4 is a positive integer. In the sequence, there is a pair of consecutive terms whose squares differ by 399. Find the largest term of the sequence.

Solution

This sort of problem rests heavily on an *intelligent guessing and testing* strategy. Yet the way in which this strategy is used may vary. So here we will show two such approaches.

The first method for our *intelligent guessing and testing* strategy is to let $a_0 = 25 - 2d$. Then, $a_1 = 25 - d$, $a_3 = 25 + d$, and $a_4 = 25 + 2d$. We now try (guess) $25^2 - (25 - d)^2 = 399$. Then, $d^2 - 50d + 399 = 0$. The discriminant is 904, so that d is not an integer and, therefore, must be rejected as a possible answer.

We now try the third and fourth elements in the sequence: $(25 + d)^2 - 25^2 = 399$. Then, $d^2 + 50d - 399 = 0$ or $(d - 7)(d + 57) = 0$, which yields $d = 7$ and $d = -57$. Using the value $d = 7$, we obtain $a_3 = 32$ and $a_4 = 39$. With the value $d = -57$, the sequence is 139, 82, 25, -32, -89. With the condition of the problem that each a_i is a *positive* integer, this result is rejected. If the problem is changed so that each a_i is an integer, then the result 139 is acceptable.

This solution is based heavily on algebra. Getting bogged down with factoring the equation can be a drawback. We will use the *intelligent guessing and testing* strategy yet another time and with less algebra involved. For this second method, we try $25^2 - a_1^2 = 399$. Then, $a_1^2 = 226$. This answer must be rejected, because a_1 is not an integer. Let us now try $a_3^2 - 25^2 = 399$. Then, $a_3^2 = 1,024 = 32^2 \cdots a_3 = 32$, and the difference between terms of this arithmetic sequence is 7. Therefore, the largest term of the sequence, $a_4 = 32 + 7 = 39$.

Notice that we could not avoid using the *intelligent guessing and testing* strategy because of the nature of the problem. Yet it is important to point out that there are often various ways in which we can employ the guess and test method.

Problem 8.20

Jack's bank charges 10¢ for each check he writes, plus a monthly service charge of 25¢ per month. Beginning in March of next year, the fee structure will be changed. Jack will be charged 8¢ for each check he writes and a monthly service charge of 50¢. The bank told Jack that this is a better fee structure for him, because of the number of checks he writes each month. What is the minimum number of checks Jack must write each month for the new fees really to be "better?"

Solution

This problem is regularly presented to students in an algebra class. The traditional method for solving this problem is to set up an inequality as follows:

Let x represent the number of checks Jack writes each month.

Under the old fee structure, Jack spent $0.10x + 0.25$ per month.

Under the new fee structure, Jack will spend $0.08x + 0.50$ per month.

For the new system to save Jack money,

$$0.08x + 0.50 < 0.10x + 0.25$$
$$8x + 50 < 10x + 25$$
$$-2x < -25$$
$$x < 12.5.$$

Because Jack cannot write a fractional number of checks, he must write a minimum of 13 checks.

Notice that this technique requires the ability to set up an inequality, as well as to solve it. Instead, let's look at this problem using our *intelligent guessing and testing strategy*. The size of the numbers seems to indicate that the number of checks will be relatively small. Let's begin with a guess of 10 checks.

Number of Checks	Original Cost	New Cost
10	$10 \times 0.10 + 0.25 = \$1.25$	$10 \times 0.08 + 0.50 = \$1.30$ (too small)
15	$15 \times 0.10 + 0.25 = \$1.75$	$15 \times 0.08 + 0.50 = \$1.70$ (all right, but ...)

All right, but is this the *minimum number?* We continue guessing and testing:

Number of Checks	Original Cost	New Cost
14	$14 \times 0.10 + 0.25 = \$1.65$	$14 \times 0.08 + 0.50 = \$1.62$
13	$13 \times 0.10 + 0.25 = \$1.55$	$13 \times 0.08 + 0.50 = \$1.54$
12	$12 \times 0.10 + 0.25 = \$1.45$	$12 \times 0.08 + 0.50 = \$1.46$

The minimum number is 13 checks.

We could also solve this problem by *logical reasoning.* Since the monthly fee goes up by 25¢ and the charge per check goes down by 2¢, Jack needs $12\frac{1}{2}$ checks to "make up" the 25¢. Thus, he must write 13 checks to be "better off."

9

Accounting for All Possibilities

Considering all the options can be an effective way to solve a problem. Although there may be instances where this strategy is not the most sophisticated procedure, it may be the simplest to use, since it is typically not very abstract. However, the issue of accounting for *all* the possibilities is crucial in the use of this strategy. If we do not have an organized procedure to account for all the possibilities, the strategy often goes awry. A table or organized list will often be the simplest method of accounting for all the possibilities. In fact, an exhaustive list will contain the answer to the problem and limits the number of possibilities to be considered. This can be seen in the mathematics application that follows and more subtly in the everyday examples that follow.

THE *ACCOUNTING FOR ALL POSSIBILITIES* STRATEGY IN EVERYDAY LIFE PROBLEM-SOLVING SITUATIONS

We often use this problem-solving strategy in everyday life without conscious awareness that the strategy is even being employed. Suppose that you are asked to attend a meeting in a hotel about 150 miles away. The way most people would decide on the best way to travel to the meeting is to list all the possible modes of travel (train, plane, car, bus, helicopter, etc.) either in writing or mentally and then select the most efficient method by elimination or direct selection (due to time, cost, etc.).

When a computer program malfunctions and we have to determine the cause, we usually begin by listing (again, perhaps mentally) the various possible reasons for the malfunction. Then, one by one, we inspect the potential trouble spots on the list until we find the one that is causing the malfunction.

A similar approach is used when we try to determine why a lamp is not functioning. We list the possible causes of the malfunction (bad wire, burned-out bulb, "dead" outlet, etc.) and then, one by one, eliminate the ones that are functioning until the "culprit" is discovered.

When people are first seated in a restaurant, they are usually handed a menu that has a selection of appetizers, salads, entrees, and desserts. From the menu, they are expected to select those dishes that will provide a complete meal. The usual procedure for most people is to read the entire menu through, *account for all the possibilities*, and then place an order that provides a balanced meal that will satisfy them. Even though we usually do not consciously realize it, we are using the accounting for all the possibilities strategy to select our dinner.

Similarly, when we settle back in an easy chair and peruse the local television guide in preparation for an evening of entertainment, we usually *account for all the possibilities* for programs that are being presented that evening. We then make a selection from among the many programs.

Obviously, in criminal cases, detectives must investigate all possibilities to solve a case. The everyday situations in which all possibilities are considered as a way of solving a problem are bountiful. There are times when a simple solution in hand is better than an elegant solution that you just cannot think of easily in the time you have for solving the problem.

The often used "process of elimination" is another example of using the *accounting for all possibilities* strategy in everyday life. For example, whenever a catastrophe such as a train or airplane crash occurs, the authorities must *account for all possibilities* to determine the cause of the accident. Then, by making a careful investigation of the accident and all its potential causes, followed by a proper elimination of events that could not have occurred, the authorities can be clear about the actual cause by its being the sole remainder in this process of elimination.

APPLYING THE *ACCOUNTING FOR ALL POSSIBILITIES* STRATEGY TO SOLVE MATHEMATICS PROBLEMS

Consider the following problem:

> If four coins are tossed, what is the probability that at least two heads will be showing?

Naturally, we can use methods of probability calculation to obtain this answer quite quickly if we recognize the appropriate "formula" to use. However, it is quite simple to list all the possibilities (the sample space) and then to highlight those that fit the requirement of at least two heads. Here is the entire list of all possibilities:

HHHH	**HHHT**	**HHTH**	**HTHH**
THHH	**HHTT**	**HTHT**	**THHT**
HTTH	**THTH**	**TTHH**	HTTT
THTT	TTHT	TTTH	TTTT

The boldface events are those that have 2 or more Hs and satisfy the given conditions. There are 11 of these; thus, the required probability is $\frac{11}{16}$.

PROBLEMS USING THE *ACCOUNTING FOR ALL POSSIBILITIES* STRATEGY

Problem 9.1

Joyce invited 17 friends to a dinner party at her house last Friday evening. She gave each guest a card with a number from 2 through 18, reserving number 1 for herself. When she had everyone paired off at the dinner table, she noticed that the sum of each couple's numbers was a perfect square. What number did Joyce's partner have?

Solution

The traditional method of solution is to guess. Students can write all the numerals from 1 through 18 and match them up until the conditions of the problem have been met. Will this method yield an answer? Probably. However, it will take a great deal of time.

Instead, let's *account for all the possibilities* by making a list of all possible number pairs from 1 through 18, whose sum is a perfect square:

1 & 3, 1 & 8, 1 & 15	10 & 6, 10 & 15
2 & 7, 2 & 14	11 & 5, 11 & 14
3 & 1, 3 & 6, 3 & 13	12 & 4, 12 & 13
4 & 5, 4 & 12	13 & 3, 13 & 12
5 & 4, 5 & 11	14 & 2, 14 & 11
6 & 3, 6 & 10	15 & 1, 15 & 10
7 & 2, 7 & 9, 7 & 18	16 & 9
8 & 1, 8 & 17	17 & 8
9 & 7, 9 & 16	18 & 7

Notice that three pairs are "fixed" (16 & 9, 17 & 8, 18 & 7), because 16, 17, and 18 cannot be combined with any other numbers to make a perfect square. Eliminate any other combinations that contain any of these six numbers. We are now left with 1 & 15, 2 & 14, 3 & 13, 4 & 12, 5 & 11, and 6 & 10, because the other numbers were already used. Thus, Joyce's dinner partner was number 15.

Problem 9.2

The two spinners shown in Figure 9.1 are spun, and the resulting numbers are added. What is the probability that the sum of the two numbers is even?

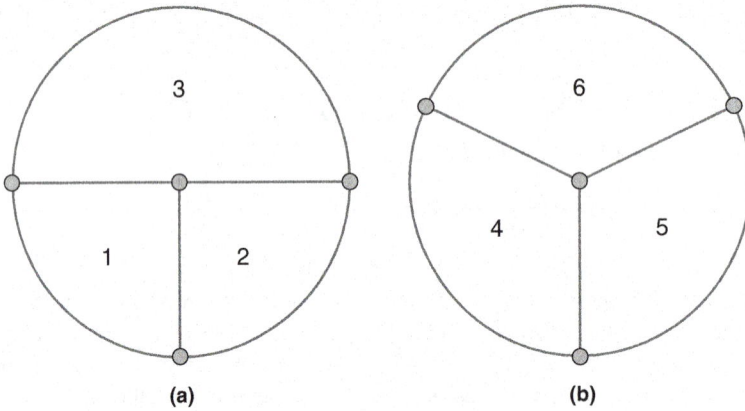

(a)   (b)

Figure 9.1

Solution

The even sums are produced by adding either two odd numbers or two even numbers. We make an adjustment in the first spinner so that we have four equal regions (see Figure 9.2).

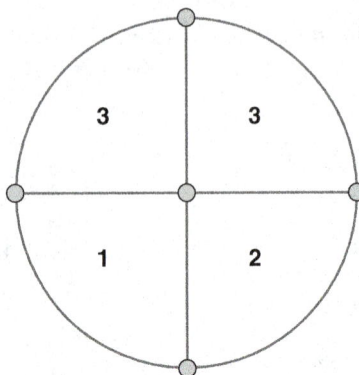

Figure 9.2

Students who are familiar with probability can solve the problem in the following manner:

$$P(3+5) + P(1+5) + P(2+4) + P(2+6)$$

where $P(3+5)$ means "probability of a 3 and a 5"

$$\left(\frac{1}{2}\right)\left(\frac{1}{3}\right) + \left(\frac{1}{4}\right)\left(\frac{1}{3}\right) + \left(\frac{1}{4}\right)\left(\frac{1}{3}\right) + \left(\frac{1}{4}\right)\left(\frac{1}{3}\right) = \left(\frac{5}{12}\right).$$

Of course, this depends on the individual student's ability to set up the probability expressions.

We can also solve this problem and *account for all the possibilities* by setting up an organized sample space:

+	4	5	6
1	5	6	7
2	6	7	8
3	7	8	9
3	7	8	9

There are 12 possibilities in the sample space, of which 5 are even. Thus, the probability of the sum being even is $\frac{5}{12}$.

We can also look at this problem from a *different point of view*. We simply need parity (i.e., both spinners showing odd numbers or both spinners showing even numbers). Consider the probability of getting an odd number on the left-hand spinner and an odd number on the right-hand spinner (see Figure 9.1): $P(\text{odd and odd}) = \frac{3}{4} \times \frac{1}{3} = \frac{1}{4}$. Now, the probability of getting two even numbers: $P(\text{even and even}) = \frac{1}{4} \times \frac{2}{3} = \frac{1}{6}$. The probability of getting two odds *or* two evens is $\frac{1}{4} + \frac{1}{6} = \frac{5}{12}$.

Problem 9.3

In triangle ABC, $\cos \angle A \times \cos \angle B \times \cos \angle C > 0$. What kind of triangle is triangle ABC?

Solution

Some students will attempt to substitute values for angles A, B, and C and resolve the problem. This usually leads to a variety of difficulties. We will solve the problem by *considering all possibilities* of types of triangles.

1. *Triangle ABC is a right triangle.* If triangle ABC is a right triangle, then one of its angles must be $90°$, and $\cos 90° = 0$. Then, $\cos \angle A \times \cos \angle B \times \cos \angle C = 0$, which contradicts the given.

2. *Triangle ABC is an obtuse triangle.* If triangle ABC is an obtuse triangle, then one of its angles (let's assume angle B) must have measure greater than $90°$, while angles A and C must both be acute. Then

cos $\angle B < 0$, while cos $\angle A > 0$ and cos $\angle C > 0$. Here, cos $\angle A \times$ cos $\angle B \times$ cos $\angle C < 0$. Again, this is a contradiction of the given.

3. *Triangle ABC is an acute triangle.* If triangle *ABC* is acute, then all its three angles must be acute. Thus, cos $\angle A > 0$, cos $\angle B > 0$, and cos $\angle C > 0$. This makes cos $\angle A \times$ cos $\angle B \times$ cos $\angle C > 0$. Thus, our triangle is an acute triangle.

Problem 9.4

Find the range of values for *x* in the triangle shown in Figure 9.3.

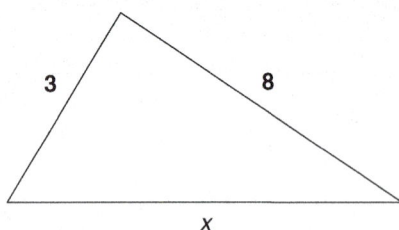

Figure 9.3

Solution

Many students faced with this problem use trial and error. They assign various values to see to what extent the triangle inequality holds true for different values of *x*.

A more organized way is to directly *consider all possibilities*. We know that the sum of any two sides of a triangle must be greater than the third side. Thus, we must consider the following three possibilities:

(a)		(b)		(c)	
	$x < 3 + 8$		$8 < 3 + x$		$3 < x + 8$
	$x < 11$		$5 < x$		$-5 < x$
			$x > 5$		$x > -5$

We can now draw a diagram to determine the intersection of these three conditions:

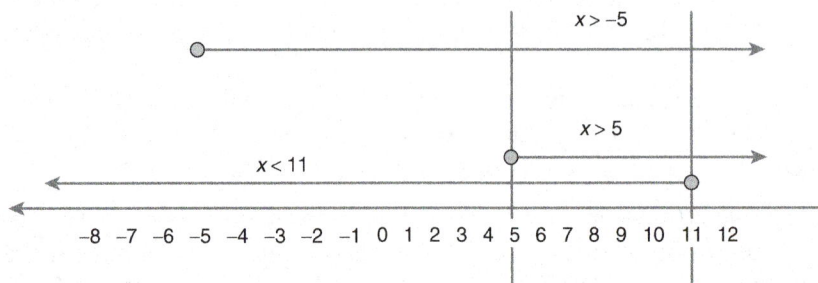

Figure 9.4

Thus, $5 < x < 11$.

We can also solve this problem by *considering extremes*. Suppose the angle formed by the sides of length 5 and 8 gets extremely large, that is, becomes 180°. Then, to preserve a triangle, $x < 3 + 8$, or $x < 11$. Now, suppose this angle approaches the other extreme, namely, 0°. Then, to preserve a triangle, $x > 5$. Therefore, $5 < x < 11$.

Problem 9.5

Given that the number 94,8*d*8 is divisible by 12, what are the possible values for *d*?

Solution

Many students approach a problem such as this by substituting the digits 0 through 9 for *d*. They then divide each of the resulting numbers by 12 to see which leave no remainder. Although this solution would yield the correct answer, it is quite time-consuming and open to error, even with a calculator.

Let's examine this problem by *considering all the possibilities* in an organized manner. If a number is divisible by 12, it must be divisible by both 3 and 4. First we find all the possible values of *d* that make 94,8*d*8 divisible by 3, and then eliminate those for which the number is not divisible by 4. If 941,8*d*8 is divisible by 3, then the sum of the digits must be a multiple of 3:

$$9 + 4 + 8 + d + 8 = 29 + d.$$

Therefore,

  d can be 1 (a digit sum of 30).

  d can be 4 (a digit sum of 33).

  d can be 7 (a digit sum of 36).

Our number must be 94,818 or 94,848 or 94,878.

To be divisible by 4, the final two digits of the number, when considered as a two-digit number, must be divisible by 4. Neither 18 nor 78 is divisible by 4. Only 48 is divisible by 4. Therefore, the only possible value for *d* that satisfies both conditions is 4.

Note: This is an excellent opportunity to discuss the tests for divisibility by various numbers. (See Posamentier, A. S., & Krulik, S. (1996). *Teachers! Prepare your students for the mathematics for SAT I: Methods and problem-solving strategies*. Thousand Oaks, CA: Corwin Press.)

Problem 9.6

The numerator of a fraction is randomly chosen from the set of odd integers {1, 3, 5, 7, 9}, and the denominator is chosen at random from the set of the first five digits {1, 2, 3, 4, 5}. What is the probability that the fraction thus formed, when expressed as a decimal, will be a terminating decimal?

Solution

There will be a limited number of fractions possible, namely, 25 (because there are 5 choices for the numerator and 5 choices for the denominator, $5 \times 5 = 25$). Students may write out all 25 fractions, convert them to decimal form using their calculators, and then determine which are terminating. This method will produce the correct answer, but is rather tedious.

Instead, let's *consider all the possibilities* with some mathematical reasoning. Fractions will terminate if the denominators contain only factors of 1, 2, or 5. Thus, we know that the 20 fractions with denominators 1, 2, 4, and 5 will all terminate. We need only examine the fractions whose denominators are 3. Consider these 5 fractions. Of the five, $\frac{3}{3}$ and $\frac{9}{3}$ terminate. Only $\frac{1}{3}$, $\frac{5}{3}$, and $\frac{7}{3}$ will not terminate. Thus, 22 of the 25 fractions terminate. The probability that the fraction will terminate is $\frac{22}{25}$.

Problem 9.7

Find the smallest integral value for x for which $\dfrac{12}{x+1}$ yields an integer.

Solution

Students usually try various values for x until they find a small one for which $\frac{12}{x+1}$ yields an integer. However, does this guarantee that it will be the *smallest*?

Let's *consider all the possibilities* by examining $(x+1)$. If $\frac{12}{x+1}$ is to give an integral answer, then $(x+1)$ must divide 12, leaving no remainder. Thus, $(x+1)$ must equal 12, 6, 4, 3, 2, 1, −1, −2, −3, −4, −6, or −12. This means that x must equal 11, 5, 3, 2, 1, 0, −2, −3, −4, −5, −7, or −13. The smallest integral value for x is −13.

Problem 9.8

On a standard die, the dots on the opposite faces have a sum of 7. How many different sums of dots on three adjacent faces are there on this standard die?

Solution

Most students will draw a die and then systematically count the dots on adjacent faces to come up with an answer. Others will list all possible combinations of dots on any three faces with no regard for whether or not they are adjacent.

We will organize the data in such a way that we can *account for all possibilities*. Whereas the sum of opposite faces is 7, the only possibilities for this to happen would be 1 and 6, 2 and 5, and 3 and 4.

Now, we know that if we consider three adjacent faces, they must share a common vertex. Because there are eight vertices, there will be eight sets of three adjacent faces. We now check to see whether or not the sets all have different sums. To do this, we select all possible sets of three by choosing one number from each of the three pairs of described opposite faces and then take their sum. To be certain that we have all the possibilities, we select them in an organized manner:

{1, 2, 3}; sum = 6	{1, 5, 3}; sum = 9	{6, 2, 3}; sum = 11
{1, 2, 4}; sum = 7	{1, 5, 4}; sum = 10	{6, 2, 4}; sum = 12
{6, 5, 3}; sum = 14	{6, 5, 4}; sum = 15.	

There are eight *different* sums.

Problem 9.9

Two families have moved into a neighborhood. Each has a rectangular backyard garden, with a perimeter of 24 yards. However, one garden has an area that is 8 yard^2 more than the other. What are the areas of the two gardens? (Consider only integral answers.)

Solution

The usual procedure most students follow is to draw the situation, place variables on the dimensions, and attempt to form equations.

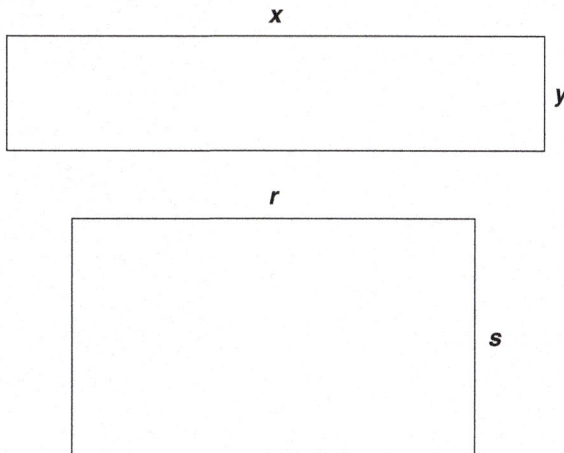

Figure 9.5

This leads to the following system of equations:

$$2x + 2y = 24$$
$$2r + 2s = 24$$
$$xy + 8 = rs.$$

Unfortunately, we have a system of three equations containing four variables. This is beyond the abilities of most high school students.

Let's solve the problem by *examining all the possibilities*. To do this, we will make an organized list of all possible cases where the perimeter is 24 and the sides are integral:

Dimensions	Area
11 × 1	11
10 × 2	20
9 × 3	27
8 × 4	32
7 × 5	35
6 × 6	36

Since the areas must differ by 8 yard^2, we look for two areas that satisfy this condition. The areas of the two gardens are 27 and 35 yard^2.

Problem 9.10

In Figure 9.6, what is the number of common tangents to exactly two circles at a time?

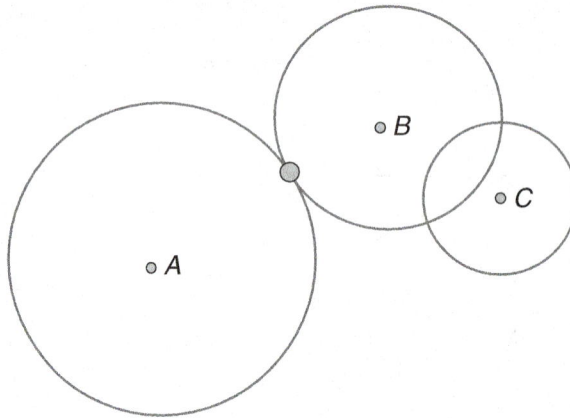

Figure 9.6

Solution

We could draw all the common tangents and count them, but we would not necessarily get them all, because the drawing would probably become too confusing. Instead, let's take the circles two at a time and *account for all the possibilities*.

Circles A and B: two external tangents + one internal tangent.

Circles A and C: two external tangents + two internal tangents.

Circles B and C: two external tangents.

Thus, there is a total of nine tangents in all. Emphasize to your students that the problem was easily resolved by accounting for all the possibilities.

Problem 9.11

Figure 9.7 shows three faces of a cube. If the six faces of the cube are numbered consecutively, what is the sum of the numbers on all six faces?

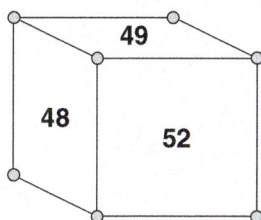

49

48

52

Figure 9.7

Solution

Most students will observe that the numbers shown on the faces of the cube begin with 48 and 49. The most usual assumption is to merely continue the sequence for six terms, arriving at 48, 49, 50, 51, 52, 53 as the numbers on the faces. Because the third face shown, namely, 52, appears in their sequence, students are usually quite content to give the sum of these six numbers, 303, as their answer.

However, the students have not *accounted for all the possibilities.* We see three of the six faces. Because we see 48, 49, and 52, there must also be a 50 and a 51. However, the sixth number could occur on either end of the sequence. Thus, there are *two* possibilities for the sixth number, either 47 or 53. This yields two possible sums, 297 or 303.

Problem 9.12

Find all pairs of consecutive whole numbers less than 25 such that their squares differ by a perfect square.

Solution

Students usually begin by forming a pair of equations as follows:

Let x represent the smaller of the consecutive numbers.

Let $x + 1$ represent the larger of the consecutive numbers.

Then,

$$(x+1)^2 - x^2 = z^2$$
$$x^2 + 2x + 1 - x^2 = z^2$$
$$2x + 1 = z^2,$$

which presents us with one equation in two variables, which most high school students cannot solve.

Since the answers are integers, this is a Diophantine equation and can be solved as follows:

$$2x + 1 = z^2.$$

Solving for x,

$$x = \frac{z^2 - 1}{2}.$$

If x is to be an integer, z must be an odd number for $z^2 - 1$ to be divisible by 2.

We now consider all possibilities for z:

If $z=1$, then $x=0$ and $(x+1)=1$	$1^2 - 0^2 = 1$	Correct
If $z=3$, then $x=4$ and $(x+1)=5$	$5^2 - 4^2 = 9$	Correct
If $z=5$, then $x=12$ and $(x+1)=13$	$13^2 - 12^2 = 25$	Correct
If $z=7$, then $x=24$ and $(x+1)=25$	$25^2 - 24^2 = 49$	Correct
If $z=9$, then $x=40$ and $(x+1)=41$	but these are greater than specified in the problem statement.	

By *accounting for all possibilities*, we were able to focus quickly on the sought-after values.

Problem 9.13

Find the number of ways in which 20 coins, consisting of nickels, dimes, and quarters, can total $3.10.

Solution

It is expected that the students will immediately try to create algebraic expressions that reflect the given information in the problem statement. Therefore, they will get

$$n + d + q = 20,$$

where n, d, and q represent the number of nickels, dimes, and quarters, so that

$$n = 20 - q - d.$$

Furthermore, $25q + 10d + 5n = 310$, which by combining the last two equations gives us

$$25q + 10d + 5(20 - q - d) = 310.$$

Then,

$$4q + d = 42 \text{ or } q = 10 + \frac{2 - d}{4}.$$

We are now at the point at which we must *account for all possibilities* for the value of d. We find that d must be even and of the form $4k + 2$.

The following chart shows the various value possibilities for k and the ensuing values for d, q, and n:

k	d	q	n
0	2	10	8
1	6	9	5
2	10	8	2
3	14	7	−1

All seems to be fine with $k = 0, 1, 2$. However, when $k = 3$, then $4k + 2 = 14$, which will not render a proper result. Thus, we have the solution to our problem by having *accounted for all possibilities.*

Problem 9.14

A mathematics teacher noted that his present age is a prime number. He observed the next time his age would be a prime number was as far in the future as the previous prime number age was in the past. How old is the mathematics teacher?

Solution

This problem does not lend itself to very many alternative methods of solution. Yet it is important that students recognize the strategy of *accounting for all possibilities.*

Primes	2		3		5		7		11		13		17		19		23		29		31		37		41	
Differences		1		2		2		4		2		4		2		4		6		2		6		4		2

Primes	43		47		53		59		61		67		71		73		79		83		89		97		101
Differences		4		6		6		2		6		4		2		6		4		6		8		4	

In so doing, a list of primes from 1 to 100 (although the mathematics teacher's age would probably only require inspecting the prime numbers between 20 and 80) reveals only two situations where three consecutive primes have a common difference. The first case, 3, 5, and 7, could not possibly be used because the mathematics teacher's age cannot be 5 years. The second case, 47, 53, and 59, seems to suggest a reasonable age range. Thus, the mathematics teacher's age would be 53.

Problem 9.15

A digit is inserted between the digits of a two-digit perfect square number to form another perfect square. Find the three-digit squares formed in this way.

Solution

An algebraic solution might be attempted here. However, it is clearly not as efficient as using our strategy of *accounting for all possibilities*.

The two-digit squares are 16, 25, 36, 49, 64, and 81.

The three-digit squares are 100, 121, 144, 169, 196, 225, 256, 289, 324, 361, 400, 441, 484, 529, 576, 625, 676, 729, 784, 841, 900, and 961.

Now we inspect the hundreds and units places of each of the three-digit squares. We notice that those that come from the two-digit numbers are 196, 225, and 841. This solves our problem.

10

Organizing Data

I t is not uncommon to find a student who, a bit baffled by a problem, emerges from this state of confusion by organizing given data from the problem situation in a way different from the way it was presented. This reorganization may be visual, or it may simply be an alternative way to look at the situation. We visually organize data when we do home budgeting and arrange bills according to category.

THE *ORGANIZING DATA* STRATEGY IN EVERYDAY LIFE PROBLEM-SOLVING SITUATIONS

This problem-solving strategy manifests itself frequently in our everyday planning processes. When faced with several tasks and the problem of how best to approach them, we tend to organize the tasks by time, place, difficulty, or some other important criterion. For example, we use the notion of organizing data when we embark on a shopping trip and want to make the best use of the time available. We might list the items to be purchased and then organize them in the order that makes the most sense to avoid crowds of people or to minimize the travel time to and between stores. Similarly, a tourist, wanting to make his sightseeing efficient, organizes the sights by location.

When we gather together the information needed to prepare our annual taxes, the way in which we organize our receipts, checks, W-2 forms, 1099 forms, and so forth becomes critical. If these papers are not placed into some organized format, it becomes impossible to fill out the tax forms properly.

The problem of passing a history test is sometimes dependent on the ability to organize data. Such organization can help to analyze concepts or to establish common issues in history, which then lead to determining a policy or principle. Just such a question could appear on a test, so that the student who has the ability to first organize data and ideas and then to analyze them is at a distinct advantage.

The organization of data is crucial for making sense out of a survey or poll taken to determine the meaning of subjects' responses. To be able to make assessments, predictions, and descriptions about a given situation is also, in large measure, dependent on the ability to organize data. There are times when the same data collected by two researchers yield two different results because of a variation in the organization of the data. The way in which data are combined and counted can make a huge difference in interpretation.

The organization of data seems to permeate most aspects of everyday life. From organizing a personal library to organizing your clothes closet or kitchen, we can much better attack a problem situation with *organized data* or information. Sometimes it is not merely an issue of it being easier to solve a problem with organized information, it is absolutely essential!

APPLYING THE *ORGANIZING DATA* STRATEGY TO SOLVE MATHEMATICS PROBLEMS

Mathematicians face data organization in very dramatic ways. Often, a reorganization of data leads to a solution in a significantly more efficient manner. For example, suppose we are asked to find the median score for the following group of 15 test scores:

$$72, 43, 98, 57, 87, 89, 67, 23, 56, 89, 91, 88, 72, 75, 66.$$

The way these scores have been listed makes it next to impossible to find the median score directly. However, if we organize the scores from lowest to highest,

$$23, 43, 56, 57, 66, 67, 72, 72, 75, 87, 88, 89, 89, 91, 98,$$

the middle or median score of 72 is readily found.

Often, a different organization can reveal a great deal about what is taking place in the problem, as well. Consider the following problem:

> Given eight dots, no three of which lie on a straight line, how many straight line segments must be drawn to connect every pair of dots with one straight line segment?

Some students may recognize that this can be approached simply as a combination problem, with two points determining each segment. Thus, the formula $_8C_2$ yields the answer 28 rather quickly. However, the reasoning behind the use of this formula as well as a view of what is taking place is lost in this quick application of a formula.

Other students will jump right in and begin by determining the eight dots and then attempting to draw straight line segments connecting the points in pairs. If they try this approach without any organization, they will soon become confused about which points have already been joined and which line segments have not yet been drawn. In other words, the diagram will become quite messy and disorganized.

Let's begin by considering a different method of *organizing the data*. We begin by drawing and labeling the eight points. Then, starting at A, how many segments are needed to join point A to each of the other points? Since there are seven other points, we need seven segments (see Figure 10.1). These are $\overline{AB}, \overline{AC}, \overline{AD}, \overline{AE}, \overline{AF}, \overline{AG}$, and $\overline{AH}$.

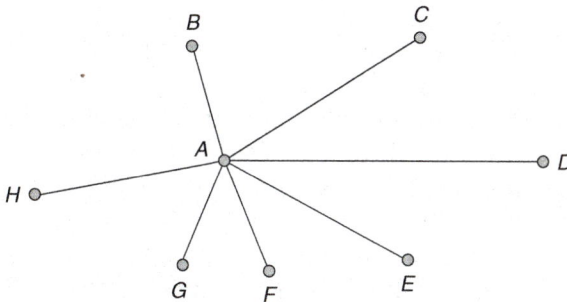

Figure 10.1

Now let's consider point B. To join B to every one of the other points, we also need seven line segments. However, one of these, namely, the segment from B to A, is the same as the one already drawn to connect A to B. Thus, because $\overline{AB}$ has already been used, we need only six new segments to connect B to every other point, namely, $\overline{BC}, \overline{BD}, \overline{BE}, \overline{BF}, \overline{BG}$, and $\overline{BH}$.

If we continue following this pattern of organization, we find the following requirements:

Five new line segments to join point C to each of the other points.

Four new line segments to join point D to each of the other points.

Three new line segments to join point E to each of the other points.

Two new line segments to join point F to each of the other points.

One new line segment to join point G to each of the other points.

Point H is already joined to each of the other points.

Thus, we need $7+6+5+4+3+2+1=28$ line segments to join all the pairs of points.

You should emphasize that a careful plan of organization often makes solving a complex problem easier and more revealing than merely jumping in without an organized plan.

PROBLEMS USING THE *ORGANIZING DATA* STRATEGY

Problem 10.1

David and Lisa are in a charity tennis tournament at the local tennis club. The first player to win either two consecutive games or a total of three games wins the match. In how many different ways can their match end?

Solution

We can begin to resolve this problem by writing out all the possible scenarios. That is, suppose Lisa wins the first game, loses the second, wins the third, wins the fourth. Alternatively, David might win the first game, lose the second, win the third, win the fourth, and so on. Obviously, there are too many ways to ensure that we'll have them all.

At first, there seem to be too many different ways to count. However, let's *organize the data* in a careful manner by making an exhaustive list of the possibilities. The first half of the list contains all situations when Lisa wins the first game. The second half of the list contains all the situations when David wins the first game.

LL	DD
LDD	DLL
LDLL	DLDD
LDLDL	DLDLD
LDLDD	DLDLL

Thus, there are 10 possible ways to end the match.

Problem 10.2

A regular dodecagon is inscribed in a unit circle. A point, P, on the circle is selected. Find the sum of the squares of the distances from P to each of the vertices.

Solution

An initial approach by many students would be to consider each of the angles in turn, based on their intercepted arcs. Examine the diagram shown in Figure 10.2.

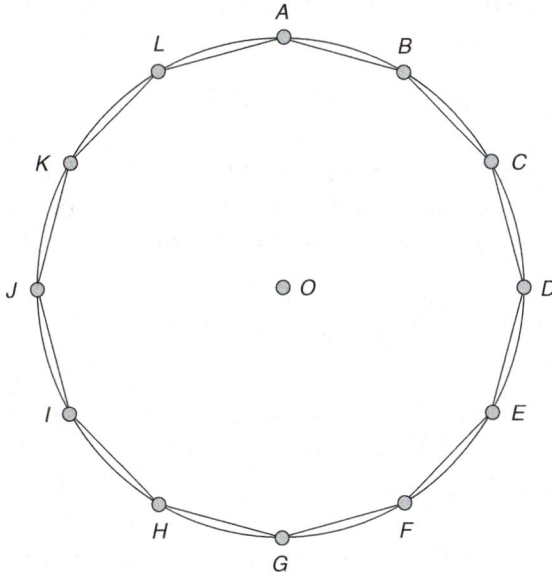

Figure 10.2

Each of the arcs contains 30°, and each angle intercepts 10 of these arcs (300°) and must therefore contain 150°. Unfortunately, this approach seems to lead nowhere.

Let's examine the problem by *organizing the data* in a slightly different manner. As we have stated, each arc contains 30°, so the points occur in diametrically opposite pairs. Now let's consider two of the distances called for in the problem, namely, $\overline{PA}$ and $\overline{PG}$ (Figure 10.3).

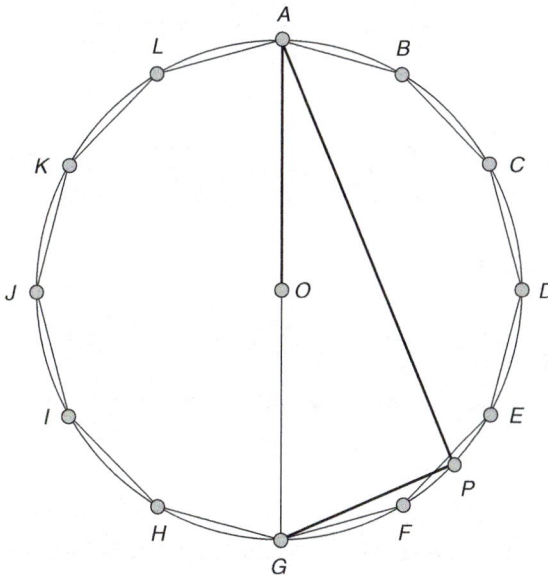

Figure 10.3

Because $\overline{AOG}$ is a diameter, triangle APG is a right triangle. Applying the Pythagorean theorem yields

$$(PA)^2 + (PG)^2 = (AG)^2 = 2^2 = 4.$$

Similarly, we conclude that $(PL)^2 + (PF)^2 = 4$, because $\triangle LPF$ is a right triangle. Organizing the data in this manner reveals six pairs of diametrically opposite points, and the sum of the squares of the distances from P is $6 \times 4 = 24$.

Problem 10.3

Find the greatest possible product of two natural numbers whose sum is 41.

Solution

Students can set up the equation $y = x(41 - x)$, where x is one of the numbers, $(41 - x)$ is the other, and y is the product. By drawing the graph, they can obtain a parabola. They can then determine the maximum point of the parabola to find the values required.

However, we can easily solve the problem by *organizing the data* in tabular form:

Numbers	Product
1 40	40
2 39	78
3 38	114
⋮ ⋮	⋮
15 26	390
16 25	400
17 24	408
18 23	414
19 22	418
20 21	420

The greatest possible product is 420.

Problem 10.4

If A apples cost D dollars, what is the cost in cents of B apples at the same rate?

Solution

There are several ways that students tackle this problem. Most often, they use numbers in place of the letters and then try to reinsert the letters to find the answer. This can easily lead to confusion and, unfortunately, to an incorrect answer. Some students have been taught to look for unit costs and proceed from there. Again, this too, may lead to confusion.

As a general rule, a problem like this can best be solved by *organizing the data* in some meaningful manner. Here, we will use proportionality together with some common sense. The proportionality is obtained by setting up the proportion with the same units of measure in each fraction:

$$\frac{A}{B} = \frac{\text{cost of } A \text{ apples}}{\text{cost of } B \text{ apples}} = \frac{100D}{x}.$$

Notice that we have used common sense to obtain the last fraction. Because the problem called for the answer in cents, we used a fraction with cents as the unit rather than dollars. Thus, when we find x, we have found the answer. The rest is simple:

$$\frac{A}{B} = \frac{100D}{x},$$

$$x = \frac{100BD}{A}.$$

Problem 10.5

Find the product of $(\tan 15°)(\tan 30°)(\tan 45°)(\tan 60°)(\tan 75°)$.

Solution

Many students will approach this problem by finding the value for each factor either with a table or with their calculators. They will then attempt to multiply the numbers to find the product. Others will simply multiply the factors as given on their calculators.

Rather than performing the multiplication as given, let's *organize the data* in a slightly different fashion. That is,

$$(\tan 15°)(\tan 75°) \times (\tan 30°)(\tan 60°) \times (\tan 45°).$$

We know that $\tan A$ and $\tan(90° - A)$ are reciprocals, so their product must equal 1. Thus,

$$(\tan 15°)(\tan 75°) = 1$$
$$(\tan 30°)(\tan 60°) = 1$$
$$(\tan 45°) = 1.$$

Therefore, the product is 1.

Problem 10.6

Find the sum of the terms in the series

$$20^2 - 19^2 + 18^2 - 17^2 + 16^2 - 15^2 + \cdots + 4^2 - 3^2 + 2^2 - 1^2.$$

Solution

The traditional method for solving this problem is to evaluate each square and then to add or subtract the appropriate terms (using a calculator, of course). Some students might even separate the series into two separate series,

$$20^2 + 18^2 + 16^2 + \cdots + 4^2 + 2^2 \quad \text{and} \quad -19^2 - 17^2 - 15^2 - \cdots - 3^2 - 1^2,$$

and then combine them.

However, using the problem-solving strategy of *organizing data*, we can view this series as

$$(20^2 - 19^2) + (18^2 - 17^2) + (16^2 - 15^2) + \cdots + (4^2 - 3^2) + (2^2 - 1^2).$$

Factoring each set of parentheses, we obtain

$$
\begin{aligned}
&(20-19)(20+19) + (18-17)(18+17) + (16-15)(16+15) + \cdots \\
&\quad + (4-3)(4+3) + (2-1)(2+1) \\
&= (1)(20+19) + (1)(18+17) + (1)(16+15) + \cdots + (1)(4+3) + (1)(2+1) \\
&= 20 + 19 + 18 + 17 + \cdots + 4 + 3 + 2 + 1 = 210,
\end{aligned}
$$

which is the required sum. This sum can be found easily by approaching the addition from *another point of view*, which is popularly attributed to Carl Friedrich Gauss in his childhood. That is to *organize the data* differently than the way it is presented by considering the sum of pairs of sums:

$$20 + 1 = 21$$
$$19 + 2 = 21$$
$$18 + 3 = 21$$
$$17 + 4 = 21$$
$$\vdots$$
$$11 + 10 = 21.$$

Then,

$$10 \times 21 = 210.$$

Problem 10.7

How many positive integers are there that are less than or equal to 1,000,000 and are perfect squares or perfect cubes?

Solution

An unsuspecting soul would list all the numbers in order, beginning with 1 and ending with 1,000,000, then circle the perfect squares and the perfect cubes, and count the results.

We can, however, use our strategy of *organizing data* to count the perfect squares as

$$1^2, 2^2, 3^2, 4^2, \ldots, 1,000^2, \text{ which is 1,000 numbers.}$$

We now must find the number of perfect cubes:

$$1^3, 2^3, 3^3, 4^3, \ldots, 100^3, \text{ which is 100 numbers.}$$

However, those numbers that are both perfect squares and perfect cubes (i.e., sixth powers) have been counted twice. They are

$$1^6, 2^6, 3^6, 4^6, \ldots, 10^6, \text{ which is 10 numbers.}$$

Therefore, the required number of numbers is $1,000 + 100 - 10 = 1,090$.

Problem 10.8

Max has between 50 and 100 pennies. When he stacks them in piles of 2, he has one penny left over. When he stacks them in piles of 3, he has one penny left over. When he stacks them in piles of 4, he has one penny left over. However, when he stacks them in piles of 5 there are no pennies left over. How many pennies does Max have?

Solution

The strategy that we will use here is clearly mapped out for us. We will *organize the data* as it was given. We shall rewrite the five pieces of data that are given:

1. When divided by 2 (or grouped by 2s), the remainder is 1.

2. When divided by 3, the remainder is 1.

3. When divided by 4, the remainder is 1.

4. When divided by 5, the remainder is 0.

5. There are between 50 and 100 coins (exclusively).

Clue 4 tells us that the number has to be a multiple of 5. Therefore, we consider all possible multiples of 5 between 50 and 100: 55, 60, 65, 70, 75, 80, 85, 90, and 95.

Clue 1 tells us that the number is an odd number (because if it were even, then there would not be a remainder of 1 when divided by 2). So we can eliminate all even numbers we considered for Clue 4 and are left with 55, 65, 75, 85, and 95.

Clue 2 gives us the following information: The number has to be one more than a multiple of 3. This leaves only two choices: 55 and 85.

Clue 3 tells us that we can eliminate 55, since 55 divided by 4 does not leave a remainder of 1.

Therefore, the only number satisfying all clues is 85. So Max has 85 pennies.

Problem 10.9

Each of the 10 court jewelers gave the king's adviser, Mr. Pogner, a stack of gold coins. Each stack contained 10 coins. The real coins weighed exactly 1 oz each. However, one and only one stack contained "light" coins, each having had exactly 0.1 oz of gold shaved off the edge. Mr. Pogner wishes to identify the crooked jeweler and the stack of light coins with just one single weighing on a scale. How can he do this?

Solution

The traditional procedure for most students is to begin by selecting one of the stacks at random and weighing it. This trial-and-error technique offers only a 1 chance in 10 of being correct. Once the students realize this, they may then attempt to solve the problem by reasoning. First of all, if all the coins were true, their total weight would be 10×10 or 100 oz. Each of the 10 counterfeit coins is lighter, so there will be a deficiency of 10×0.1 or 1 oz. However, thinking in terms of the overall deficiency doesn't lead anywhere, because the 1-oz shortage will occur regardless of which stack the counterfeit coins are in.

Let us try to solve the problem by *organizing the data* in a different fashion. We must find a method to vary the deficiency in a way that permits us to identify the stack from which the counterfeit coins are taken. Label the stacks 1, 2, 3, 4, ..., 9, 10. Now, take one coin from Stack 1, two coins from Stack 2, three coins from Stack 3, four coins from Stack 4, and so on. We now have a total of $1 + 2 + 3 + 4 + \cdots + 8 + 9 + 10 = 55$ coins. If they were all true, the total weight would be 55 oz. If the deficiency is 0.5 oz, then there were 5 light coins, taken from Stack 5. If the deficiency is 0.7 oz, then there were 7 light coins, taken from Stack 7, and so on. Thus, Mr. Pogner can readily identify the stack of light coins and, consequently, the jeweler who had shaved each coin.

Problem 10.10

A hungry hunter came across two shepherds getting ready to eat. The first shepherd had three loaves of bread and the second one had five loaves of bread, all of the same size. The hunter had no bread, but he did have 80¢ to contribute to the "pot." The loaves of bread were then divided equally among the three. How should the two shepherds divide the money?

Solution

Students usually try to solve this problem by attempting to find a set of equations. This is an extremely difficult process, and probably doomed to failure. The other traditional approach is to use a trial-and-error strategy, again, usually without much success.

To facilitate a solution, we *organize our data* into a table, considering the eight loaves of bread as a sort of "shepherd's pot."

	Shepherd 1	Shepherd 2	Hunter
Amount given to the "pot"	3 loaves	5 loaves	no loaves
Share taken from the "pot"	$\frac{8}{3}$ loaf	$\frac{8}{3}$ loaf	$\frac{8}{3}$ loaf
Amount left in the "pot" (for the hunter)	$\frac{1}{3}$ loaf	$\frac{7}{3}$ loaf	

Whereas the hunter paid 80¢ for his $\frac{8}{3}$ loaves, each loaf is worth 30¢. Because each loaf is worth 30¢ (as paid by the hunter), the first shepherd receives $\frac{1}{3}$ of 30¢ or 10¢ for his contribution, while the second shepherd receives $\frac{7}{3}$ of 30¢ or 70¢ for his contribution.

Problem 10.11

Find the numerical value of the expression

$$\left(1-\frac{1}{4}\right)\left(1-\frac{1}{9}\right)\left(1-\frac{1}{16}\right)\left(1-\frac{1}{25}\right)\cdots\left(1-\frac{1}{225}\right).$$

Solution

The usual first attempt by a student faced with this problem is to simplify the expressions in each of the 14 parentheses to get

$$\left(\frac{3}{4}\right)\left(\frac{8}{9}\right)\left(\frac{15}{16}\right)\left(\frac{24}{25}\right)\cdots\left(\frac{224}{225}\right).$$

They then try to change each fraction to a decimal (with a calculator) and multiply the results (again with their calculators). It is obviously a very cumbersome calculation.

An alternative method would be to *organize the data* in a different way. This will permit us to look at the problem from a *different point of view* (reinforcing what we have said many times before, namely, it often takes more than one single strategy to solve a problem) and hope to see some sort of *pattern* that will enable us to simplify our work:

$$\left(1^2 - \frac{1}{2^2}\right)\left(1^2 - \frac{1}{3^2}\right)\left(1^2 - \frac{1}{4^2}\right)\left(1^2 - \frac{1}{5^2}\right)\cdots\left(1^2 - \frac{1}{15^2}\right).$$

We now factor each parenthetical expression as the difference of two perfect squares, which yields

$$\left(1 - \frac{1}{2}\right)\left(1 + \frac{1}{2}\right)\left(1 - \frac{1}{3}\right)\left(1 + \frac{1}{3}\right)\left(1 - \frac{1}{4}\right)\left(1 + \frac{1}{4}\right)\left(1 - \frac{1}{5}\right)\left(1 + \frac{1}{5}\right)\cdots$$
$$\left(1 - \frac{1}{15}\right)\left(1 + \frac{1}{15}\right)$$
$$= \left(\frac{1}{2}\right)\left(\frac{3}{2}\right)\left(\frac{2}{3}\right)\left(\frac{4}{3}\right)\left(\frac{3}{4}\right)\left(\frac{5}{4}\right)\left(\frac{4}{5}\right)\left(\frac{6}{5}\right)\cdots\left(\frac{13}{14}\right)\left(\frac{15}{14}\right)\left(\frac{14}{15}\right)\left(\frac{16}{15}\right).$$

A *pattern* is now evident, and we may "cancel" throughout the expression. As a result, we are left with $\left(\frac{1}{2}\right)\left(\frac{16}{15}\right) = \left(\frac{8}{15}\right)$.

Problem 10.12

The coefficients of the quadratic equation $x^2 + bx + c = 0$ are determined by throwing a fair die twice. The first outcome is b; the second outcome is c. What is the probability that the equation will have real roots?

Solution

There are 36 possible combinations of the two throws of the die. Traditionally, students will substitute all 36 pairs of numbers for b and c, form the equations, and then solve each to see which equations have real roots. Whereas not all the roots will be integral, this process will involve repeated use of the quadratic formula, which takes an inordinate amount of time. Obviously, this will be a long and tedious process, even though, if done correctly, it should eventually yield the correct results.

Let's *organize our data* to show all the possible combinations:

1, 1	2, 1	3, 1	4, 1	5, 1	6, 1
1, 2	2, 2	3, 2	4, 2	5, 2	6, 2
1, 3	2, 3	3, 3	4, 3	5, 3	6, 3
1, 4	2, 4	3, 4	4, 4	5, 4	6, 4
1, 5	2, 5	3, 5	4, 5	5, 5	6, 5
1, 6	2, 6	3, 6	4, 6	5, 6	6, 6

Now, we can make use of the discriminant to see if any pattern exists. For the roots to be real, $b^2 - 4ac$ must be nonnegative; that is, $b^2 - 4ac \geq 0$. Obviously, all the pairs that have 1 as the coefficient of b will not yield real roots, because $1 - 4(1)(c)$ will be negative. Similarly, of the pairs beginning with 2, only 2, 1 provides us with real roots. In fact, it quickly becomes apparent that the following pattern "works":

1, 1	2, 1	3, 1	4, 1	5, 1	6, 1
1, 2	2, 2	3, 2	4, 2	5, 2	6, 2
1, 3	2, 3	3, 3	4, 3	5, 3	6, 3
1, 4	2, 4	3, 4	4, 4	5, 4	6, 4
1, 5	2, 5	3, 5	4, 5	5, 5	6, 5
1, 6	2, 6	3, 6	4, 6	5, 6	6, 6

Thus, there are 19 pairs that yield real roots out of 36 possibilities. The probability is $\frac{19}{36}$, or 52.8%.

Problem 10.13

How many triangles are in Figure 10.4?

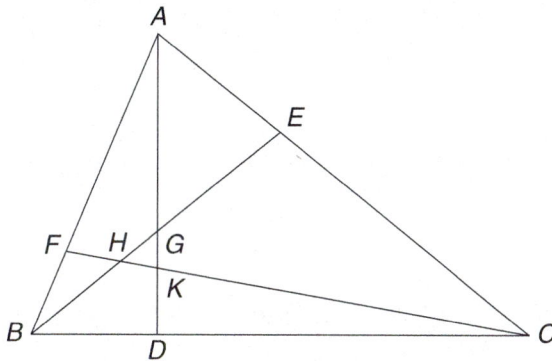

Figure 10.4

Solution

The traditional method, or that which "might be expected by the teacher," involves formal counting methods. These involve calculating the combinations that can be formed by the 6 lines and excluding those combinations that result in concurrency. Hence, the number of combinations of 6 lines taken three at a time yield $_6C_3 = 20$. From this we subtract the three concurrencies (at the vertices). Thus, there are 17 triangles in the figure.

If students attempt to count the triangles in the figure, they could very likely miss some of them in their counting. It is obvious that they need some method of organizing the information to obtain an accurate answer.

Let's try to simplify the problem by reconstructing the figure, gradually adding the lines as we go, and counting from this form of organized data. That is, counting the triangles created by the addition of each additional part of the figure.

Start with the original triangle, *ABC*. Thus, we have exactly 1 triangle.

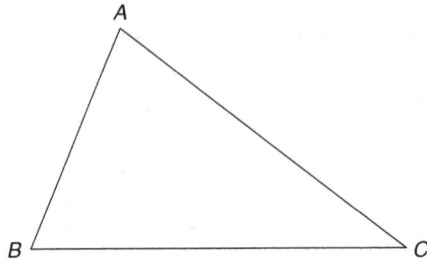

Figure 10.5

Now consider the triangle *ABC* with one interior line segment, $\overline{AD}$. We now have 2 new triangles, *ABD* and *ADC*.

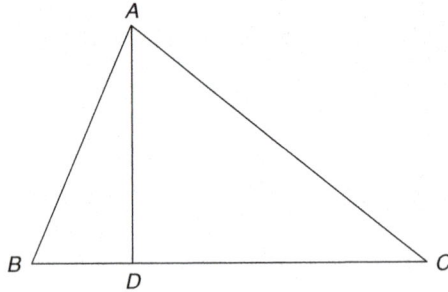

Figure 10.6

Now add the next interior line segment, $\overline{BE}$, and count all the new triangles that use $\overline{BE}$ as a side.

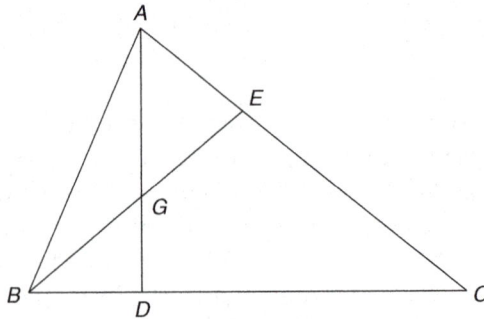

Figure 10.7

Continue in this manner, adding line segment $\overline{CF}$. Again count the new triangles that use part of $\overline{CF}$ as a side.

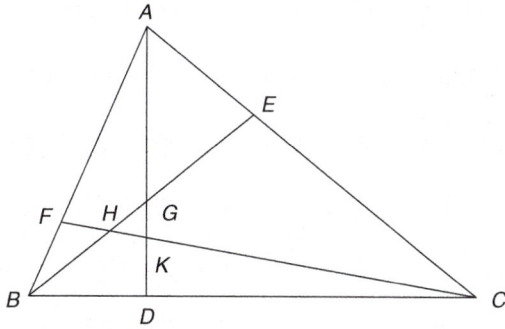

Figure 10.8

Let's put these results into a table:

	Added Line Segment	New Triangles Formed
Figure 10.5	0	1 (ABC)
Figure 10.6	$\overline{AD}$	2 (ABD, ADC)
Figure 10.7	$\overline{BGE}$	5 (ABG, BGD, AGE, BEC, ABE)
Figure 10.8	$\overline{CKHF}$	9 (FBH, AFC, BHC, AFK, KDC, AKC, FBC, HKG, EHC)
Total		17

There are 17 triangles in the figure.

Problem 10.14

Given the sequence of integers 1, 2, 2, 3, 3, 3, 4, 4, 4, 4, 5, 5, 5, 5, 5, ..., where each positive integer, n, occurs in a grouping of n consecutive terms, how many terms are needed so that the sum of the reciprocals is 500?

Solution

At first glance, the problem as posed appears to require some extensive number crunching. The traditional solution would, therefore, involve an inordinate amount of calculation. We must seek an alternate solution. Let's organize the data in a slightly different format. That is, we'll follow the wording in the original problem and write the sum of the reciprocals, but by *organizing the data* in a way that will enable us to solve the problem more easily:

$$\frac{1}{1}, \frac{1}{2}, \frac{1}{2}, \frac{1}{3}, \frac{1}{3}, \frac{1}{3}, \frac{1}{4}, \frac{1}{4}, \frac{1}{4}, \frac{1}{4}, \ldots$$

Now help your students see the pattern that has emerged by examining the fractions in "clusters":

$$\frac{1}{1} = 1 \quad \text{(one term)}$$
$$\frac{1}{2} + \frac{1}{2} = 1 \quad \text{(two terms)}$$
$$\frac{1}{3} + \frac{1}{3} + \frac{1}{3} = 1 \quad \text{(three terms)}$$
$$\frac{1}{4} + \frac{1}{4} + \frac{1}{4} + \frac{1}{4} = 1 \quad \text{(four terms)},$$

and so on.

Thus, for every grouping of n consecutive terms in the original series, the sum of the reciprocals equals 1. Now the problem is easily resolved. We are really looking for the sum of the first 500 integers from 1 through 500. That is, $250(501) = 125{,}250$. The problem was easily solved once we organized the data in a more meaningful manner.

Problem 10.15

Evaluate the expression

$$(211 \times 555) + (445 \times 789) + (555 \times 789) + (211 \times 445).$$

Solution

The traditional method is to follow the indicated arithmetic instructions and evaluate the expression. With the help of a calculator the problem becomes considerably easier. However, there are times when even an arithmetic problem can be shortened if we can *organize the data* to our advantage. We notice that several numbers appear more than once. Let's use this to make our work simpler.

We factor as follows:

$$555(211 + 789) + 445(211 + 789)$$
$$= 555(1{,}000) + 445(1{,}000)$$
$$= (555 + 445)(1{,}000)$$
$$= (1{,}000)(1{,}000), \quad \text{which equals } 1{,}000{,}000.$$

Problem 10.16

Four married couples belong to a theater club. The wives' names are Alice, Barbara, Christa, and Edith. The husbands' names are Al, Frank, Fred, and Ernest. Who is married to whom? Use the following clues to determine the couples.

1. Al is Edith's brother.
2. Edith and Fred were once engaged, but "broke up" when Edith met her present husband.
3. Christa has a sister, but her husband is an only child.
4. Alice is married to Ernest.

Solution

Students will usually begin by making guesses at who the couples are and then seeing if their guesses fit the clues. However, this will yield an answer only if the students guess right, usually after several incorrect trials.

We can *organize the data* in a table and then mark off the clues one at a time to see what is happening. Have students prepare a table similar to the following:

	Alice	Christa	Barbara	Edith
Al				
Frank				
Fred				
Ernest	YES	×	×	×

The fourth clue tells us that Alice and Ernest are married. We put a "YES" in that cell, and an × in all the other cells in that row and column:

	Alice	Christa	Barbara	Edith
Al	×			
Frank	×			
Fred	×			
Ernest	YES	×	×	×

The first clue tells us that Al could not be married to Edith:

	Alice	Christa	Barbara	Edith
Al	×			×
Frank	×			
Fred	×			
Ernest	YES	×	×	×

We continue in a like manner, using one clue at a time. The final result:

	Alice	Christa	Barbara	Edith
Al	×	×	YES	×
Frank	×	×	×	YES
Fred	×	YES	×	×
Ernest	YES	×	×	×

Thus, Al is married to Barbara, Frank is married to Edith, Fred is married to Christa, and Ernest is married to Alice.

Problem 10.17

Find the value of the expression

$$20 - 19 + 18 - 17 + 16 - 15 + 14 - 13 + 12 - 11.$$

Solution

An obvious way to solve this problem is to punch the numbers into your calculator. Assuming that you punch in all the numbers correctly, you should arrive at the correct answer, 5.

However, we can solve this problem rather quickly by *organizing the data* in the following way. We can group the numbers in pairs as follows:

$$(20 - 19) + (18 - 17) + (16 - 15) + (14 - 13) + (12 - 11)$$
$$= 1 + 1 + 1 + 1 + 1$$
$$= 5.$$

Problem 10.18

You are given a number composed of the numbers from 1 through 1,998 written next to one another:

123456789101112131415161718...1995199619971998.

From this very large number, we delete all the zeros, yielding a new number. What is the sum of digits of this resulting number?

Solution

Typically, a student faced with this problem would set out to find the sum of these digits—a daunting task, at best. It is clear that we will need a clever problem-solving strategy to accomplish this task with a minimum amount of effort. The key is to *organize the data* in a more manageable fashion. We begin by taking the sum of the first 9 digits as follows:

$$1 + \cdots + 9 = 45 = S_1.$$

The sum of the digits for the numbers 10 to 99 is dealt with by organizing the sum of the 10s digits numerals and the sum of the units digits numerals as follows:

The digit sum, S_1, of the numbers from 1 to $9 = 45$.

The digit sum of the numbers from 10 to $99 =$
$10 \times (1 + \cdots + 9) + 9 \times S_1 = 10 \times 45 + 9 \times 45 = 855.$

The total digit sum, S_2, of the numbers from 1 to 99 is the sum of the previous two sums: $S_2 = 45 + 855 = 900.$

Similarly, the digit sum, S_3, of the numbers from 100 to 999 is found by taking the sum of the hundredths digit numerals (which is 100 times each of the numerals 1 through 9), plus 9 times the sum from 1 to 99:

$$S_3 = 100 \times S_1 + 9 \times S_2 = 100 \times 45 + 9 \times 900 = 12{,}600.$$

To get the digit sum, S_4, of the numbers from 1 to 999, we add the sum S_3 to the sum S_2, which is

$$S_3 + S_2 = 12{,}600 + 900 = 13{,}500 = S_4.$$

We now consider the digit sum, S_5, of the numbers 1,000 through 1,999. The thousands digit is used 1,000 times for a sum of $1 \times 1{,}000 = 1{,}000$. Therefore, the digit sum, S_5, of the numbers from 1,000 to 1,999 is

$$S_5 = 1{,}000 + S_4 = 1{,}000 + 13{,}500 = 14{,}500.$$

The digit sum, S_6, of the numbers from 1 to 1,999 is

$$S_6 = S_5 + S_4 = 14{,}500 + 13{,}500 = 28{,}000.$$

Therefore, the digit sum of the numbers from 1 to 1,998 is

$$S_6 - (1 + 9 + 9 + 9) = 28{,}000 - 28 = 27{,}972.$$

Problem 10.19

The basement of an apartment building has six tanks of oil. A measuring gauge for the oil stored in the basement is set up to measure five tanks at a time. Following are the results of these measurements:

Without tank A there were 2,000 liters of oil.

Without tank B there were 2,200 liters of oil.

Without tank C there were 2,400 liters of oil.

Without tank D there were 2,600 liters of oil.

Without tank E there were 2,800 liters of oil.

Without tank F there were 3,000 liters of oil.

How much oil is there in each tank?

Solution

This problem can be solved algebraically by setting up six equations and solving them simultaneously:

$$B + C + D + E + F = 2,000$$
$$A + C + D + E + F = 2,200$$
$$A + B + D + E + F = 2,400$$
$$A + B + C + E + F = 2,600$$
$$A + B + C + D + F = 2,800$$
$$A + B + C + D + E = 3,000.$$

The task would be a bit more cumbersome than the typical high school student is accustomed to. We can use our strategy of *organizing data* in a way that will make the solution relatively simple.

Consider the following chart, where we organize the data from the problem:

Measurements	Tank A	Tank B	Tank C	Tank D	Tank E	Tank F	Total
1		×	×	×	×	×	2,000
2	×		×	×	×	×	2,200
3	×	×		×	×	×	2,400
4	×	×	×		×	×	2,600
5	×	×	×	×		×	2,800
6	×	×	×	×	×		3,000

From the table, we can easily see that the vertical sums, that is, $5A + 5B + 5C + 5D + 5E + 5F = 15,000$.[1] Therefore, by taking one fifth of both sides of this equation, we get $A + B + C + D + E + F = 3,000$. Multiplying both sides by 4, we get $4A + 4B + 4C + 4D + 4E + 4F = 12,000$. However, measurement 6 gave us $A + B + C + D + E = 3,000$, which when multiplied by 4 gives $4A + 4B + 4C + 4D + 4E = 12,000$. This implies that tank $F = 0$.

Similarly, for measurement 5: $A + B + C + D + F = 2,800$, but since $F = 0$, it follows that $A + B + C + D = 2,800$, yet we have from the table that $A + B + C + D + E + 0 = 3,000$. Therefore, E must be 200. Following this same line of reasoning we get $D = 400$, $C = 600$, $B = 800$, and $A = 1,000$. The preceding chart enabled us to organize the data in a manageable form so that we could then logically solve the problem.

Note: We did use our logical reasoning strategy here as well.

Problem 10.20

Which of the following, (a) or (b), has the larger total?

(a)	(b)
987654321	1
87654321	12
7654321	123
654321	1234
54321	12345
4321	123456
321	1234567
21	12345678
1	123456789

Solution

Students can actually perform the addition and determine which is the larger sum. However, the unusual array in (b) makes this difficult to do by hand. Calculators, too, are quite difficult to use because of the odd arrangements of the digits. In addition, there are 9 digits in some of the addends, and most calculators will not accept more than 8 digits.

Let's examine these arrays using our *organizing data* strategy. Compare the digits column by column. In the units column, for example, the 9 in (b) is matched by nine 1s in (a). In the 10s column, (a) has eight 2s, while (b) has two 8s. Similarly for the digits in the other places. The two sums are the same.

---

1. The $5A$ term represents 5 times the quantity in tank A.

11

Logical Reasoning

When dealing with friends and colleagues, we find that what we say will often evoke a certain response. That response can then lead to another, and so on. When we try to predict a conversation scenario or a potential discussion/argument, we are, in effect, using logical reasoning. That is, if you say *A*, then it is expected that the response will be *B*. This then will lead to statement *C*, which will likely be responded to with statement *D*. This sort of logical reasoning, done effectively, can help immensely with interpersonal relationships and can help solve (or perhaps avoid) problems before they arise. We do this often without being aware of the actual process. However, in mathematics, we more formally make our students aware of this thinking process. We try to guide them or train them to think logically. Whereas it can be argued that inductive thinking (i.e., going from several specific examples to a generalization) is more natural, the logical form of reasoning requires some practice.

THE *LOGICAL REASONING* STRATEGY IN EVERYDAY LIFE PROBLEM-SOLVING SITUATIONS

In everyday life situations, we typically rely on logical reasoning to plan a strategy for a work plan, or we may use it to argue a point with a colleague or boss. The strength of an argument is often dependent on the validity of the logical reasoning used. This can often mean the difference between success and failure in court proceedings. It can affect success or advancement on the job. Status is gained when you convince your boss that you have a more efficient way to conduct a process than was previously the case. The success or failure of a business deal can depend on your facility with *logical reasoning*.

Even in the most elementary situations, we make use of this strategy. For example, if you arrange to meet someone the day after tomorrow, you rely on the fixed order of the days to deduce that; because today is Thursday, the day after tomorrow must be Saturday.

APPLYING THE *LOGICAL REASONING* STRATEGY TO SOLVE MATHEMATICS PROBLEMS

Logical reasoning in a mathematical setting can be as simple as having to figure out the least number of bottles needed to carry home 10 qt of water, when there are 1-qt, 2-qt, and 1-gal bottles available. To minimize the number of bottles, we would reason that we need to maximize the size of the bottles. Therefore, two 1-gal bottles and one 2-qt bottle would be the correct answer. This sort of logical reasoning can be applied to many mathematical situations.

PROBLEMS USING THE *LOGICAL REASONING* STRATEGY

Problem 11.1

A domino can cover exactly 2 adjacent squares on a standard checkerboard. Thus, 32 dominoes will exactly cover the 64 squares on the checkerboard shown in Figure 11.1. Suppose we now remove one square from each of the two diagonally opposite corners of the checkerboard (Figure 11.2) and remove one domino as well. Can you now cover this "notched" checkerboard with the 31 remaining dominoes? Why or why not?

Solution

One way to solve this problem is to obtain a checkerboard, remove the corner squares as shown, then take 31 dominoes and do it! However, this can be rather messy and time-consuming, since there are many ways we can place the dominoes on the board.

Instead, let's apply our strategy of *logical reasoning* to solve the problem. Notice that 1 domino covers exactly 2 squares either horizontally or vertically, one of which is black and the other white. On the 64-square checkerboard, there were 32 white and 32 black squares in an alternating pattern to be covered. This was easily done. In the notched checkerboard, however, we have removed 2 squares of the same color, black. This leaves us with 30 black squares and 32 white squares. Since a domino must always cover one of each color, it is impossible to completely cover the notched checkerboard with the 31 dominoes.

Figure 11.1

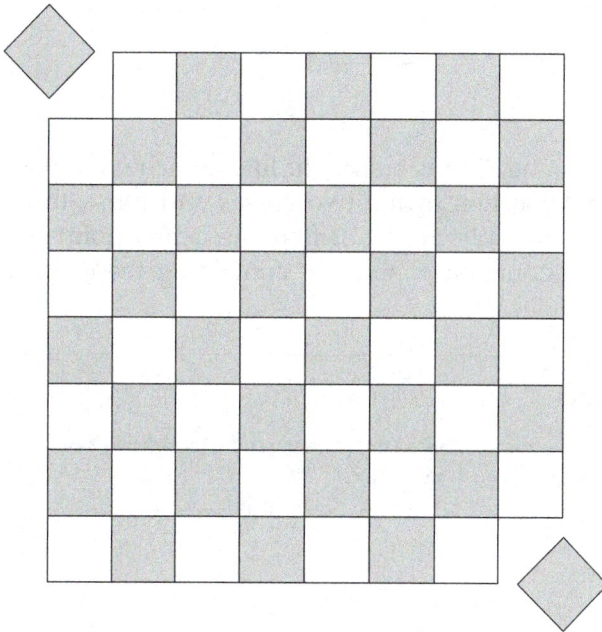

Figure 11.2

Problem 11.2

Find the equation of the line that contains the common chord of the two circles given by the equations

$$(x-5)^2 + (y+2)^2 = 15$$
$$(x-4)^2 + (y+1)^2 = 9.$$

Solution

We could plot the graphs of these two circles on the same set of axes, find the coordinates of their points of intersection, and then, once we have the coordinates of two points, use the $y = mx + b$ form to write the equation of the common chord that joins these two points.

However, let's use *logical reasoning*. Solving a pair of equations simultaneously means finding the points common to the graphs of both equations. So, if we add or subtract these two equations, the graph of the resulting equation must contain all points common to the original two equations.

Simplifying the original equations, we obtain

$$x^2 + y^2 - 10x + 4y + 14 = 0$$
$$x^2 + y^2 - 8x + 2y + 8 = 0.$$

Subtracting yields

$$-2x + 2y + 6 = 0$$
$$y = x - 3.$$

The graph of this equation is a straight line, which must pass through the two points of intersection of the two circles and must, therefore, contain their common chord. We need not find the actual points of intersection, because only the equation of the line containing these points was called for in the problem.

Problem 11.3

How many palindromic numbers (those that read the same in both directions, such as 131) are there between 1 and 1,000?

Solution

We begin to solve the problem by *organizing the data* of the problem. There are 9 single-digit palindromic numbers. There are 9 two-digit numbers that are palindromes (11, 22, 33, ...). To create three-digit palindromes, we will use some *logical reasoning*. We can have 9 possible "outside" digits and 10 possible "middle" digits. This gives us 90 three-digit palindromes. Thus, there are $9+9+90=108$ palindromic numbers between 1 and 1,000.

By using our strategy of *organizing data* together with *logical reasoning*, we could have solved the problem by noting the number of palindromes in each of the following intervals:

Interval	Number of Palindromes
1–9	9
10–99	9
100–199	10
200–299	10
300–399	10
400–499	10
500–599	10
600–699	10
700–799	10
800–899	10
900–999	10

for a total of 108 palindromes.

See Problem 3.19 for an additional solution to this problem.

Problem 11.4

Brünnhilde has $20 in quarters. She also has five times as many nickels as quarters. How much money does Brünnhilde have in nickels?

Solution

The typical solution involves determining how many quarters are required to have $20. That is, with 4 quarters to the dollar, Brünnhilde has $20 \times 4 = 80$ quarters. Then, if she has five times as many nickels, she will have $5 \times 80 = 400$ nickels. At 5¢ each, this is $5 \times 400 = 2,000$¢, or $20 in nickels.

Using *logical reasoning*, we need only to reason that each quarter equals five nickels. Because Brünnhilde has "five times as many nickels as quarters," she must have the same amount of money in nickels as she does in quarters, or $20 in nickels.

Problem 11.5

The month of February had five Sundays in 2004. In which other years during the 21st century will the month of February again have five Sundays?

Solution

February can only have five Sundays if February 1st falls on a Sunday *and* the year is a leap year. We use the strategy of *logical reasoning* to determine that both of these conditions are met every 28 years because there are 7 different days in the week and every 4 years we have a leap year. The least common multiple of 7 and 4 is 28. Therefore, $2004 + 28 = 2032$ will be the next year with five Sundays in February.

It follows that $2032 + 28 = 2060$ will also be such a year, as well as $2060 + 28 = 2088$.

Problem 11.6

Find all real values for x that satisfy the equation

$$4 - \frac{3}{x} = \sqrt{4 - \frac{3}{x}}.$$

Solution

The traditional method begins by squaring both sides,

$$16 - \frac{24}{x} + \frac{9}{x^2} = 4 - \frac{3}{x},$$

which yields

$$12x^2 - 21x + 9 = 0$$
$$3(4x - 3)(x - 1) = 0$$
$$x = \frac{3}{4} \text{ or } x = 1.$$

This is a solution that requires careful algebraic manipulation to avoid error.

However, we can solve this problem in a much easier manner by using our *logical reasoning* strategy. In the real number system, there are only two numbers whose value equals the value of their square root. These are 0 and 1. Therefore,

$$4 - \frac{3}{x} = 1 \text{ or } 4 - \frac{3}{x} = 0$$

$$x = 1, x = \frac{3}{4}.$$

A check of these answers by substitution into the original equations is necessary.

Problem 11.7

Solve the following equation for x and y, where x and y are real:

$$(x - y^2)^2 + (x - y - 2)^2 = 0.$$

Solution

The typical student approach would be to square both terms:

$$x^2 - 2xy^2 + y^4 + x^2 - 2xy - 4x + y^2 + 4y + 4 = 0.$$

If we collect like terms, we obtain

$$2x^2 - 2xy^2 - 2xy - 4x + y^4 + y^2 + 4y + 4 = 0.$$

At this point, most students simply give up! After all, they really have not spent much time working with problems involving a single equation with two variables.

However, let's use *logical reasoning* along with our knowledge of our number system. An equation of the form $a^2 + b^2 = 0$ (where a and b are real numbers) is true if and only if $a = 0$ and $b = 0$. Thus,

$$x - y^2 = 0 \text{ and } x - y - 2 = 0$$
$$x = y^2 \text{ and } x = y + 2.$$

Substituting for x, we obtain

$$y^2 = y + 2$$
$$(y + 2) - y^2 = 0$$
$$y^2 - y - 2 = 0$$
$$(y - 2)(y + 1) = 0$$
$$y = 2, \quad y = -1$$
$$x = 4, \quad x = 1.$$

A check of these answers by substitution into the original equations is necessary.

Problem 11.8

Ruth, Stan, Ted, Una, Vicky, and Walt are going to dinner to celebrate Vicky's and Walt's graduation from high school. Each person's meal costs the same amount. Vicky and Walt are being treated for their own meal, but each must chip in equally for his or her share of the others' meal. How much should each person pay if the total bill was $108.00?

Solution

The typical student solution is algebraic:

$$\$108 \div 6 = \text{a cost of } \$18.00 \text{ per meal.}$$

Let $2x$ represent the amount each person pays for Vicky and Walt. Then,

Ruth pays $\$18 + 2x$

Stan pays $\$18 + 2x$

Ted pays $\$18 + 2x$

Una pays $\$18 + 2x$

Vicky pays x

Walt pays x

$$72 + 10x = 108$$
$$10x = 36$$
$$x = 3.6.$$

Vicky and Walt each paid \$3.60; everyone else paid $\$18 + \$7.20 = \$25.20$.

Let's try to solve this problem using our problem strategy of *logical reasoning*. We know that Vicky paid $\frac{1}{5}$ of Walt's meal, or $\frac{1}{5}$ of $\$18 = \$3.60$. At the same time, Walt paid $\frac{1}{5}$ of Vicky's meal or \$3.60, for a total of \$7.20. If we subtract the \$7.20 from the total bill of \$108, we have \$100.80 left for the remaining four people to share. Dividing \$100.80 by 4 we obtain \$25.20 per person, the amount paid by Ruth, Stan, Ted, and Una. Vicky and Walt each paid \$3.60.

Problem 11.9

When a certain integer is divided by 15, the remainder is 7. Find the sum of the remainders if we divide the same integer by 3 and then by 5.

Solution

Traditionally, students attack a problem of this type with an algebraic approach. That is, if a number is divisible by 15 with a remainder of 7, it must be of the form $15k + 7$. At this point, students usually disregard the algebraic approach and examine several numbers that leave a remainder of 7 when divided by 15. These might include 22, 37, 52, and so forth. Of course, this may lead to an answer, but it will not determine if the answer they obtain is true for *all* numbers of that form.

We can solve the problem by using our strategy of *logical reasoning*. Let's begin at the point where we have expressed the number in its general form, $15k+7$. Now, when we divide this number by 5, we divide $15k$ by 5 and 7 by 5. Dividing $15k$ by 5 leaves no remainder; dividing 7 by 5 leaves a remainder of 2. Now we divide $15k+7$ by 3. Dividing $15k$ by 3 leaves no remainder; dividing 7 by 3 leaves a remainder of 1. Thus, the sum of the remainders is $2+1$ or 3, and the problem is solved.

More formally, this would be done by beginning with $x \equiv 7 \bmod 15$, which implies $x = 15t+7$. Then, $15t+7 \equiv \alpha \bmod 3$, which implies that $\alpha = 1$, and $15t+7 \equiv \beta \bmod 5$, which implies that $\beta = 2$. Again $2+1=3$.

Problem 11.10

Mrs. Shuttleworth sold 51 jars of her homemade jam in exactly 3 days. Each day she sold 2 more jars than she sold on the previous day. How many jars did she sell on each day?

Solution

Most students can approach the problem from an algebraic point of view:

x denotes the number of jars sold on the first day.

$x+2$ denotes the number of jars sold on the second day.

$x+4$ denotes the number of jars sold on the third day.

$$x + (x+2) + (x+4) = 51$$
$$3x + 6 = 51$$
$$3x = 45$$
$$x = 15.$$

She sold 15 jars on the first day, 17 jars on the second day, and 19 jars on the third day.

Now, let's look at this problem from the point of view of *logical reasoning*. She sold 51 jars on 3 days, an average of 17 jars per day. Because the difference between the number sold on each day is a constant, the 17 represents the number sold on the "middle" day. Thus, on the day previous, she sold $17-2$ or 15 jars, and on the day following, she sold $17+2$ or 19 jars.

Problem 11.11

A Girl Scout troop baked a batch of cookies to sell at the annual bake sale. They made between 100 and 150 cookies. One fourth of the cookies were lemon crunch, and one fifth of the cookies were chocolate macadamia nut. What is the largest number of cookies the troop could have baked?

Solution

Most students will approach the problem algebraically as follows:

x represent the total number of cookies.

$\frac{x}{4}$ represents the number of lemon crunch cookies.

$\frac{x}{5}$ represents the number of chocolate macadamia nut cookies.

$x - \frac{x}{4} - \frac{x}{5}$ represents the remainder of the cookies baked.

Then,

$$100 < \frac{x}{4} + \frac{x}{5} + \left[x - \frac{x}{4} - \frac{x}{5}\right] < 150$$
$$2{,}000 < 5x + 4x + 20x - 5x - 4x < 3{,}000$$
$$2{,}000 < 20x < 3{,}000$$
$$100 < x < 150,$$

which we already knew. As a result, this approach appears to lead nowhere.

Let's attack this problem with *logical reasoning*. Because the number of cookies must be exactly divisible by 4 and by 5, it must be divisible by 20. Furthermore, because the number lies between 100 and 150, it must be either 120 or 140. Thus, the maximum number of cookies they could have baked is 140, and the problem is solved.

Problem 11.12

A standard deck of 52 playing cards is randomly split into 2 piles with 26 cards in each. How does the number of red cards in one pile compare with the number of black cards in the other pile?

Solution

We can represent the situation symbolically as follows:

B_1 represents the number of black cards in Pile 1.

B_2 represents the number of black cards in Pile 2.

R_1 represents the number of red cards in Pile 1.

R_2 represents the number of red cards in Pile 2.

Then, because the total number of black cards equals 26,

$$B_1 + B_2 = 26.$$

Whereas the total number of cards in Pile 2 equals 26,

$$R_2 + B_2 = 26.$$

By subtraction, $B_1 - R_2 = 0$ and $B_1 = R_2$. Thus, the number of red cards in one pile equals the number of black cards in the other pile.

Although this solution leads to the correct answer, let's try to solve this problem using our *logical reasoning* strategy. Take all the red cards in Pile 1 and switch them with the black cards in Pile 2. Now, all the black cards will be in one pile and all the red cards in Pile 2. Therefore, the number of red cards in one pile and the number of black cards in the other pile had to be equal to begin with.

Problem 11.13

If $\dfrac{1}{x+5} = 4$, what is the value of $\dfrac{1}{x+6}$?

Solution

Traditionally, the student faced with this problem will seek to find the value of x by solving the original equation. If we solve this equation for x, we obtain $x = -\frac{19}{4}$. Then, we substitute for x in the fraction expression $\frac{1}{x+6}$ and obtain $\frac{4}{5}$. Of course, this will involve some rather cumbersome algebraic and arithmetic manipulations.

Using our *logical reasoning* strategy, we can approach the problem differently. If $\frac{1}{x+5} = 4$, we can take the reciprocals of both sides and obtain $x + 5 = \frac{1}{4}$. We now add 1 to both sides, giving us $x + 6 = \frac{5}{4}$. We again take the reciprocals of both sides and obtain

$$\frac{1}{x+6} = \frac{4}{5}.$$

Problem 11.14

In a 10-team sports league, each team plays each of the other teams 10 times. When the season ends, there are no ties in the standings, and each team is the same number of games ahead of the team immediately following in the standings. What is the maximum number of games the last-place team could have won?

Solution

Students should begin by determining the total number of games played by the 10 teams during the season. There will be $10(9 + 8 + 7 + 6 + 5 + 4 + 3 + 2 + 1)$ or 450 games played altogether. This can also be found by taking $_{10}C_2$ or 45 (the number of games each team plays when they play every other team once), and then multiplying by 10.

Students can now approach the problem algebraically as follows:

Let n denote the number of games won by the last-place team.

Let d denote the consecutive difference between games won by each team.

Hence,

$$n + (n + d) + (n + 2d) + (n + 3d) + \cdots + (n + 8d) + (n + 9d) = 450$$
$$10n + 45d = 450$$
$$2n + 9d = 90.$$

For n to be a maximum, d must be a minimum. We know that $d \neq 0$, because there were no ties in the standings. The minimum value for d would be 2:

$$2n + 18 = 90$$
$$2n = 72$$
$$n = 36.$$

The maximum number of games the last-place team could have won would be 36.

We can also solve the problem using the *logical reasoning* strategy. We know there were 450 games played in all. With 10 teams in the league, the "middle" teams (i.e., numbers 5 and 6) must win $\frac{1}{5}$ of them, or 90 games between them. Furthermore, they must play as close to .500 as possible. Thus, the 5th place team won 46 games; the 6th place team won 44. With a common difference of 2, the 10 teams must have won, respectively, 54, 52, 50, 48, 46, 44, 42, 40, 38, and 36 games. The last-place team won a maximum of 36 games.

Problem 11.15

If a and b are both integers, how many ordered pairs (a, b) will satisfy the equation $a^2 + b^2 = 10$?

Solution

Students may attempt to draw an accurate graph of a circle, center at the origin and radius $\sqrt{10}$. They will then examine their graph to see where it crosses the grid lines at lattice points. Of course, this requires a carefully drawn diagram, large enough to read the coordinates of the points accurately.

Let's see if we can use our *logical reasoning* strategy instead. Because we are working with integers for a and b, we must look for solutions in which

a^2 and b^2 are whole numbers. Any number with an absolute value greater than 3 would give a square greater than 10. We need only examine those perfect squares less than or equal to 10, meaning we must examine only $a = 1$, 2, or 3. If $a = 1$ $(a^2 = 1)$ and $b = 3$ $(b^2 = 9)$, we have a set that satisfies the equation. The only values that will satisfy the equation are $a = 1$ and $b = 3$ or their symmetric opposites, $a = 3$ and $b = 1$. However, because we are dealing with squares, we may also consider both positive and negative answers. There are eight pairs of answers that will satisfy the equation. We prepare an *organized list* to be certain that we have *accounted for all the possibilities*:

$$(+1, +3), (+1, -3), (-1, +3), (-1, -3), (+3, +1),$$
$$(+3, -1), (-3, +1), \text{ and } (-3, -1).$$

Problem 11.16

The four points A(3, 3), B(5, 7), C(8, 7), and D(12, 3) are the vertices of a trapezoid. The points A′, B′, C′, and D′ are found by multiplying the abscissas of A, B, C, and D, respectively, by -1. Find the difference in the number of square units in the areas of trapezoid ABCD and trapezoid A′B′C′D′.

Solution

Obviously, the problem can be resolved by students finding the areas of each of the trapezoids and then finding their difference. This takes time.

It is easier to solve this problem by examining it using *logical reasoning*. Examine the operator $x \rightarrow x'$. Whereas this results in a reflection in the y axis of the original figure, it effects no change in area. Notice that all the multiplication by -1 does is shift the coordinates to the opposite side of the y axis. It does nothing to the size or shape of the original figure. Thus, the difference in the areas is 0.

Problem 11.17

One of the following numbers is exactly equal to 13!. Which is it?

a. 6,227,020,800

b. 6,227,028,000

c. 6,227,280,000.

Solution

Traditionally, students will try to resolve this problem by turning to their calculators and entering the factors of 13!. The factors are

13, 12, 11, 10, ... , 3, 2, 1. This is a time-consuming process. Certainly if the calculator has a "!" (factorial) key, then the problem becomes trivial. However, the problem-solving strategy we use here is still instructive and useful.

We will use the *logical reasoning* strategy. Let's examine the factors of $13! = 13, 12, 11, 10 \cdots 5, 4, 3, 2, 1$. Because the only factors that can produce products of 10 are the 10, 5, and 2, the 13! will end with two zeros. Therefore, the only possibly correct choice above is (a).

Problem 11.18

The four digit number *x*56*y*, where *x* and *y* are the first and last digits, respectively, is divisible by 9. What is the value of $x + y$?

Solution

Typically, a student simply will try various values for x and y to see which enable divisibility by 9. Although this is a form of guessing and testing, it is not sufficient. It must be combined with *logical reasoning* from the given information.

Recall that for a number to be divisible by 9, the sum of the digits of the number must be a multiple of 9. Therefore, $x + 5 + 6 + y = 9M$, or $x + y + 11 = 9M$. The largest $x + y$ can be is $9 + 9 = 18$, but $18 + 11 = 29$, and 29 is not a multiple of 9. Can we obtain 27? Then $x + y$ would have to be 16. The next smaller multiple of 9 counting back from 27 would be 18. Then $x + y = 7$. A lower multiple of 9 would be too small to work. There are no others. Thus, $x + y = 16$, or 7.

Problem 11.19

Find all pairs of prime numbers whose sum equals 999.

Solution

Many students will begin by taking a list of prime numbers and trying various pairs to see if they obtain 999 for a sum. This is obviously very tedious as well as time-consuming, and students would never be quite certain that they had considered all the prime number pairs.

Let's use our *logical reasoning* strategy to solve this problem. To obtain an odd sum for two numbers (prime or otherwise), exactly one of the numbers must be even. Because there is only one even prime, namely, 2, there can be only one pair of primes whose sum is 999, and that pair is 2 and 997.

Problem 11.20

Henry is driving to the local shopping mall, a distance of 2 miles. He drives the first mile at exactly 30 mph and then realizes that he will be late for his appointment and decides to drive faster. At what speed must he drive the second mile to average 60 mph for the 2 miles?

Solution

Students will probably begin by setting up a table to organize their data using the rate $\times$ time $=$ distance relationship:

Rate	Time	Distance
30	$\dfrac{1}{30}$	1
x	$\dfrac{1}{x}$	1

$$\frac{\text{total distance}}{\text{total time}} = \text{average rate}$$

$$\frac{2}{\dfrac{1}{30} + \dfrac{1}{x}} = 60$$

$$2 = 2 + \frac{60}{x}$$

$$\frac{60}{x} = 0,$$

which is impossible.

Let's use our *logical reasoning* strategy. For a 2-mile trip to be completed at an average speed of 60 mph, it must take 2 min. At 30 mph, Henry has already taken 2 min to drive the first mile. It would be impossible to average 60 mph for the entire 2 miles.

Problem 11.21

Rudy offers to bet Christie that the product of the number of runs scored by the New York Mets in each game of the 1998 baseball season is less than the sum of the runs. Should Christie take the bet?

Solution

Students may wish to obtain a record book and examine the actual number of runs scored by the New York Mets in the 1998 season. Using a calculator, they can then actually find the product and sum of the numbers of runs scored by the team. Obviously, this will be very time-consuming and quite possibly inaccurate. Others may reason that the product of the numbers is most likely to be greater than the sum.

However, if we apply our *logical reasoning* strategy, we can reason as follows. It is highly probable that the New York Mets were shut out at least once during their 162-game season. Therefore, the product of the number of runs scored would be 0. Thus, Christie should not take the bet.

Problem 11.22

A wooden cube is 3 in. on each edge. Mr. Twain wishes to cut it into smaller cubes, each 1 in. on an edge. After each cut, he may stack the pieces of wood any way he wishes prior to making the next cut. What is the smallest number of cuts he must make?

Solution

Many students will attempt to draw a diagram to solve the problem. Others may actually obtain a wooden (or paper) cube and go through the problem, attempting to find a smaller number of cuts.

However, let's make use of our *logical reasoning* strategy. No matter how the pieces are stacked, it will still take a total of 6 cuts to create the cube in the center. Thus, the minimum number of cuts required will be 6.

Problem 11.23

Max has fewer than 100 comic books in his collection. He decided to donate one half of his collection to the children's hospital. He then puts 10 aside for himself. He then divides the rest equally among 4 friends. How many comic books could he have in his original collection?

Solution

It is reasonable to begin by letting x represent the number of comic books Max has in his original collection. Following the events of the statement of the problem, he gives half after his donation $(\frac{x}{2})$ to the hospital and then keeps 10 for himself before dividing the remainder $(\frac{x}{2} - 10)$ equally among his friends, who then get

$$\frac{(\frac{x}{2} - 10)}{4} = \frac{x - 20}{8}.$$

Using logical reasoning, we find that this fraction must be a positive integer. To make this the smallest positive integer, we have $x = 28$. The next greater value of x would have to be 36. For each successive value of x that would allow the fraction to be a positive integer, we would increase x by 8 until we reach 92, our highest acceptable value, since the problem told us that there were fewer than 100 comic books.

So the acceptable values of x are 28, 36, 44, 52, 60, 68, 76, 84, and 92.

Let's use our *logical reasoning* strategy and *work backwards*. The minimum number of comic books Max could give to each friend is 1. Having four friends means he gave away 4 comic books. Max kept 10, giving a total of 14 books. But this is one-half of his collection, so the smallest number he could have under these circumstances would be 28. Similarly, if we assume that Max gave each friend 2 comics, $4 \cdot 2 = 8$, then $8 + 10 = 18$, and $2 \cdot 18 = 36$. If we continue in this manner, we get the sequence: 28, 36, 44, 52, 60, 68, 76, 84, 92, as before.

Afterword

As I was reading the proof pages of this book, I was reminded of my high school days when, as members of the mathematics club, a number of us students were challenged every week to solve difficult problems presented by our faculty advisor. I am surprised now to note that, however unconsciously, we students were led, many years ago, to adopt many of the same strategies described in this book.

As I continued thinking about those "good old days," one problem in particular kept bubbling up from the depths of my subconscious: What is the probability, call it P, that two numbers (positive integers) chosen at random will be relatively prime, that is, will have no common divisor greater than unity? As I struggled to recover my ancient solution to this problem, I decided finally to analyze the problem in accordance with the principles described in this book. First, to be relatively prime it is necessary and sufficient that the two numbers, call them M and N, not have the common factor p, where p is any prime number whatsoever. To find this probability, let us solve a simpler analogous problem (Chapter 4), the case that $p = 2$. To find the probability that M and N do not have the factor 2 in common, we adopt a different point of view (Chapter 3) and ask instead for the probability that M and N *do* have the factor 2 in common, that is to say, are both even. Since the probability that M is even is $\frac{1}{2}$ and the probability that N is even is also $\frac{1}{2}$, the probability that M and N (independently chosen) are both even is $\frac{1}{2} \times \frac{1}{2} = \frac{1}{2^2}$, whence the probability that they are *not* both even is $1 - \frac{1}{2^2}$. In short, the probability that M and N do not have the factor 2 in common is $1 - \frac{1}{2^2}$.

It is now easy to see (Chapter 4) that the same argument holds when $p = 3$ or 5, or, more generally, when p is any prime number. We conclude that the probability that M and N are not both divisible by the same prime p is simply $1 - \frac{1}{p^2}$. It follows that the probability P that M and N have no prime factor p in common, that is, are relatively prime, is simply the infinite product

$$P = \left(1 - \frac{1}{2^2}\right)\left(1 - \frac{1}{3^2}\right)\left(1 - \frac{1}{5^2}\right) \cdots = \prod_p \left(1 - \frac{1}{p^2}\right) \qquad \text{[A.1]}$$

taken over all primes p, and this is the solution I was looking for.

Or was it? The more I thought about this solution, the more convinced I became that this was *not* the solution I was looking for. I simply had no recollection whatsoever of this strange looking formula (Equation A.1). I therefore set about looking for a different solution, the one that I had found many years ago.

Again, denoting by P the probability that the greatest common divisor (g.c.d.) of M and N is unity, we adopt a different point of view (Chapter 3) and ask for the probability (call it P_g) that the g.c.d. of M and N is g, where g is an arbitrary positive integer. For g to be the g.c.d. of M and N, g must, first of all, divide M, and g must also divide N. The probability that M is a multiple of g is $\frac{1}{g}$, and the probability that N is a multiple of g is also $\frac{1}{g}$. Hence, the probability that g divides both M and N is $\frac{1}{g^2}$. However, since g is the g.c.d. of M and N, the g.c.d. of the integers M/g and N/g is unity and the probability of this event has already been called P. Hence, the probability that the g.c.d. of M and N is g is simply P/g^2. However, the g.c.d. of M and N *must* be some number. We conclude that

$$\sum_{g=1}^{\infty} \frac{P}{g^2} = P \sum_{g=1}^{\infty} \frac{1}{g^2} = 1,$$

where

$$P = \frac{1}{\displaystyle\sum_{g=1}^{\infty} \frac{1}{g^2}} = \frac{1}{\frac{1}{1^2} + \frac{1}{2^2} + \frac{1}{3^2} + \frac{1}{4^2} + \cdots}, \qquad [\text{A.2}]$$

where the sum is taken over all positive integers g, which should be compared with Equation A.1. Now, Equation A.2 does have a familiar ring to it, and I am now convinced that this formula is the one I derived some 65 years ago.

So now we have found not one, but two answers (Equations A.1 and A.2) to our original problem, and it is not at all obvious that these answers are identical. Well, one thing leads to another, and our work so far suggests the following:

Challenge. Prove that

$$\prod_p \left(1 - \frac{1}{p^2}\right) = \frac{1}{\displaystyle\sum_{g=1}^{\infty} \frac{1}{g^2}}, \qquad [\text{A.3}]$$

where the infinite product is taken over all primes p and the infinite sum is taken over all positive integers g.

To prove Equation A.3, we again adopt a different point of view (Chapter 3) and, taking reciprocals, replace Equation A.3 by the equivalent

$$\prod_p \left(\frac{1}{1 - \frac{1}{p^2}}\right) = \sum_{g=1}^{\infty} \frac{1}{g^2}. \qquad [\text{A.4}]$$

Recalling the formula for the sum of an infinite geometric series with common ratio $\frac{1}{p^2}$,

$$1 + \frac{1}{p^2} + \frac{1}{p^4} + \cdots = \sum_{n=0}^{\infty} \frac{1}{p^{2n}} = \frac{1}{1 - \frac{1}{p^2}} \qquad [A.5]$$

for each prime p, Equation A.4 is itself replaced by the equivalent

$$\prod_p \left(1 + \frac{1}{p^2} + \frac{1}{p^4} + \cdots \right) = \sum_{g=1}^{\infty} \frac{1}{g^2}. \qquad [A.6]$$

Recall the fundamental theorem of arithmetic that every integer is a product of primes in one and only one way. It follows that by carrying out the indicated multiplications on the left-hand side of Equation A.6, the summands on the left range, without duplication, over the products of all powers of the squares of the reciprocals of primes, are therefore themselves the reciprocals of squares and are to be found among the terms on the right-hand side. Again invoking the fundamental theorem of arithmetic, we conclude that, conversely, every summand on the right-hand side of Equation A.6 is to be found, once and only once, on the left-hand side. This concludes the proof of Equations A.6, A.4, and A.3.

We remark in passing that the formula

$$1 + \frac{1}{2^2} + \frac{1}{3^2} + \cdots = \frac{\pi^2}{6}, \qquad [A.7]$$

well known to students of calculus, implies that

$$P = \frac{6}{\pi^2}, \qquad [A.8]$$

which, finally, is *the* satisfactory solution to our original problem.

An interesting check of the formula in Equation A.8 is to choose, at random, several hundred pairs of integers (M, N) and count the number of pairs (M, N) that are relatively prime. Dividing this number by the total number of pairs (M, N) yields an estimate for P. How does this estimate agree with Equation A.8? Can we, in this way, find an estimate for π? Can you generalize this problem to the case that n integers chosen at random are relatively prime or have the greatest common divisor g?

As I continued to think about the problem-solving strategies described in this book, I began to wonder whether any of them had, in fact, played a role in my own work. As it happens, I have devoted the past 50 years of my life to the attempt to solve a single problem: the determination of crystal structures from the X-ray scattering experiment. When a beam of X-rays strikes a crystal, it is scattered by the crystal in many different (observed) directions and with different (measured) intensities yielding what is known as the diffraction pattern of the crystal. The diffraction pattern determines the crystal structure, that is, the arrangement of the atoms in the crystal. The problem of going from the observed diffraction pattern to the crystal structure (for 40 years considered at best intractable, at worst unsolvable) may be formulated in purely mathematical terms. Thus, one anticipates that the problem-solving strategies described in this book may find useful application in the solution of the crystal structure problem, and this expectation is, in fact, realized.

It is, of course, not possible in this brief account to describe the nature of these strategies in great detail. Suffice it to say that the original problem was earlier replaced by an equivalent, simpler one (Chapter 4), the so-called phase problem of X-ray crystallography. It is essential to observe that this reformulation of the original problem previously led the crystallographic community to the erroneous conclusion that the problem was an unsolvable one, even in principle. One of the first contributions that my colleague, Jerome Karle, and I made (by adopting a different point of view) was to demonstrate that the phase problem was not only solvable, at least in principle, but actually greatly overdetermined. Owing to this overdetermination, stemming from the redundancy of the experimentally observed data, a statistical approach was called for. This necessitated the derivation of joint probability distributions of several random variables. Because of the complexity of these distributions and their derivations, it turned out to be advantageous first to solve a simpler problem (Chapter 4)— the derivation of the analogous probability distribution of a single random variable. Once this was done, the extension to the general case of several random variables was straightforward. In time, this work led to extremely powerful and routine methods for the determination of crystal and molecular structures that have important implications for structural chemistry and molecular biology.

It should, perhaps, also be mentioned that two other problem-solving strategies, consideration of extreme cases (Chapter 5) and making drawings (Chapter 6), played the important role of yielding insights into the nature of the solution that were not otherwise transparent.

Although the mathematical underpinning of this eventual Nobel Prize–winning work was, for the most part, done in the years 1947 to 1955, and the first applications were made in the mid-1950s, the Nobel Prize (in chemistry) itself was not awarded until 1985. The delay was probably due to the fact that the full importance of this work in applications to structural chemistry and the life sciences was not fully appreciated until the late 1970s and early 1980s, when the appropriate software and more powerful computers became widely available. In any case, I place a great deal of importance on my penchant for problem solving, and my familiarity with the problem-solving strategies highlighted in this very useful book enabled me to have the honor of being the first mathematician to win a Nobel Prize.

This book very cleverly demonstrates applications of the 10 most prevalent problem-solving strategies, not only in the context of mathematics but also as they may be used in everyday life situations. This way the reader can begin to get accustomed to the broader application of these important problem-solving techniques beyond their use in mathematics. Once readers witness the power of these strategies in the mathematical context, and see their use in everyday life, they might begin to expand their application to other fields.

Problem solving in general, whether it is used to solve mathematical problems at the school level, or in serious research that may lead to major medical breakthroughs, or simply to solve problems we encounter during our daily lives, is an indispensable skill that every well-educated person should acquire. There are some gifted people who have attained these skills in a natural way. Yet the vast majority of us requires some training to develop proper problem-solving skills. Providing this training is perhaps one of the most important responsibilities resting with our educators. All too often students "pick up" problem-solving skills through experience or as a by-product of doing exercises in mathematics or science classes. Watching the teacher or the textbook author plow through some problem situations can also lead to some lasting spin-offs. However, with this book the teacher is provided (or one might even say, "spoon fed") the tools essential for any problem-solving situation.

It could be said that all problem solving is merely a combination of the 10 problem-solving strategies presented in this book. In some cases, these techniques, applied independently of others, can provide the key to a clever (or elegant) solution. Other times, a solution may require a series of these techniques to tickle out the solution to a problem. From my long experience with problem solving, I find it absolutely essential that teachers familiarize themselves with the 10 problem-solving strategies presented in this book, make them a part of their personal arsenal of mathematical tools, and then regularly incorporate them into their teaching, whenever they appropriately fit.

I hope these brief remarks will persuade the reader that problem solving is not only fun, but, at least occasionally, even important.

—Herbert A. Hauptman, PhD
Nobel Laureate in Chemistry, 1985

Sources for Problems

Abraham, R. M. (1932). *Winter nights entertainments*. London: Constable. (Reprinted as *Easy-to-do entertainments and diversions with coins, cards, string, paper and matches*. New York: Dover, 1961)

Ainley, S. (1977). *Mathematical puzzles*. London: Bell.

Alcuin (attrib.). Propositions Alcuini doctoris Caroli Magni Imperatoris ad acuendos juvenes. (Translated and annotated by John Hadley and David Singmaster (1992). Problems to sharpen the young. *Mathematical Gazette*, 76(475), 102–126.

Alexanderson, G. L., Klosinski, L. F., & Larson, L. C. (1985). *The William Lowell Putnam Mathematical Competition—Problems and solutions: 1965–1984*. Washington, DC: Mathematical Association of America.

Allen, L. (1991). *Brainsharpeners*. London: New English Library (Hodder & Stoughton).

ApSimon, H. (1984). *Mathematical byways*. New York: Oxford University Press.

ApSimon, H. (1990). *More mathematical byways in ayling, beeling and ceiling*. New York: Oxford University Press.

Aref, M. N., & Wernick, W. (1986). *Problems and solutions in Euclidean geometry*. New York: Dover.

Artino, R. A., Galione, A. N., & Shell, N. (1982). *The contest problem book IV*. Washington, DC: Mathematical Association of America.

Barbeau, E., Klamkin, M., & Moser, W. (1976). *1001 problems in high school mathematics*. Montreal: Canadian Mathematical Congress. (Also reprinted in 1978, 1980, 1985)

Barr, S. (1965). *A miscellany of puzzles*. New York: Crowell.

Barr, S. (1969). *Second miscellany of puzzles*. New York: Macmillan. (Reissued as *Mathematical brain benders*. New York: Dover, 1982)

Barry, D. T., & Lux, J. R. (1984). *The Philips Academy Prize Examination in mathematics*. White Plains, NY: Dale Seymour.

Bates, N. B., & Smith, S. M. (1980). *101 puzzle problems*. Concord, MA: Bates.

Berloquin, P. (1976). *100 geometric games*. New York: Scribner's. (Retitled as *Geometric games*. London: Unwin, 1980)

Berloquin, P. (1976). *100 numerical games*. New York: Scribner's.

Berloquin, P. (1977). *100 games of logic*. New York: Scribner's. (Retitled as *Games of logic*. London: Unwin, 1980)

Berloquin, P. (1985). *The garden of the sphinx*. New York: Scribner's.

Birtwistle, C. (1971). Mathematical puzzles and perplexities. London: Allen & Unwin.

Brandes, L. G. (1975). *The math wizard* (Rev. ed.). Portland, ME: J. Weston Walch.

Bridgman, G. (1981). *Lake Wobegon math problems* (Rev. and enlarged ed.). Minneapolis, MN: Author.

Brousseau, A. (1972). *Saint Mary's College mathematics context problems*. Palo Alto, CA: Creative Publications.

Bryant, S. J., Graham, G. E., & Wiley, K. G. (1965). *Nonroutine problems in algebra, geometry, and trigonometry*. New York: McGraw-Hill.

Bryant, V., & Postill, R. (1980). *The Sunday Times book of brain teasers—Book 1*. London: Unwin. (Also published as *The Sunday Times book of brainteasers*. New York: St. Martin's Press, 1982)

Bryant, V., & Postill, R. (1983). *The Sunday Times book of brain teasers—Book 2*. Englewood Cliffs, NJ: Prentice-Hall.

Burkill, J. C., & Kundy, H. M. (1961). *Mathematical scholarship problems*. London: Cambridge University Press.

Butts, T. (1973). *Problem solving in mathematics*. Glenview, IL: Scott, Foresman.

Canadian Mathematical Society. *Crux mathematicorum*. Ottawa, Ontario, Canada: Author.

CEMREL. (1975). *Elements of mathematics book, problem book* (2 vols.). St. Louis, MO: Author.

Charosh, M. (1965). *Mathematical challenges*. Washington, DC: National Council of Teachers of Mathematics.

Clarke, B. R. (1994). *Puzzles for pleasure*. New York: Cambridge University Press.

Clarke, B. R., Gooch, R., Newing, A., & Singmaster, D. (1993). *The daily telegraph book of brain twisters No. 1*. London: Pan.

Conrad, S. R., & Flegler, D. (1992). *Math contests for high school* (2 vols.). Tenafly, NJ: Math League Press.

Conrad, S. R., & Flegler, D. (1992). *Math contests grades 7 and 8* (2 vols.). Tenafly, NJ: Math League Press.

Conrad, S. R., & Flegler, D. (1994). *Math contests grades 4, 5, and 6* (2 vols.). Tenafly, NJ: Math League Press.

Dorofeev, G., Potapov, M., & Rozov, N. (1973). *Elementary mathematics: Selected topics and problem solving*. Moscow: Mir.

Dorrie, H. (1965). *100 great problems of elementary mathematics*. New York: Dover.

Dowlen, N., Powers, S., & Florence, H. (1987). *College of Charleston mathematics contest books*. White Plains, NY: Dale Seymour.

Dudney, H. E. (1926). *Modern puzzles* (New edition, nd [1936]). New York: Pearson.

Dudney, H. E. (1932). *Puzzles and curious problems* (Revised by J. Travers, 2nd [1936]). London: Nelson.

Dudney, H. E. (1941). *A puzzle mine* (J. Travers, Ed.). Nelson: London.

Dudney, H. E. (1958). *The Canterbury puzzles*. New York: Dover.

Dudney, H. E. (1967). *536 puzzles and curious problems* (M. Gardner, Ed.). New York: Scribner's. (Contains almost all of modern puzzles and puzzles and curious problems).

Dudney, H. E. (1970). *Amusements in mathematics*. New York: Dover.

Dunn, A. (1964). *Mathematical bafflers*. New York: McGraw-Hill.

Dunn, A. F. (1983). *Second book of mathematical bafflers*. New York: Dover.

Dynkin, E. B., & Uspenskii, V. A. (1963). *Multicolor problems*. Lexington, MA: Heath.

Edwards, J. D., King, D. J., & O'Halloran, P. J. (1986). *All the best from the Australian Mathematics Competition*. Melbourne, Australia: Ruskin.

Emmet, E. R. (1976). *Mind tickling brain teasers*. Buchanan, NY: Emerson.

Emmet, E. R. (1976). *The Puffin book of brain teasers*. London: Puffin.

Emmet, E. R. (1977). *A diversity of puzzles*. New York: Barnes & Noble.

Emmet, E. R. (1977). *Puzzles for pleasure*. Buchanan, NY: Emerson.

Emmet, E. R. (1979). *The great detective puzzle book*. New York: Barnes & Noble.

Emmet, E. R. (1980). *The island of imperfection puzzle book*. New York: Barnes & Noble.

Emmet, E. R. (1984). *The Penguin book of brain teasers*. New York: Viking. (Compiled from Emmet's posthumous notes by David Hall and Alan Summers)

Emmet, E. R. (1993). *Brain puzzler's delight*. New York: Sterling.

Emmet, E. R., & Eperson, D. B. (1988). *Patterns in mathematics*. Oxford, UK: Blackwell.

Engel, A. (1998). *Problem-solving strategies*. New York: Springer-Verlag.

Filipiak, A. S. (1942). *Mathematical puzzles*. New York: Bell.

Fisher, L., & Kennedy, B. (1984). *Brother Alfred Brousseau Problem Solving and Mathematics Competition, Introductory division*. White Plains, NY: Dale Seymour.

Fisher, L., & Medigovich, W. (1984). *Brother Alfred Brousseau Problem Solving and Mathematics Competition, Senior division*. White Plains, NY: Dale Seymour.

Friedland, A. J. (1970). *Puzzles in math and logic*. New York: Dover.

Frohlichstein, J. (1962). *Mathematical fun, games and puzzles*. New York: Dover.

Fujimura, K. (1978). *The Tokyo puzzles* (M. Gardner, Ed.). New York: Scribner's.

Gamow, G., & Stem, M. (1958). *Puzzle-math*. London: Macmillan.

Gardner, M. (1959). *Arrow book of brain teasers*. New York: Scholastic.

Gardner, M. (1959). *The Scientific American book of mathematical puzzles and diversions*. New York: Simon & Schuster. (Revised, with new afterword and references, as *Hexaflexagons and other mathematical diversions*. Chicago: University of Chicago Press, 1988)

Gardner, M. (1961). *The second Scientific American book of mathematical puzzles and diversions*. New York: Simon & Schuster.

Gardner, M. (1966). *Martin Gardner's new mathematical diversions from Scientific American*. New York: Simon & Schuster. (Reprinted in 1983 by the University of Chicago Press)

Gardner, M. (1967). *The numerology of Dr. Matrix*. New York: Simon & Schuster.

Gardner, M. (1969). *Perplexing puzzles and tantalizing teasers*. New York: Simon & Schuster.

Gardner, M. (1969). *The unexpected hanging and other mathematical diversions*. New York: Simon & Schuster. (Revised ed. in 1991 by the University of Chicago Press)

Gardner, M. (1971). *Martin Gardner's sixth book of mathematical games from Scientific American*. San Francisco: Freeman. (Reprinted in 1983 by the University of Chicago Press)

Gardner, M. (1975). *Mathematical carnival*. New York: Knopf. (Revised ed. in 1989 by the Mathematical Association of America)

Gardner, M. (1976). *The incredible Dr. Matrix*. New York: Scribner's. (Contains all of *The numerology of Dr. Matrix*)

Gardner, M. (1977). *Mathematical magic show*. New York: Knopf. (Revised ed. in 1990 by the Mathematical Association of America)

Gardner, M. (1977). *More perplexing puzzles and tantalizing teasers*. New York: Archway (Pocket Books).

Gardner, M. (1978). *Aha! Insight.* New York: Scientific American & Freeman.

Gardner, M. (1979). *Mathematical circus.* New York: Knopf. (Revised ed. in 1992 by Mathematical Association of America)

Gardner, M. (1981). *Science fiction puzzle tales.* New York: C. N. Potter.

Gardner, M. (1982). *Aha! Gotcha.* New York: Freeman.

Gardner, M. (1983). *Wheels, life and other mathematical amusements.* New York: Freeman.

Gardner, M. (1985). *The magic numbers of Dr. Matrix.* Buffalo, NY: Prometheus. (Contains all of *The incredible Dr. Matrix*)

Gardner, M. (1986). *Entertaining mathematical puzzles.* New York: Dover.

Gardner, M. (1986). *Knotted doughnuts and other mathematical entertainments.* New York: Freeman.

Gardner, M. (1986). *Puzzles from other worlds.* New York: Vintage (Random House).

Gardner, M. (1987). *Riddles of the sphinx.* Washington, DC: New Mathematical Library, Mathematical Association of America.

Gardner, M. (1988). *Time travel and other mathematical bewilderments.* New York: Freeman.

Gardner, M. (1989). *Penrose tiles to trapdoor ciphers.* New York: Freeman.

Gardner, M. (1992). *Fractal music, hypercards and more.* New York: Freeman.

Gardner, M. (1994). *My best mathematical and logical puzzles.* New York: Dover.

Garvin, A. D. (1975). *Discovery problems for better students.* Portland, ME: Weston Walch.

Gleason, A. M., Greenwood, R. E., & Kelly, L. M. (1980). *The William Lowell Putnam Mathematical Competitions. Problems and solutions: 1938–1964.* Washington, DC: Mathematical Association of America.

Goebel, J. A. (1992). *Contest problem book: Problems and solutions from the North Carolina Mathematics League, 1981–1989.* White Plains, NY: Dale Seymour.

Gould, P. (1992). *Senior challenge '85–'91. Mathematical education on Merseyside.* Liverpool, UK: University of Liverpool.

Gould, P., & Porteous, I. (1984). *Senior challenge '80–'84. Mathematical education on Merseyside.* Liverpool, UK: University of Liverpool.

Graham, L. A. (1959). *Ingenious mathematical problems and methods.* New York: Dover.

Graham, L. A. (1968). *The surprise attack in mathematical problems.* New York: Dover.

Greitzer, S. L. (1978). *International Mathematical Olympiads 1959–1977.* Washington, DC: Mathematical Association of America.

Haber, P. (1957). *Mathematical puzzles and pastimes.* Mount Vernon, NY: Peter Pauper.

Halmos, P. R. (1991). *Problems for mathematicians young and old (Dolciani Mathematical Expositions #12).* Washington, DC: Mathematical Association of America.

Higgins, A. M. (1971). *Geometry problems.* Portland, ME: Weston Walch.

Hill, T. J. (1974). *Mathematical challenges II—Plus six.* Washington, DC: National Council of Teachers of Mathematics.

Holton, D. (1988–1990). *Problem solving series* (15 vols.). Leicester, UK: Mathematical Association.

Honsberger, R. (1978). *Mathematical morsels*. Washington, DC: Mathematical Association of America.

Honsberger, R. (1997). *In Polya's footsteps: Miscellaneous problems and essays*. Washington, DC: Mathematical Association of America.

Hunter, J. A. H. (1957). *Figures for fun*. London: Phoenix House.

Hunter, J. A. H. (1965). *Fun with figures*. New York: Dover.

Hunter, J. A. H. (1965). *Hunter's math brain teasers*. New York: Bantam. (Corrected and enlarged as *Mathematical brain teasers*. New York: Dover, 1976)

Hunter, J. A. H. (1966). *More fun with figures*. New York: Dover.

Hunter, J. A. H. (1979). *Challenging mathematical teasers*. New York: Dover.

Hunter, J. A. H. (1983). *Entertaining mathematical teasers and how to solve them*. New York: Dover.

Kahan, S. (1978). *Have some sums to solve: The compleat alphametics book*. Farmingdale, NY: Baywood.

Kahan, S. (1994). *At last!! Encoded totals second addition: The long awaited sequel to "Have some sums to solve."* Farmingdale, NY: Baywood.

Kahan, S. (1996). *Take a look at a good book: The third collection of additive alphametics for the connoisseur*. Farmingdale, NY: Baywood.

Kendall, P. M. H., & Thomas, G. M. (1962). *Mathematical puzzles for the connoisseur*. London: Griffin; New York: Apollo (Crowell).

King, T. (1927). *The best 100 puzzles solved and answered*. London: Foulsham.

Kinnaird, W. C. (Ed.). (1946). *Encyclopedia of puzzles and pastimes*. New York: Grosset & Dunlap.

Klamkin, M. S. (1986). *International Mathematical Olympiads, 1979–1985*. Washington, DC: Mathematical Association of America.

Klee, V., & Wagon, S. (1991). *Old and new unsolved problems in plane geometry and number theory*. Washington, DC: Mathematical Association of America.

Konhauser, J. D. E., Velleman, D., & Wagon, S. (1996). *Which way did the bicycle go?* Washington, DC: Mathematical Association of America.

Kordemsky, B. A. (1972). *The Moscow puzzles* (M. Gardner, Ed.). New York: Scribner's.

Krechmer, V. A. (1974). *A problem book in algebra* (V. Shiffer, Trans.). Moscow: Mir.

Krulik, S., & Rudnick, J. A. (1980). *Problem solving: A handbook for teachers*. Boston: Allyn & Bacon.

Krulik, S., & Rudnick, J. A. (1996). *The new sourcebook for teaching reasoning and problem solving in junior and senior high schools*. Boston: Allyn & Bacon.

Kürschak, J. (1963). *Hungarian problem book I and II* (based on the Eötvös Competitions, 1894–1905 and 1906–1928) (E. Rapaport, Trans.). New Mathematical Library, Washington, DC: Mathematical Association of America.

Kutepov, A., & Rubanov, A. (1975). *Problems in geometry* (O. Meshkov, Trans.). Moscow: Mir.

Kutepov, A., & Rubanov, A. (1978). *Problem book: Algebra and elementary function* (L. Levant, Trans.). Moscow: Mir.

Larson, L. C. (1983). *Problem solving through problems*. New York: Springer-Verlag.

Lehoczky, S., & Rusczyk, R. (1994). *The art of problem solving, Volume 1: The basics*. Stanford, CA: Greater Testing Concepts.

Lenchner, G. (1983). *Creative problem solving in school mathematics*. Boston: Houghton Mifflin.

Loyd, S. (1914). *Sam Loyd's cyclopedia of 5,000 puzzles, tricks and conundrums.* New York: Bigelow; New York: Lamb. (Reprint in 1976 by Corwin Press, New York).

Loyd, S. (1927). *Sam Loyd's tricks and puzzles* (Vol. I). New York: Experimenter Publishing.

Loyd, S. (1928). *Sam Loyd and his puzzles.* New York: Barse.

Loyd, S. (1959). *Mathematical puzzles of Sam Loyd* (Vol. 1). New York: Dover.

Loyd, S. (1960). *Mathematical puzzles of Sam Loyd* (Vol. 2). New York: Dover.

Luckács, C., & Tarján, E. (1968). *Mathematical games.* New York: Walker.

Morris, I. (1969). *The Riverside puzzles.* New York: Walker.

Morris, I. (1970). *The lonely monk and other puzzles.* Boston: Little, Brown.

Morris, I. (1972). *Foul play and other puzzles of all kinds.* New York: Vintage (Random House).

Moscovich, I. (1984). *Super-games.* London: Hutchinson.

Moscovich, I. (1991). *Fiendishly difficult math puzzles.* New York: Sterling.

Moscovich, I. (1991). *Fiendishly difficult visual perception puzzles.* New York: Sterling.

Moser, W., & Barbeau, E. (1976). *The Canadian Mathematics Olympiads 1969–1975.* Montreal, Quebec, Canada: Canadian Mathematical Congress.

Moser, W. O. J., & Barbeau, E. J. (1978). *The first ten Canadian Mathematics Olympiads (1969–1978).* Montreal, Quebec, Canada: Canadian Mathematical Society.

Mosteller, F. (1965). *Fifty challenging problems in probability.* New York: Dover.

Mott-Smith, G. (1954). *Mathematical puzzles for beginners and enthusiasts.* New York: Dover.

Newton, D. E. (1972). *One hundred quickies for math classes.* Portland, ME: Weston Walch.

Phillips, H. (1932). *The week-end problems book.* London: Nonesuch.

Phillips, H. (1933). *The playtime omnibus.* London: Faber & Faber.

Phillips, H. (1934). *The sphinx problem book.* London: Faber.

Phillips, H. (1936). *Brush up your wits.* London: Dent.

Phillips, H. (1937). *Question time.* London: Dent. (Also New York: Farrar and Rinehart, 1938)

Phillips, H. (1945). *Ask me another.* London: Ptarmigan.

Phillips, H. (1945). *Hubert Phillips's heptameron.* London: Eyre & Spottiswoode.

Phillips, H. (1945). *Something to think about.* London: Ptarmigan. (With additional foreword, one problem omitted, and 11 problems added, London: Max Parrish, 1958)

Phillips, H. (1947). *Playtime.* London: Ptarmigan.

Phillips, H. (1950). *The Hubert Phillips annual 1951.* London: Hamish Hamilton.

Phillips, H. (1960). *Problems omnibus* (Vol. 1). London: Arco.

Phillips, H. (1961). *My best puzzles in logic and reasoning.* New York: Dover.

Phillips, H. (1961). *My best puzzles in mathematics.* New York: Dover.

Phillips, H. (1962). *Problems omnibus* (Vol. 2). London: Arco.

Phillips, H., Shovelton, S. T., & Marshal, G. S. (1961). *Caliban's problem book.* New York: Dover.

Polya, G., & Kilpatrick, J. (1974). *The Stanford mathematics book.* New York: Teachers College Press.

Posamentier, A. S. (2002). *Advanced Euclidean geometry.* Emeryville, CA: Key College.

Posamentier, A. S. (1996). *Students! Get ready for the mathematics for SAT 1: Problem-solving strategies and practice tests*. Thousand Oaks, CA: Corwin Press.

Posamentier, A. S., & Krulik, S. (1996). *Teachers! Prepare your students for the mathematics for SAT 1: Methods and problem-solving strategies*. Thousand Oaks, CA: Corwin Press.

Posamentier, A. S., & Hauptman, H. A. (2006). *100+ Great Ideas for Introducing Key Concepts in Mathematics*. Thousand Oaks, CA: Corwin Press.

Posamentier, A. S., & Jaye, D. (2006). *What Successful Math Teachers Do, Grades 6–12*. Thousand Oaks, CA: Corwin Press.

Posamentier, A. S., Jaye, D., & Krulik, S. (2007). *Exemplary Practices for Secondary Math Teachers*. Alexandria, VA: Association for Supervision and Curriculum Development.

Posamentier, A. S., & Salkind, C. T. (1996). *Challenging problems in algebra* (rev. ed.). New York: Dover.

Posamentier, A. S., & Salkind, C. T. (1996). *Challenging problems in geometry* (rev. ed.). New York: Dover.

Posamentier, A. S., & Sheridan, G. (1984). *Math motivators: Pre-algebra, algebra, and geometry*. Menlo Park, CA: Addison-Wesley.

Posamentier, A. S., & Stepelman, J. (2006). *Teaching secondary school mathematics: Techniques and enrichment units* (7th ed.). Upper Saddle River, NJ: Pearson, Merrill/Prentice Hall.

Posamentier, A. S., & Wernick, W. (1988). *Advanced geometric constructions*. Palo Alto, CA: Dale Seymour.

Ransom, W. R. (1955). *One hundred mathematical curiosities*. Portland, ME: Weston Walch.

Rapaport, E. (1964). *Hungarian problem book* (2 vols.). New York: Random House.

Reis, C. M., & Ditor, S. Z. (Eds.). (1988). *The Canadian Mathematics Olympiads (1979–1985)*. Ottawa, Ontario, Canada: Canadian Mathematical Society.

Ruderman, H. D. (1983). *NYSML-ARML Contests 1973–1982*. Norman, OK: Mu Alpha Theta.

Rusczyk, R., & Lehoczky, S. (1994). *The art of problem solving, Volume 2: And beyond*. Stanford, CA: Greater Testing Concepts.

Salkind, C. T. (1961). *The contest problem book*. New York: Random House.

Salkind, C. T. (1966). *The MAA problem book II*. New York: Random House.

Salkind, C. T., & Earl, J. M. (1973). *The MAA problem book III*. New York: Random House.

Saul, N. A., Kessler, G. W., Krilov, S., & Zimmerman, L. (1986). *The New York City Contest problem book*. White Plains, NY: Dale Seymour.

Shell Centre for Mathematics Education and the Joint Matriculation Board. (1982). *Problems with patterns and numbers*. Manchester, UK: Author.

Shklarsky, D. O., Chentzov, N. N., & Yaglom, I. M. (1962). *The USSR Olympiad problem book*. San Francisco: W. H. Freeman.

Shklarsky, D. O., Chentzov, N. N., and Yaglom, I. M. (1979). *Selected problems and theorems in elementary mathematics* (V. M. Volosov & I. G. Volsova, Trans.). Moscow: Mir.

Shortz, W. (1991). *Will Shortz's best brain busters*. New York: Times Books (Random House).

Shortz, W. (1993). *Brain twisters from the First World Puzzle Championships*. New York: Times Books (Random House).

Sierpinski, W. (1964). *A selection of problems in the theory of numbers*. London: Pergamon/Macmillan.

Sierpinski, W. (1970). *250 problems in elementary number theory*. New York: Elsevier.

Sitomer, H. (1974). *The new mathlete problems book*. Valley Stream, NY: Nassau County Interscholastic Mathematics League.

Smith, D. P., Jr., & Fagan, L. T. (1961). *Mathematics review exercises* (4th ed.). Boston, MA: Ginn.

Snape, C., & Scott, H. (1991). *How puzzling*. Cambridge, UK: Cambridge University Press.

Soifer, A. (1987). *Mathematics as problem solving*. Colorado Springs, CO: Center for Excellence in Mathematics Education.

Sole, T. (1988). *The ticket to heaven and other superior puzzles*. London: Penguin.

Steinhaus, H. (1963). *One hundred problems in elementary mathematics*. New York: Pergamon.

Straszewicz, S. (1965). *Mathematical problems and puzzles from the Polish Mathematical Olympiads* (J. Smsliska, Trans.). New York: Pergamon.

Trigg, C. W. (1967). *Mathematical quickies*. New York: McGraw-Hill.

Ulam, S. M. (1960). *Problems in modern mathematics*. New York: Wiley.

Vakil, R. (1996). *A mathematical mosaic: Patterns and problem solving*. Burlington, Ontario, Canada: Brendan Kelly.

Vout, C., & Gray, G. (1993). *Challenging puzzles*. Cambridge, UK: Cambridge University Press.

Wall, H. S. (1963). *Creative mathematics*. Austin: University of Texas Press.

Wells, D. G. (1979). *Recreations in logic*. New York: Dover.

Wells, D. (1982). *Can you solve these?* Norfolk, UK: Stradbroke.

Williams, W. T., & Savage, G. H. (1940). *The Penguin problems book*. London: Penguin.

Williams, W. T., & Savage, G. H. (1940). *The Strand problems book*. London: Newnes.

Williams, W. T., & Savage, G. H. (1944). *The second Penguin problems book*. London: Penguin.

Williams, W. T., & Savage, G. H. (1946). *The third Penguin problems book*. London: Penguin.

Yaglom, A. M., & Yaglom, I. M. (1964, 1967). *Challenging mathematical problems with elementary solutions* (2 vols.). San Francisco: Holden-Day.

Readings on Problem Solving

Ackoff, R. L. (1978). *The art of problem solving.* New York: Wiley.

Adams, J. L. (1974). *Conceptual blockbusting.* San Francisco: Freeman.

Andre, T. (1986). Problem solving and education. In G. Phye & T. Andre (Eds.), *Cognitive classroom learning.* Orlando, FL: Academic Press.

Arnold, W. R. (1971). Students can pose and solve original problems. *The Mathematics Teacher, 64,* 325.

Averbach, B., & Chein, O. (1980). *Mathematics: Problem solving through recreational mathematics.* San Francisco: Freeman.

Barbeau, E. J. (1997). *Power play.* Washington, DC: Mathematical Association of America.

Bransford, J. D., & Stein, B. S. (1984). *The ideal problem solver.* New York: Freeman.

Brown, S. I., & Walter, M. I. (1983). *The art of problem posing.* Hillsdale, NJ: Lawrence Erlbaum.

Butts, T. (1985). In praise of trial and error. *The Mathematics Teacher, 78,* 167.

Charles, R., & Lester, F. (1982). *Teaching problem solving: What, why, and how.* White Plains, NY: Dale Seymour.

Chipman, S., Segal, J., & Glaser, R. (1985). *Thinking and learning skills: Vol. 2. Research and open questions.* Hillsdale, NJ: Erlbaum.

Cofman, J. (1990). *What to solve? Problems and suggestions for young mathematicians.* New York: Oxford University Press.

Cofman, J. (1995). *Numbers and shapes revisited: More problems for young mathematicians.* New York: Oxford University Press.

Costa, A. (1984, November). Mediating the metacognitive. *Educational Leadership,* 57–62.

Curcio, F. (Ed.). (1987). *Teaching and learning: A problem-solving focus.* Reston, VA: National Council of Teachers of Mathematics.

Derry, S. J., & Murphy, D. A. (1986). Designing systems that train learning ability: From theory to practice. *Review of Educational Research, 56*(1), 1–39.

Emmet, E. R. (1981). *Learning to think.* Verplanck, NY: Emerson.

Fisher, R. B. (1981). *Brain games.* London: Fontana.

Fixx, J. F. (1978). *Solve it!* New York: Doubleday.

Frederiksen, N. (1984). Implications of cognitive theory for instruction on problem solving. *Review of Educational Research, 54*(3), 363–407.

Gardner, M. (1978). *Aha! Insight.* New York: Scientific American & Freeman.

Gardner, M. (1982). *Aha! Gotcha.* San Francisco: Freeman.

Gifted Students [Special issue]. (1983). *The Mathematics Teacher, 76.*

Gordon, W. J. J. (1961). *Synectics—The development of creative capacity.* New York: Harper & Row.

Hadamard, J. (1954). *The psychology of invention in the mathematical field.* New York: Dover.

Heiman, M., Narode, R., Slomianko, J., & Lochhead, J. (1987). *Thinking skills: Mathematics, teaching.* Washington, DC: National Education Association.

Herr, T., & Johnson, K. (1994). *Problem-solving strategies: Crossing the river with dogs.* Berkeley, CA: Key Curriculum Press.

Honsberger, R. (1970). *Ingenuity in mathematics.* New Mathematical Library, Washington, DC: Mathematical Association of America.

Honsberger, R. (1973). *Mathematical gems* (Vol. 1, Dolciani Mathematical Expositions #1). Washington, DC: Mathematical Association of America.

Honsberger, R. (1976). *Mathematical gems* (Vol. 2, Dolciani Mathematical Expositions #2). Washington, DC: Mathematical Association of America.

Honsberger, R. (1978). *Mathematical morsels* (Dolciani Mathematical Expositions #3). Washington, DC: Mathematical Association of America.

Honsberger, R. (1979). *Mathematical plums* (Dolciani Mathematical Expositions #4). Washington, DC: Mathematical Association of America.

Honsberger, R. (1985). *Mathematical gems III* (Dolciani Mathematical Expositions #9). Washington, DC: Mathematical Association of America.

Honsberger, R. (1991). *More mathematical morsels* (Dolciani Mathematical Expositions #10). Washington, DC: Mathematical Association of America.

Hough, J. S. (Ed.). (1984). *Problem solving. Newsletter* (Vols. 1–5). Philadelphia: Franklin Institute Press.

Hughes, B. (1975). *Thinking through problems.* Palo Alto, CA: Creative Publications.

Jensen, R. J. (1987). Stuck? Don't give up! Subgoal-generation strategies in problem solving. *The Mathematics Teacher, 80,* 614.

Karmos, J., & Karmos, A. (1987). Strategies for active involvement in problem solving. In M. Heiman & J. Slomianko (Eds.), *Thinking skills instruction: Concepts and techniques* (pp. 99–110). Washington, DC: National Educational Association.

Kluwe, R. (1987). Executive decisions and regulation of problem solving behavior. In F. Weinert & R. Kluwe (Eds.), *Metacognition, motivation and understanding.* Hillsdale, NJ: Lawrence Erlbaum.

Krulik, S. (Ed.). (1980). *Problem solving in school mathematics, 1980 yearbook.* Reston, VA: National Council of Teachers of Mathematics.

Krulik, S., & Rudnick, J. (1987). *Problem solving: A handbook for teachers* (2nd ed.). Boston: Allyn & Bacon.

Krulik, S., & Rudnick, J. (1989). *Problem solving: A handbook for senior high school teachers.* Boston: Allyn & Bacon.

Krulik, S., & Rudnick, J. (1993). *Reasoning and problem solving: A handbook for elementary school teachers.* Boston: Allyn & Bacon.

Krulik, S., & Rudnick, J. (1995). *The new sourcebook for teaching reasoning and problem solving in elementary schools.* Boston: Allyn & Bacon.

Krulik, S., & Rudnick, J. (1996). *The new sourcebook for teaching reasoning and problem solving in secondary schools.* Boston: Allyn & Bacon.

Mason, J. (1978). *Learning and doing mathematics.* Milton Keynes, UK: Open University Press.

Mason, J., with Burton, L., & Stacey, K. (1985). *Thinking mathematically.* Reading, MA: Addison-Wesley.

Mayer, R. (1986). Mathematics. In R. Dillon & R. Sternberg (Eds.), *Cognition and instruction.* Orlando, FL: Academic Press.

Mayer, R., Larkin, J., & Kadane, J. (1984). A cognitive analysis of mathematical problem solving ability. In R. Sternberg (Ed.), *Advances in the psychology of human intelligence* (Vol. 2, pp. 231–273). Hillsdale, NJ: Lawrence Erlbaum.

McKim, R. H. (1980). *Thinking visually: A strategy manual for problem solving.* White Plains, NY: Dale Seymour.

Moses, S. (1974). *The art of problem-solving.* London: Transworld.

Mottershead, L. (1978). *Sources of mathematical discovery.* Oxford, UK: Blackwell.

Mottershead, L. (1985). *Investigations in mathematics.* Oxford, UK: Blackwell.

Nickerson, R. (1981, October). Thoughts on teaching thinking. *Educational Leadership,* 21–24.

Nickerson, R., Perkins, D., & Smith, E. (1985). *The teaching of thinking.* Hillsdale, NJ: Lawrence Erlbaum.

Noller, R. B., Heintz, R. E., & Blaeuer, D. A. (1978). *Creative problem solving in mathematics.* Buffalo, NY: D. O. K. Publishers.

Polya, G. (1945). *How to solve it.* Princeton, NJ: Princeton University Press.

Polya, G. (1954). *Introduction and analogy in mathematics.* Princeton, NJ: Princeton University Press.

Polya, G. (1954). *Patterns of plausible inference.* Princeton, NJ: Princeton University Press.

Polya, G. (1962). *Mathematical discovery* (2 vols.). New York: Wiley. (Combined ed. with foreword by Peter Hilton, bibliography extended by Gerald Alexanderson, and index extended by Jean Pedersen, New York: Wiley, 1981)

Posamentier, A. S., & Schulz, W. (Eds.). (1996). *The art of problem solving: A resource for the mathematics teacher.* Thousand Oaks, CA: Corwin Press.

Posamentier, A. S., & Stepelman, J. (1999). *Teaching secondary school mathematics: Techniques and enrichment units* (5th ed.) Columbus, OH: Merrill/Prentice Hall.

Reeves, C. A. (1987). *Problem solving techniques helpful in mathematics and science.* Reston, VA: National Council of Teachers of Mathematics.

Schoenfeld, A. H. (1983). *Problem solving in the mathematics curriculum.* Washington, DC: Mathematical Association of America.

Schoenfeld, A. H. (1985). *Mathematical problem solving.* Orlando, FL: Academic Press.

Segal, J., Chipman, S., & Glaser, R. (Eds.). (1985). *Thinking and learning skills, Vol. I: Relating instruction to research.* Hillsdale, NJ: Lawrence Erlbaum.

Silver, E. A. (Ed.). (1985). *Teaching and learning mathematical problem solving.* Hillsdale, NJ: Lawrence Erlbaum.

Simon, M. A. (1986). The teacher's role in increasing student understanding of mathematics. *Educational Leadership, 43*(7), 40–43.

Skemp, R. R. (1971). *The psychology of learning mathematics.* Baltimore, MD: Penguin.

Soifer, A. (1987). *Mathematics as problem solving.* Colorado Springs, CO: Center for Excellence in Mathematics Education.

Soifer, A. (1994). *Colorado Mathematical Olympiad: The first ten years and further explorations.* Colorado Springs, CO: Center for Excellence in Mathematics Education.

Topoly, W. (1965). An introduction to solving problems. *The Mathematics Teacher, 58,* 48.

Troutman, A., & Lichtenberg, B. P. (1974). Problem solving in the general mathematics classroom. *The Mathematics Teacher, 67,* 590.

Walter, M. I., & Brown, S. I. (1977). Problem posing and problem solving. *The Mathematics Teacher, 70,* 4.

Whirl, R. J. (1973). Problem solving—Solution or technique? *The Mathematics Teacher, 66,* 551.

Winckelgren, W. A. (1974). *How to solve problems.* San Francisco: Freeman.

CORWIN PRESS

The Corwin Press logo—a raven striding across an open book—represents the union of courage and learning. Corwin Press is committed to improving education for all learners by publishing books and other professional development resources for those serving the field of PreK–12 education. By providing practical, hands-on materials, Corwin Press continues to carry out the promise of its motto: **"Helping Educators Do Their Work Better."**

CPSIA information can be obtained
at www.ICGtesting.com
Printed in the USA
FSOW03n1528060117
29267FS

9 781412 959704